PRIXTURIOUS

A TRUE LIFE NOVEL

The Dictionary of Good Sir

"Prixturious – Prix-tur-ious - Definition – A group of people who share the same *Prick* gene and all work together to make an innocent persons life, *Torturous*. All should be pitied, Karma's a coming"

TO DAVE, HOPE YOU ENJOY IT MATE AND ALL THE BEST FOR THE FUTURE.

Michael Elwood

(Address details withheld)

29th November 2018

Cleveland Police Chief Constable

Central Ticket Office, Ash House, Princeton Drive

Thornaby

Stockton   On   Tees
TS17 6AJ

Dear Cleveland Police Chief Constable

Firstly, I hope you are well, Good Sir?

I write in good heart and spirit. However, I find myself quite vexed, the offense that I have been accused of is not quite as simple as first thought and after, and I can assure you Good Sir, a thorough and fair assessment of all the facts and evidence from the 04/10/18 @ 5.03pm, that in fact I do not have all the um, facts.

* Please note the officer's name is ineligible on ticket, so because I can, I have called him Tim. *

The well-intentioned but a little dim, Officer Tim who offered his kind advice to me that day, was well intentioned, though Officer Tim had some difficulty in his statement he gave me just after the incident. His Story went something along these lines….

Officer Tim – "You were doing 38 in a 30 you know?"

Good Sir "How did you know I was doing 38?"

Officer Tim "Err well I could see on the electronic speed sign on the lamp post, but I got the gun on you as you came off the roundabout"

Good Sir "What speed was that?"

Officer Tim "35"

This brings into focus a few inconsistencies and questions.

1. How did the officer know what the electronic speed sign was displaying? When the device does not display the speed of oncoming vehicles to anything at its rear but in fact only to the front as you approach the device and the officer was parked behind said device?

2. I never once looked at the speedometer during the alleged offence and cannot be certain of my speed. However, I did pay a lot more attention to the police officer and at no time did I see the officer hold a speed detection device?

3. If the speed the officer with the 'speed detection device' recorded 35mph then why would my ticket say 38mph?

4. Is the officer using the 'electronic speed detection sign' as evidence or the 'speed detection device?' which he wasn't holding? It's all triflingly confusing I say.

I have a couple of requests that the **Outstanding and Honourable Individuals** at Cleveland Police could help with.

1. A Statement from Officer Tim who issued the ticket for the alleged offense.

2. All calibration certification of electronic devices involved before and after the alleged incident and of course the evidence itself from the 'Speed Detection Device' and 'Public Speed Display Warning Device on Lamppost'

3. As I have previously stated I have no idea what my speed was so cannot in all good

conscience admit to a crime without seeing the evidence against me in this scenario, I respectfully ask under the Freedom of Information Act 2000 to see any and all evidence against me including but not limited to electronic, photographic and paper based evidence, after which if satisfied, I would of course pay the fine and collect 3 points. If not satisfied then I will of course roll the dice, pass go and proceed straight to an honorable duel in court.

I trust we can resolve this to both our and the public's interest. I know the good work Cleveland Police do, the top awards won in most every category, the highest arrest rates amongst some of the lowest crime rates figures in any place called Cleveland on earth. Superb! ('Disclaimer' 'Best Named Cleveland Police Force in the World' needs considerable research and should in no way be taken as fact).

Yours Sincerely

Michael Elwood - Good Sir, Leader of Men, Founder and Chairman of 'The Party of Perpetual Annoyance Against Plonker Policing' (The 4 P's for short.)

The letter above was sent 28 days after receiving the letter from the police. Below is a transcript of the resulting trial after Cleveland Police would not cancel the ticket. I admit I enjoyed the experience so much I had a lot fun writing it but is a true account by and large of how it went down that day. The story is told from the unique perspective of the Arsehole that lives in me.

PRIXTURIOUS

PART ONE – THE COURT CASE

Chapter One - Arseholes Modus Operandi

Hello, I will introduce myself, my name is Arsehole, I live in the depths of the brain and most people with this infliction are more than capable of controlling said Arsehole. However, our subject today, my Good Sir is in constant conflict with his Arsehole, me. When people first meet Good Sir, I'm not initially very noticeable, never the less and unfortunately for him, I'm a very dominating part. I swear a lot, I say exactly what I want to, I'm grumpy and I complain a lot, I hate everybody, I am angry, narcissistic and maybe a little psychotic. Good Sir does have some power over me. Indeed he is a constant pain in our arse, always apologizing and being nice, opening doors for people, putting people at ease and making even the shyest of people talkative, he's a modern day gentleman, the Annabelle. He tries to be a good person, sees the best in people, is always kind and that's his problem you see, people see that as a weakness to exploit and it would be but for the Arsehole part of him, me, I make sure it is in fact, just a length of rope to see what happens and what they do with it, I have a very long memory and I take all the credit for the high quality and trust worthy-ness of Good Sirs friends, who strangely, love me just as much as him. (Umm) My Good Sir is very outgoing and I hate him if I'm honest. But he's my Good Sir and I need the Nancy so fuck it, I'm stuck with him. So before we proceed with the trial, below is an example of one of Good Sirs and his Arsehole's, erm, indiscretions. Told from Good Sirs point of view.

The scene location today is outside a rather jolly B&Q in a town somewhere in little England and situated outside in the car park, in a little mobile food trailer is Arseholes latest victim, who we will call Vic. Good Sir, "Hello Good Sir! Can I have a bacon and sausage butty please?" Vic "Sure no problem" At this point Arsehole notices the bacon on the hot plate with the fat cut off, as a flash of biblical rage descends upon him, Arsehole, very un-gentlemanly, barges me out of the way, now just a bystander and unable to do anything about it, firmly in charge now, Arsehole "Mate? Why do you cut the fat off the bacon??" Vic looks at Arsehole for a few seconds and says "Because my customers prefer it that way" Ah, the standard reply. You see, Arsehole knows fine well why he cuts the fat off of the bacon for he has had this very same argument in every eatery he's ever been to that cuts the bloody fat off, you know the bit that adds flavour and a nice texture to any bacon butty and it's a, as Arsehole with his own brand of class would say "A fucking diabolical liberty" in his opinion, just because it doesn't cook before the meat part on a hot plate, unless you turn the gas up and use more fat. Arsehole "No you don't, you do it to save time and gas!" Vic doesn't say anything and just looks at Arsehole like he's a well, Asshole. Arsehole continues "Turn the heat up, use more fat, add 50p and you wouldn't have to cut the best part of the whole bloody butty off" Good Sir has no idea if Vic ever took Arseholes advice for he has been to that same jolly B&Q many times since but still embarrassed, he has never had the courage to go and buy one. Arsehole would have no problem, but alas, when Good Sir is just marauding about his daily tasks, Arsehole is usually tightly locked up in his cage. He watches Vic put bacon and sausage in a dry bun "And another thing Pal, what's the deal with no butter on me butty n all?" Vic's face has now turned to pure hate. Vic says through gritted teeth that he has 'Margarine' Arsehole, don't! "Margarine!?" Jesus wept "Yeah mate I'll have a bit of plastic on me butty no problem" Arsehole takes the butty without any butty and pays, still fuming with indignation, he walks away. Good Sir, feeling sorry for poor old Vic now "Arsehole was there any need for that? I'm surprised he didn't throw the wall paper scraper at your head, I would have done, the man's just trying to earn a living" Arsehole. "Deborah! Stop being a pussy, it boils my piss and needed to be said it's the best bloody part and you never know he might have learned something" Good Sir sighs "No Arsehole, he just thinks you're a Dickhead"...

Chapter Two

The Trial – Arsehole's Redemption

Good Sir has decided that Good Ol' Arsehole here should narrate the story. I've told Good Sir he will probably regret that decision but fuck it I'm game. So we will get right to it. All the names have been changed and the following story, although based on truth, is purely from memory and can in no way be taken as fact. The events and comments will be messed up in order and the replies between characters not totally accurate. Everything is to the best of Good Sirs knowledge but there will be some/mostly/unintentional/intentional /everything in between, inaccuracies throughout. Please take a little pinch of salt with it. By this time reader, you should have read the letter concerning PC Tim that Good Sir wrote to his superiors. If you haven't then stop, you complete dickhead and read it. For the rest of you who put the effort in, do continue, you're in for an absolute fucking doozy and not completely accurate transcript of the god dam trial. Good Sir wanted the court minutes but unavailable apparently. Of course any issues with accuracy, we are always available to receive the court minutes and problem solved. We would in fact, donate our left testicle and even consider the right to compare the two, true story. We genuinely don't think they will be that far off and have been as honest as it's possible to be from memory, every Arsehole narrative is actually based on, loosely, a thought that popped into my head or feeling felt at that particular time, obviously I've used some artistic license in those bits but everything that was said in open court dialogue was indeed said at some point in one form or another and the facts of what happened and all the skulduggery, unbelievably, really did happen too.

Good Sir vs. The Establishment. 2pm.
Elwood Vs Ragina

Good Sir is sat outside of court room five, when he is approached by a court official, the court room has moved to court room 3 and there is a delay. 2.30pm - PC Tim arrives but does not go into the witness room and sits close by to where Good Sir and his Arsehole are pacing up and down and have been for the last 10 minutes, practising the role of a defence barrister. Good Sir "PC Tim is it?" It's been 9 months since we've seen him. PC Tim "Yeah"
Good Sir "Excellent! Really glad you could make it" As Good Sir or was it me? Imagines he's suddenly Jason Statham, grabs PC Tim and with head crushed by bicep, ribcage, forearm, in one fluid squeeze and twist of the arm, snaps the lying c@&t's neck. Had you looked at Good Sir at this very moment, you would have noticed him twitch at the thought of the satisfying cracking noise, shnortle a little, as his eyebrows raised slightly in pleasure at the thought.

Really enjoying himself now, every time Good Sir turns around in the PCs direction, the usually nice guy was just staring at PC Tim and pacing towards him, turning, pacing away, turning, you get the picture, over and over again, hands behind his back and with a smirk of righteousness on his face that must of made him look a little unhinged...That was me...For the lying bastards part he looked quite nervous, red faced and could not look at Good Sir for very long. His uncomfortable-ness delighted Good Sir and I. You see Good Sir wasn't nervous or anxious, no, Good Sir was excited and with righteousness on his side, even I have to admit I was starting to enjoy this too. Suddenly, PC Tim proceeded to remove his copy of his witness statement from a folder, with the finesse and care of a professor removing a priceless scroll from the ages. Good Sir, slowing his paces down and paying extra attention to PC Dickhead now, he got the feeling that the PC was looking at His/The Authors witness statement for the very first time, maybe/could have been/it's possible.

2.35pm - The Trial.
The Usher was an attractive and quite short blonde woman who was a very nice lady...not mine...and always smiling, we will call her Sweetheart...also not mine...who helped school Good Sir on how to conduct himself and address the court, also explaining that today the court will be heard by a

district judge and not the usual 3 magistrates. I asked if this was normal procedure. She said yes. To this day we both have no clue if she was right. I mentioned the fact I should of took this to crown court as I knew I'd win with 12 of my peers and of that I have no doubt. Sweetheart smiled and looked like she agreed, though mixed with relief that she was not going to miss today's show after Good Sir teased Sweetheart with his performance in the preliminary hearing when she was last his usher! But that's another story. I think there will be three quite pissed off, now not going to be present, magistrates too.
Usher "Come on in Good Sir" We're only in! He's feeling the excitement now.
Usher "Just stand there please Good Sir" as she led and pointed Good Sir to the Defence bench. The other people present were a beautiful and rather sexy blonde who was taking the court minutes, we will call her Foxy...That's mine...Ma'm and not Ma'am but Ma'm, why I hear you ask? Because I don't like the extra 'a' and find it completely unnecessary and it just doesn't need to be there, according to the dictionary of Good Sir anyway and if the Oxford Dictionary would like to set up a debate on the

matter then I will of course fight my case vigorously. Ma'm the district judge, also a nice lady who Good Sir would class as "Lovely"...Jesus wept... and then the err... He looks to his side and takes in the lady from the prosecution, every fold and every crease, quite a short and erm, stocky woman with jet black, witch like hair, down to her jaw line, and wearing an all black suit, his shock was quickly replaced with his first instinctive thought."Fuck me love, you need to get laid!" So for the duration of the trial, we will call her 'Needs to get laid' or NGL for short.

Good Sir, unable to hide his sickening goodness-ness, thought "I bet she's a lovely woman any other time though" Good Sir has asked me to tell you, prosecution lady wasn't horrible, she didn't look like a witch...much...and I have no doubt in different circumstances she and I would get on like a house on fire, probably. However she's one of the villains of the story so, tough, the thoughts were genuine thoughts and a reaction to one of my court duel opponents and was a first Arsehole reaction, that under normal circumstances would never be vocalized or heard but alas, if I've offended you, prosecution lady, then I'm very

sorry my dear, as no offence is or indeed was, intended.
Good Sir "Hello Ma'm"...I can tell straight away Ma'm, the district judge, was a last minute change and knows absolutely fuck all about this case.
Ma'm "Hello Good Sir" Ma'm went through my name, you sure you don't want legal counsel, the fact they had spelt my name wrong with two L's instead of one and is it a problem. "No, Ma'm, not one bit, especially if it means I don't get my day in court" Ma'm looks at NGL
Ma'm - "Are you ready?"
NGL "Yes I'll call PC Tim in" Good Sir. WTF! "Erm hang on Ma'm, I thought I could address the court first and explain my side and then give the prosecutor the opportunity to withdraw the charge to save PC Tim the risk of committing perjury on the witness stand?"
Ma'm - "It doesn't work like that, the prosecution calls first then you can question him"
Good Sir "Forgive me Ma'm you might need some patience with me today concerning court procedure and I'm thankful for any impartial help Ma'm can give me" Fuck! Again, Good Sir doesn't have a Scooby if she was right. We get the right to address the court first? Don't we? Even

says so in the defence pack, he's Good Sirs star witness and if it wasn't for Good Sir he wouldn't even be here but he has only been planning and rehearsing for it to go in that order, this is going to throw the fucker, I know it. Good Sir has only been in the room for 5 minutes and now has to go straight into a cross examination, double fuck. Deep breath as PC Tim walks in. NGL asks PC Tim his name then asks PC Tim to tell the court his statement. This will take PC Tim all of 3 minutes. He's going to fuck it up the Nancy, I know it. He's feeling the nerves now, out of sequence to what he's been practising. Good Sir has told me to give the TWAT ABOUT TO COMMIT PERJURY a shortened overview of his statement. He basically just told His/The Authors witness statement rather than what actually happened, PC Tim or whoever actually wrote it had the nerve to add to His/The Authors witness statement, which He/The Author wrote 5 months after the alleged offence, and added two blatant and very unnecessary lies, which Good Sir only found out about two days prior to the trial when he received his defence pack, CPS dirty tricks as always. PC Tim/The Author had added the lies he was holding a Unipar Sl1700 speed detection device whilst travelling down the road with the '38mph speed' and again at '35mph' when coming off of the roundabout that PC Tim was situated at but of course Good Sir knows he didn't have one and was blatantly not holding anything and arms firmly inside the van. YOU FUCKING LYING SCIVVY C@&T FACE C@&T. PC Tim you have just committed perjury on the witness stand, oh dear, oh dear, *oh Dear!* Actually would have been quicker to just print the bloody statement. Arsehole shouts at Good Sir "Nancy! Jump over the counter, grab him by the hair and crack his head off of the witness stand a dozen times, nobody would blame you, we can do the time" Good Sir "Calm down Arsehole, as nice as that would be, we just can't"

Arsehole "Pussy!"

Good Sir "Piss off!"

The best way to describe Good Sir and his Arseholes relationship is, metaphorically speaking, Arsehole is "Slim Shady" and Good Sir "Dr Dre" The prosecutor had no questions for PC Tim. Ma'm "Ok Good Sir it is now your turn to cross examine the witness" This is going to go so fucking wrong.

Good Sir "Hello PC Tim, how are you today?"

PC Tim "Hello, yes fine thank you"
Good Sir "That's good PC Tim. Can I please take you back to the beginning when you first witnessed me on ————- road? Can you confirm to the court that after the speed bump and a slight kink in the road that said road is as straight as a die for at least 1 mile? PC Tim "Yes I can confirm this" Good Sir "Would you also confirm that in that particular area of the ports there are no features on the road except for the roundabout at the end where you were parked on and you were directly in my line of sight to the point that I would have had nothing else to look at except you?" PC Tim. "Yes that would also be correct" Good Sir. "The thing is PC Tim, if we go back to the conversation we had after you pulled me over you never once mentioned the fact you had a speed detection device pointed at me to gain the 38mph figure did you? If you remember correctly, when I questioned you about how you came to that figure you said it was the electronic speed detection device you got the figure from that was situated on the lamppost that wasn't facing you? I assumed you meant it flashed on my windscreen and reflected on it for a split second and with the numbers backwards and half a mile away from

your position?" Ma'm interrupts "You need to let the officer answer a question before you ask another question, Good Sir" He looks up at Ma'm "Sorry Ma'm I'm leading up to one I promise" You've just asked three you prat. PC Tim, as I was about to point out to you that the lamppost speed sign was inadmissible you quickly added your little white lie about getting me with your fictional speed gun at 35mph between the two roundabouts. Is that correct?"
PC Tim "No that is not correct as the sign doesn't face me and I did tell you I used my gun"
He goes quiet, he then looks PC Tim direct in the eyes, with anger, disgust and indignation he thinks "YOU FUCKING LYING LITTLE BASTARD!" Yes you did sorta, but I know you are lying you lanky streak of piss because I know you didn't have a gun! For a split second and to my absolute surprise, I thought Good Sir was actually going to pounce and bounce PC Tim's head off of the witness stand and with the, awesome to watch aggression of Vinny Jones in the classic, Lock Stock car door, bad head scene. I'm starting to warm to my Good Sir but he needs to calm down, the numpty isn't good at thinking when angry. Good Sir "PC Tim that is an out and out lie, you

have just committed perjury on the witness stand, so we did not have the conversation that I said we had?" PC Tim "No" Good Sir "I was facing you for the entirety of that journey to the roundabout that you were parked on and you did not have a gun, we both know that, PC Tim stop lying and tell the truth! So when you shouted at me to slow down did you have the gun on me between the roundabout you are on and the next roundabout?" Good Sir originally thought PC Tim must of meant the second roundabout and the entrance to PD Ports, because that was the only time PC Tim was out of sight and he couldn't possibly mean any other time as I know and he knows he never had a gun. Good Sirs entire defence revolved around it being that way and the fact PC Tim was behind him too quickly to have had any chance to get a gun on me and you never, ever do 35mph anyway as the turn in to the yard is only 200 yards further from the roundabout, it's a tight bend coming off and in my rear wheel drive car you'd of been sideways, erm, I assume. That was until two days prior when Good Sir received PC Tims/The Authors witness statement and read the little ripper. What a Revelatory, Bombshell piece of Dynamite that was and turned a boring

Saturday in to a thoroughly exciting one. A proper, spit your coffee out, "HOLY SHIT! THIS CHANGES EVERYTHING!" moment. It was no wonder I only received the defence pack two days prior. I have to say, Good Sir and I didn't even know we needed a defence pack until it arrived, that's the level of organisation and research involved on our part. We just looked at the thick envelope that landed on the mat on Saturday morning with the court stamp on it, one of Good Sir's dogs, Bear was sniffing the envelope and looked at him as if to say "I don't like it Boss, smells funny"

"I know son that'll be all the lies and despair you're smelling, from the morally confused hell that is the CPS" As always Bear looked at Good Sir with his familiar confused look, head to one side, ears raised and tongue sticking out slightly, if he possessed eyebrows and one could move them, then an eyebrow would undoubtedly be raised. We picked it up, also confused but extremely intrigued too, like "Hello, what's this? Best get the kettle on then"...

..."I'm telling the truth and yes I did"

Good Sir "The thing is PC Tim, I had you in my rear view mirror, which is magnified x 2 and

could see you better than when I approached you the first time and once again PC Tim...*YOU DID NOT HAVE IN YOUR POSSESSION, A SPEED DETECTION DEVICE DID YOU PC TIM?"*
PC Tim *"Yes I did"* What an out and out, lying c@&t.
Good Sir "Just admit it! You were as unaware of my speed as I was and you were just using your training and counting between two points?" PC Tim, "That's wrong I was holding the device" Good Sir, feeling that familiar, biblical rage, he fights the urge to "FUCKING KILL THE LYING CU" At this point I need to explain what happened to Good Sir, he/or me/or both got so angry the idiot lost his train of thought and couldn't remember where he was going with the questioning, it only took one minute of babbling utter shite to get back on track and only Ma'm looked up for a second with an eye brow raised, good lad. Except at that moment Good Sir noticed PC Tim had a smirk on his face. Doubly angry now, he then proceeded to lose his way for the second time, for fuck sake, I knew he'd fuck this up. However, at this point Arsehole here, with the speed of The Flash and the power of the Hulk came to Good Sirs rescue and mentally nutted

Good Sir into a jail in his brain and took over this amateur and shit wannabe barrister. Neither of us can remember what Good Sir said or the line of questioning he so royally fucked up on. Now with me in control, blind rage was replaced with a calm and calculated anger, this is the complete opposite to how we usually play our roles, I looked up and took a deep breath. Come to daddy you c&@t.
Arsehole "PC Tim, you know as well as I do that in fact you have been lying this entire time, I know it and you know it, fact. Unfortunately for you, what started out that day as a little white lie to secure the ticket then turned into something much, much bigger. You remember the letter I sent to your superiors?"
Ma'm looks at NGL "What letter?"
Good Sir. "Ma'm, I sent a letter to PC Tim's superiors explaining what happened and to give PC Tim the opportunity not to compound his lies any further, do the right thing and tell the truth. I was very careful to leave his name and badge number out of the letter and spare him the embarrassment and to make it easy for PC Tim to then do the right thing, he obviously choose not to do that Ma'm"
I'm getting into this now.

Ma'm "Erm okay"

At this point I am paying no heed to Good Sir. Had I listened I would have heard Good Sir shout "SHE HASN'T READ THE FUCKING LETTER YOU PRICK, MAKE HER READ THE FUCKING LETTER!!!" Good Sir although confident, tenacious and clever in his own way is also thick as fuck 'in his own way' too and is sadly not blessed with the quick witted-ness that is so badly needed in a defence barrister, it seems I am the former, plus I do not possess the latter either. Indeed, Good Sir and I come up with our most witty and funny comebacks three days after any argument and whilst in the bath or on the bog of inspiration. Arsehole, now forgetting the original question, we've no idea, you can see why we'd love the court minutes in our possession now. "PC Tim, you've lied to me, you've lied to your superiors, you've lied to the CPS, you've lied in your witness statement and *NOW ON THE WITNESS STAND!"*

Good Sir and I, are suspicious that PC Tim's superiors and the CPS are well aware that PC Tim did not have a gun that day and in fact are probably/maybe/it's possible been the very people who advised PC Tim/The Author to add the extra

lies in His/The Authors witness statement. I can even see PC Tim, having read the letter, probably tried to get the ticket cancelled, but they could not let him do that, could they? *"THAT IS PERJURY PC TIM, JUST ADMIT THE TRUTH YOU DID NOT HAVE A GUN THAT DAY!?"*
I'm getting loud now and right into it, like an orchestra starting softly and then building to a crescendo finale.
PC Tim "I did"
Arsehole *"PC TIM, YOU DID NOT HAVE A GUN MAN, TELL THE TRUTH!"*
PC Tim *"I AM!"*
Arsehole (twice as loud) *"BUT YOU NEVER PC TIM, JUST TELL THE TRUTH!"*
PC Tim "I am telling the truth" Arsehole, screaming with anger now and just like the lawyers on the TV when they exert massive, impassioned but still professional and controlled pressure on the star witness or defendant, screaming so loud now and with maximum aggression, I'm pretty sure any people in or around any of the other courts on this floor can hear this.
"PC TIM!! TELL THE DAM TRUTH! YOU ARE AN OUT AND OUT LIER, AN ABSOLUTE

DISGRACE, YOU DO NOT DESERVE TO REPRESENT THE INSTITUTION THAT YOU DO. YOU ARE AN EMBARRASSMENT TO THE BADGE YOU HOLD, YOU SHOULD BE ASHAMED TO CALL YOURSELF A POLICE MAN! YOU HAVE LIED THROUGHOUT THIS WHOLE EPISODE, IN YOUR WITNESS STATEMENT AND NOW COMMITTED PERJURY ON THE WITNESS STAND! WHAT A DISGRACE YOU ARE! YOU SHOULD BE THROUGHLY ASHAMED OF YOURSELF MAN, PC TIM JUST ADMIT THE TRUTH!" PC Tim *"I'M TELLING THE TRUTH!"* Arsehole *"PC TIM YOU ARE AN OUT AND OUT LIER MAN!"* Arseholes performance was like that of a seasoned Old Bailey barrister, it was magnificent for Good Sir to watch, still locked in his mental prison and for a second he thought Arsehole was actually going to break the dishonest prick, everybody in the room was a little startled not least PC Dickhead. As Arsehole flopped into his chair, emotionally drained, shaking with anger, his heartbeat thumping in his chest and disappointed not to break PC Tim but bloody well exhilarated at the same time, he looked up at Ma'm, his judge, his jury but somehow his angel too. Although

Ma'm had a brilliant poker face, Arsehole could tell she actually believed him over PC Tim...or did she?...After what felt like 10 minutes but was probably only 10 seconds he looked Ma'm in the eyes. Arsehole, with a palpable disgust in his voice "I HAVE No further questions for...with a snarl...PC TIM, Ma'm" She asks the PC to stand down. His eyes were burning in to PC Tim as he walked past his position and if looks could actually injure and maim then with any justice, PC Tim's head would explode with bits of brain and shattered bone hitting everyone in the court room, whilst the rest of his body would spontaneously combust and turn to ash, as Ma'm, Foxy, Sweetheart and NGL screamed in abject terror, I would just be sat there, bathing in his blood and guts whilst laughing hysterically but alas, looks, unfortunately cannot do that so that did not happen. Such a shame.

Chapter Three - Arseholes Regret

Somewhere far off in the distance I can hear a faint voice, I recognise it but I can't quite hear what it is saying. The voice starts getting louder. Good Sir like a whisper "AR, ARS, ARSE,

ARSEH, ARSEHOLE!!" Suddenly Good Sir bursts in and he is back in the game *"NO YOU PRICK DON'T LET HIM LEAVE THE STAND!! WHAT HAVE YOU DONE!?"* Arsehole "Hello Pricilla, back in the game are we? And calm down you twat that's a bit ungrateful, you should be thanking me, what's the problem? Good Sir "We needed to ask the twat about the gun, that was really important and I was working up to that!"
Arsehole "Oh shit I remember you reading the instructions, I forgot about that but fuck off you were working up to a hiding to nowhere and without me, you disrespectful c@&t, you'd be dead in the water and should be kissing our feet, I call the left one, kiss it!" Oh fuck, they were rather important questions I didn't ask, the instructions for the Unipar SI1700 device tells you that it saves to a rather large memory and records the speed, direction of travel, atmospheric conditions but more importantly the exact time and date. This means it would have had two entries for that day and at that time. The data would need to be manually deleted if not then downloaded to a laptop which would be routine you would of thought? Umm, good questions to ask and quite pivotal to Good Sirs defence.

Fuckerty...fuckerty...fuck...fuck! Good Sir, now firmly back in control, as if a switch was flicked, he is instantly calm and gentlemanly again, Ma'm looks at him and asks him if he would like to take the witness stand?
Good Sir looks at Ma'm and says "Is that the proper and right thing to do Ma'm?"
He was unsure whether he should just stay at the defence bench. Ma'm nods at Good Sir.
Good Sir "Then that's what we shall do"
Ma'm smiles and I can tell is really starting to warm to Good Sir, you can thank me for that too. Sweetheart usher, greets Good Sir with her usual character-full and big beautiful smile. Even I have to admit I was quite fond of her too at this point. Now who's the Nancy?
Sweetheart "Good Sir, you can swear on the bible or use the other quote"
Good Sir. "I'm not religious at all so the other one" Good Sir can't remember the quote so fuck it we've left it out.
Good Sir "Finally I can tell my side of the story Ma'm. I ask that you put yourself in my shoes for the duration of my statement and give me the same respect afforded to a serving police officer and presumed to be telling the truth."

"PC Tim did not have a gun that day. He simply did not. I was facing him the whole time coming down Teesport road and he just did not. Fact. Nor after I exited the roundabout he was on. Fact. As you heard earlier, If PC Tim was holding a speed gun then I would have seen him pointing it at me coming down Teesport road and just after in my rear view mirror, and more than accepted the ticket, but he simply did not. I would not of taken it this far, nine months this has been dragging on for, all the work, effort and energy put in to this" Clearly nowhere near enough Good Sir.
"Indeed, if PC Tim actually had a speed detection device and there is no doubt I would have seen, had he one, I would of hopped, skipped and jumped into a speed awareness course, grateful for the fact I wasn't getting 3 points and higher insurance premiums! I think everybody here can see I'm being honest"
I can confirm that the soft c@&t that is Good Sir is indeed one of the most truthful of people, but with his inability to control me and saying whatever we are thinking, it constantly gets the prat in trouble.
Good Sir "The fact he's added unnecessary lies in his whiteness statement, lied in fact, throughout

this whole episode and with the passion and conviction that I have displayed, I should have, at the least, created some doubt to PC Tim's witness statement. The content in my letter" (That Ma'm still hasn't read) "Was a true account of what happened and written 2 days after the incident in preparation for the incoming letter from the police. I simply would not have done that had he been holding a speed detection device. He never had his arms above the van doors and they were inside the whole time. Not to mention that it took PC Tim"...Or the Author... "5 months to write his witness statement and then needlessly lied further. I'm here today Ma'm to fight for what is right and try to prevent an injustice. I expect you to side with PC Tim" You prat, what did you say that for? "Because he is a serving police officer and afforded the respect to be automatically assumed to be telling the truth, which I find quite ridiculous. Though admittedly, he's not the brightest of officers" Speak for yourself Good Sir …"and probably why he works for the transport police. The simple fact is, other than his training PC Tim was as unaware of my speed as I was, if PC Tim perceived me to be speeding and that's all it would of been, his perception, then PC Tim

should have, like any good copper, given me a metaphorical clip around the ear and sent me on my way, that would of had a far more desirable affect on me than what has transpired since, I think we can all agree. Though I realise it's my word against his and I don't have any other proof and know, all he had to do was stick to his story, I just hope you can see that I am genuine and truthful. Thank you, Ma'm"
Ma'm looks at NGL and asks if she has any questions?
NGL "Hello Good Sir, can I ask about the speed detection device you say Officer Tim wasn't holding?"
Good Sir butts in at this point
Good Sir "Sorry NGL but there's no point with that line of questioning because there is no version of this where it's possible for PC Tim to have had a gun in his possession, end of story, I know you are just trying to protect your man NGL" She looks at me and shakes her head.
NGL "Ok Good Sir, can I ask how it was that you never looked at your speedometer on that day?"
Good Sir "Very simple, twelve hour night shifts are not the best for the body clock, I was on my 4th you basically are a zombie for the first couple

of hours until your third cup of coffee, the lights are on but you're not really with it, so minor things like watching your speedometer on a straight road with nothing ahead of you"...Except the twat sat on the roundabout "or looking at a lamppost speed detection device are really very low on the attention scale"

NGL "Why then, when the PC shouted at you to slow down did you not look at your speedometer?"

Good Sir "Because I was too busy looking at the burke in my rear view mirror and sat on the roundabout who had just shouted at me and is the other reason I know PC Tim didn't have a gun"

NGL "Good Sir would you say you were watching the road?"

Good Sir "Watching the road?"

"As in, was I looking in the distance as far as possible?" NGL "I mean, were you concentrating on the road?"

Good Sir knows fine well what NGL means but is really enjoying himself so continues being a twat. Good Sir "NGL, define watching the road? Do you mean watching the asphalt? Or do you mean looking as far in the distance as possible, concentrating on what's ahead of you and in this case and the only thing to look at, at the end of the road and therefore the end of my sight line was PC Tim"

NGL "So you were not concentrating on the road then Good Sir?"

Good Sir "NGL, I fear we a going around in circles on this one, you're driving inexperience is definitely coming to the fore"

Good Sir removes himself from the witness stand and in a brilliantly dramatic move bends down and sweeps his arms out to an imaginary road.

"NGL you do not watch the 'road' you watch what is ahead of you, and that was PC Tim" Moving his arms in a parallel forwards and backwards motion, like a cop directing traffic, then rising to his feet.

NGL "So you're saying you WERE watching the road then, Good Sir?"

Good Sir "Yes, that's correct" As he inserts himself back into the witness box. If looks could injure and maim then the look NGL was giving Good Sir meant it would have been his head exploding and body spontaneously combusting.

NGL, looking pissed off and now, quite sinister, she sits down and turns to Ma'm

"No further questions Ma'm"

Good Sir, now thankful that looks don't actually injure and maim, hears Ma'm say
"You may return to your seat Good Sir"
Good Sir "Thank you Ma'm"
I have to point out that, at the time Good Sir and I, were completely unaware of what he had just achieved. I'd like to think we were quick enough to come up with that on our feet but alas we didn't even realise what Good Sir had done until he wrote it down. What accidental gold that was.

Good Sir walks back to his seat smiling at Foxy and Sweetheart and ignoring NGL, Foxy who is now looking at him with her head slightly facing down towards her keyboard but looking up at Good Sir with her big eyes that sparkle in the court lights and with a barely suppressed smile, more a seductive smirk, yes please, madam, he turned his head and looked to sweetheart who as always greeted Good Sir with the biggest of smiles, clearly enjoying her day at work today and probably a little more than usual I would say, he sits down. Suddenly the TV screens in the court room flicker on, startling Good Sir, he looks at Ma'm then NGL "What's all this about then?" He's worried now that NGL has some fantastic

video evidence of some sort that I'm unaware of. The original version of my ticket flashes up. "Why are we looking at this NGL?"
"It's the speeding ticket Good Sir"
NGL stating the bleeding obvious.
"Yes I can see that and I have my copy right here, so again why are we looking at it?"
"Well Good Sir why does the ticket say 38mph?"
Good Sir Shnortles quite loudly and chuckles.
"Well NGL, let's be honest now, PC Tim isn't the brightest and clearly forgot his story about the 35mph with the fictional speed gun, mere seconds later when writing the ticket"
NGL looks at me as if to say "I can't really argue their Good Sir" Thanks NGL. The screen goes of and Ma'm thinks for a moment.
Ma'm "Okay Good Sir can you please stand"
Judgment day, come on Ma'm do the right thing.
Ma'm "Ok Good Sir, here's what I think, I believe that you genuinely believe that PC Tim did not have a speed detection device that day…"
Good Sir hopelessly dejected and pleadingly, he knows where this is going, he interrupts Ma'm.
"But Ma'm I promise you, he did not, there must be some part of you that believes me??" He says it with the desperation of an innocent man who

knows he faces the gallows. I can tell she does really believe us but I suspect her hands might/could/it's possible, be tied on this one. Ma'm "...but unfortunately Good Sir, my job is to find reasonable doubt..."
Good Sir, gets half a sentence out when suddenly Foxy looks up and with the grace of Marlin Munro lifts her perfectly manicured finger to her lips and with a seductive, all knowing smile, mouths, "Ssshhhh" Good Sirs jaw drops slightly. Arsehole butts in "Good Sir!" He is now mesmerised by Foxy and in a trance.
Arsehole "You are going commando remember dickhead and you're stood up, what are you, a fucking teenager" I have to point out that Good Sir can't wear boxers with the trousers he's wearing as they are quite tight and they give him a permanent wedgy, you see. "Get a grip of yourself man, quick look at NGL!" In a flash Good Sir turns his head from Foxy and looks at NGL, suddenly, Good Sir has a mild look of surprise, mixed with confusion on his face as he was instantly repelled and at the same time, righteousness scurried back as if from NGL herself, like a plague of rats looking for safety on a sinking ship, Y'all really are running to the

waves boys, this boat of righteousness is done for but the honourable captain always stays with his sinking ship, maybe those metaphorical rats of righteousness are really sacrificing themselves to comfort their doomed captain. Now firmly back in the game but surprised that that actually worked. Ma'm continues… "Without more substantial evidence, I'm inclined to believe PC Tim unfortunately Good Sir"
Good Sir and I are gutted.
Good Sir "Well Ma'm I think that is the wrong decision obviously and justice today has not been served, if you actually had put yourself in my shoes, like I asked then you cannot fail to see I'm being genuine and believe me, though I expected this decision to be honest. Would I do the same again in the same situation? Yes, dam right I would Ma'm and because it was the right thing to do and that's stand up for justice" Good Sir looks at Ma'm and then NGL and suddenly asks her "NGL, where are the logs for the…" He looks for name in notes "The Unipar S1700 device, there should have been two…" Too late mate and really, I'm sorry. Ma'm interrupts "Good Sir why did you not ask PC Tim this while he was on the witness stand?" Good Sir now thinking "Good fucking

question Ma'm" but didn't actually reply, Ma'm continued "Unfortunately my decision has been made. Good Sir, can I ask are you working at the moment?" Good Sir "Unfortunately Ma'm I have been out of work for sometime after my business failed and I've been battling back ever since, to be honest Ma'm I'm struggling to feed myself at the moment, though I should be back in gainful employment very soon" As a writer hopefully.
Ma'm "I'm very sorry to hear this Good Sir" Good Sir? Or Arsehole? Or both?
"Don't worry Ma'm I'll be back and have I no doubt in my mind I'll be successful, this is just a failure and a lot of life lessons on my journey to get there. Hindsight is a wonderful thing Ma'm and Ma'm that's the first lie I've told today!" That last bit Good Sir can't remember if he actually said or if it was in the bath two days later and what he wished he said, the gimp.
Ma'm looks at NGL and quietly asks her for the court costs figure. NGL "£630 Ma'm" Ma'm thinks for a moment then looks at Good Sir with the devil in her eyes but sympathy in her heart.
Ma'm "Ok Good Sir I'm going to give you the 3 points and a £40 fine is the lowest I can go but you will also have to pay £230 court costs, would

payment in 3 months be ok for you, Good Sir?" Probably not, it's actually not bad really when you think about it. It's like the star of the show buying a ticket to his own play, you perform to your best, please the judges and it's free or fuck up and forget your lines and you pay for the privilege! Its high stakes, drama gambling and it's a bargain for the day we've had and compared to the West End quite cheap in comparison, I should imagine. Good Sir "Yes no problems Ma'm as soon as I'm able I will set up a repayment plan"

Ma'm "Ok Good Sir that's no problem" Good Sir opens his arms wide and smiles directly to Foxy and Ma'm.

Good Sir "Well it's been an absolute pleasure to meet you all today!" What Good Sir received back from Foxy and Ma'm can only be described as big, beaming smiles that really did reach their eyes, if NGL wasn't there then hugs all round without a doubt, what a fucking Nancy but she was, so he turned to her and said "Even you NGL" She completely ignored him and refused to look in his direction, the sour cow. He loved it. Unfortunately Sweetheart was behind me but the smart monies on her displaying an even bigger beaming smile than these two. Good Sir continued

"I've thoroughly enjoyed myself today and it was totally worth taking the risk though I think all of you believed me, I wasn't going to be allowed to win let's at least be realistic, I just wanted to see what PC Tim was going to do on the stand, would he keep to his story and continue his lies or would he tell the truth, this intrigued the hell out of me. I might not be able to prove it but I know and more importantly, PC Tim knows that he committed perjury this day and he knows that I know and that's good enough for me. But what an experience! Righteousness allowed me to enjoy it today Ma'm, as much as I did. Make no mistake though this is an injustice and I'm disappointed to lose but I thank you all and hope everyone has a really great evening!" Good Sir suddenly remembers to ask Ma'm about the court minutes. Ma'm says that "They don't do court minutes in magistrates court"

Good Sir looks at Foxy, confused, jaw drops slightly, mesmerised again, remembers he's stood up, then quickly looks at NGL "Well what's Foxy been doing all this time then?" Risking it, he turns back to face her. Foxy looks down at her keyboard and nobody answers. Some skulduggery going on

here, in fact from the very bloody beginning I fear. Good Sir is not quite finished though.
"Oh Ma'm can you do me one last favour? Can you get a message to PC Tim for me please? Ma'm "Erm" Good Sir "Just a message Ma'm and it's this, I want PC Tim to learn a valuable lesson from this whole episode and leave him with this quote from a great philosopher of modern times, his name escapes me though" Pause for effect, Good Sir coughs
"Impressing your superiors, colleagues and hitting targets should always come second to being Good Police" Wow deep, about 7 months ago that one and again in the bath, no, no I'm wrong, it was on the bog of inspiration, this time. Ma'm looks at him with an eyebrow raised and confused look on her face, but nevertheless she nods, everybody else just blinks at me, all the while with slightly bemused looks. Now if PC Tim ever reads this and PC Tim I really hope you do. If you don't know what that quote means, copy rights Good Sir, then you really shouldn't be a copper PC Tim but I'll still help you out, it means "Sometimes being a good person is more important than using a pure copper instinct to be an overzealous twat and is preferable in some circumstances" Copy

rights Good Sir. PC Tim clearly does in fact suffer from the same Arsehole infliction as Good Sir but plainly PC Tim's condition is a lot more chronic than his, or is it? Good Sir as he starts to walk away, turns and with one last big smile and wave, all returned again by Ma'm, Foxy and now Sweetheart, he says "Good bye girls, what an absolute pleasure" He turns and walks out of the court room, he really should of turned back around and bowed at this point and after that performance who could blame him. This was one of the best experiences of his life and as Good Sir and his Arsehole walked out of the court room with their collective head held high, bursting with energy and on one of the biggest highs of our collective life, we both mentally screamed at the same time "absolutely fucking loved it!" He walked down the steps to the ground floor, nodding and smiling at all the surprised and bemused looking G4S security guards, clearly ready to mobilise with all the angry shouting and as he exited the building, chest puffed out, head held high and with the air, the grace, the pride and the dignity of a man who knows, beyond any doubt *"HE DID NOT HAVE A GUN, YOU FUCKING LYING CU…"*

The End

From this point Reader, there are some very, quite long words from me but if you have put the time in, well done and I thank you, I hope you enjoyed it, ergo nobody would blame you for not reading the rest of my babble. Have a great evening Reader, Sincerely, however the rest of you, or if you've now thought about it and are thinking "Umm I want to hear what he's got to say actually, fuck it I'll stick around" Outstanding! Thank you Good Sir/Ma'm and let the good times roll.

Chapter Four
Glorious Ol'Bastard Ranting

Hello, I hope you have enjoyed Good Sirs & his Arseholes trial transcript. I hope it's obvious that Good Sir and his Arsehole are a caricature of the author and he isn't actually mentally ill. A little nuts? Yes definitely, though aren't we all? I believe, one cannot truly be one's self until you just accept and embrace your nuttiness. Although I was obviously disappointed to lose my case I know that ultimately I did the right thing by fighting it. When you realise that some very wrong skulduggery that was performed all the way through. Dishonest and lying PC, fabricated witness statement, false testimony and perjury on the witness stand and not to mention wrongful conviction. It's definitely not very good reading is it? Not to also mention the red tape entanglement efforts to put me off all the way through. Let's not forget, taking advantage of an inexperienced member of the public's lack of court procedural knowledge. I genuinely don't think the police expected it to go all the way to court. When I look back they seemed quite worried to be honest with you and just kept digging a hole. The Police seriously misjudged my pig headedness, hatred of skulduggery, pride and shear love of adventure and the never to be underestimated, Fuck it & Fuck Em Philosophy of Life. Too many people roll over and just accept the charge and that needs to change. Police need to learn that they are people first and coppers second, they are not above the law themselves and need to be brought to account and kept honest. It is they who should be on the side of justice and the police seem to have forgotten that. The least you could expect if a copper is to nick you is for the collar to be fair and square and after following due process. "Bang to rights". "It's a Fair Cop Guv" This case was not about the speed awareness course or the 3 points and £100 fine or whether, I was actually speeding or not, no they don't matter one bit and are not the bloody point at all. It is about something much more important than that. It is about right and wrong. It's about, due process and above all, Justice. I have absolutely no regrets. What can we learn from my experience? Always take it to crown court and a jury of your peers, if I had, I have no doubt I'd of won and so I bloody well should have too. Always put the effort in leading up to the trial. The 7 P's, Proper, Preparation, Prevents, Piss, Poor, Performance...I count 6. Is it really a clever and useful riddle, do you think?

I know I really could have prepared better but fuck it, it wouldn't have been anywhere near as good if I had. God forbid that I might have actually won. I have to be honest and explain that from the time the letter was sent I really didn't give it much thought from that point on and every now and then I would get letters that were just an annoyance and reminders of all the bullshit. My life since the day I met PC Tim changed dramatically and I had a new business that I believed would be the making of me and quickly lost any interest in the PC Tim and all of his own making, Bullshit Drama. However my business failed, for various reasons, a book in and of its self and all within 6 months. I then lost my head for a couple of months but luckily I found the mental strength to come through it and just in the nick of time for the bloody trial! Whatdoyaknow! It was just meant to be PC Tim. So other than some hours day dreaming about how it could possibly go down, I only actually put a total of around 4 hours research, reading defence packs, filling out forms, sending emails and that includes the preliminary hearing and for the trial. Though, the original letter took a good 20hrs to write. I'm definitely just a "Fuck it, I'll just have a crack at it, see what happens" kind of guy. If you can find the strength to see it through and can defend yourself then I highly recommend it. I feel like I've had a insight to the working life of a defence barrister, a really diabolically shit one mind! I believe I now have a little experience into what it's like and why they never complain about the boring parts of court life. What a buzz.

Chapter Five - The Factualish and Well Argued bit

Speeding is a fact of life but it's not the problem on our roads, no, that's reserved for bad anticipation, poor observation and not concentrating, the "Sorry mate didn't see you" brigade and can be blamed for most accidents and as another great philosopher of our times once said "Speed doesn't kill it's coming to a stop suddenly, that's what gets you" Rather than speeding alone which is only attributed directly to 7% of accidents and the others above are many multiple times higher. The police have the moral high ground and use it to justify the number of people caught. However, the public are not stupid and knows it is all bullshit, especially when they see 'Police' in camera vans on motorway bridges and all the other dodgy tactics used. Don't get me started on "Smart" Motorways. Make no mistake the speeding prosecution business is just that, a business and a highly profitable one at that, it is protected in countries the world over, by the police and the courts and why it's vitally important for them to keep the status quo and actively crush actions like mine to discourage the public. "Oh but we don't get the money it goes straight to the government and they decide what to do with it!" That might be true but anyone who can read between the lines realises the government just gives it straight bloody back, obviously they do because if they didn't then the police would not enforce speeding with quite as much gusto. That is not to say I am for speeding per say, especially in 30 zones, near schools, parks, built up areas, accident black spots etc, no if you get caught in urban and residential zones then you are bang to rights and should be prepared for the consequences if a bobby catches you but as long as the rule of law and proper procedure has been followed, who can argue? Though just like you I also live in the real world.

I'll let you in to a little secret, on our motorways there's a club, a lot of drivers don't even realise they are members but the name for this group of road users is "The 90MPH Club" In a broad mix of roles involved in why the club members drive so much on motorways and back roads, couriers, sales reps, railway workers, road workers, engineers, doctors, mangers, directors, executives the list just goes on, all drive up and down the motorways doing many thousands of miles a year and always at 85/90/95mph, here comes the controversial bit and I believe it whole heartedly. The club members are the safest drivers on our roads if that's you, you will be nodding now, welcome to the club, you will understand straight away what I mean but if not and you are actually, a lefty, remain voting snowflake, 45 in a 60 kinda driver, foaming at the mouth with indignation at the controversy of it all and are 'offended' Not one fuck given, then you have a duty to read on and hear me out, you might even learn something. The clubs drivers are the safest on the road not because of the speed they drive, although it is important but because they are the only drivers who are properly concentrating on the road ahead, scanning as far in the distance as possible, always anticipating and observing what's happening at all times, at the same time with cat like instincts for what's behind, on gantries or parked on bridges or in lay-by's, it even combats tiredness. They are, metaphorically speaking, Maverick and Goose and the Police the Russian MiG-28s both very skilled and professional drivers. You develop instincts like in this following example "Being able to anticipate the prat in the slow lane doing around 65mph thinking about his tea, coming up to a lorry and he hasn't even twigged, he's going to brake in about 2 seconds, his indicator will come on and he will pull out seconds later, without looking and right in to the club members path but in a split second club members have anticipated this and 3 seconds ago, have already moved over to the fast lane, the members instinctively knowing what idiot driver was going to do before he did and idiot driver never even knew they were there" This example and many like it happen regularly to the club member and they are so used to anticipating other road users, they never seem to be involved in any crashes themselves, indeed they are usually past any developing hazards before they happen. I believe the members all suffer from the same Arsehole infliction. They can be angry drivers especially at poor driving or not being acknowledged by a fellow driver for a good turn, for club members this is a particular big cause for Arsehole to come to the fore, just acknowledge us you ignorant bastards. That said the members are more than prepared for getting caught, especially if it's a "Fair cop Guv" Members in reality, rarely do get caught.

However, we do get the odd idiot driver trying to join the club but natural selection and/or the police usually sort that particular membership problem out so all's good on that front. Unfortunately, speeding is used as a target based cash cow exercise and that's because the 'Sorry mate didn't see you' crew are much harder to catch and fine but result in many, many times more accidents.

Chapter Six - To the Establishment, Police, CPS, PC Tim and the Girls

Just imagine if this story inspires people and you suddenly get just a thousand more people wanting to experience being a 'Fucking Terrible Barrister' clogging the courts up and suddenly it starts to cost a lot of money because if I'm paying £230 court costs, who pays the other £400? God forbid that you actually win! Suddenly the high profit making speeding business is an unviable and loss making one and all the public needed was the inspiration to stand up and be counted and make it happen. If this story inspires people to do the right thing or missed the point completely of why I did it and do it just for the craic, I'm not saying you should do that without just cause mind and has made you, the Reader chuckle in the process then it has definitely been a worthwhile endeavour and my absolute pleasure, Reader. Though something tells me you might be one of the lucky few who get to read this. No adulation and celebrity life for Good Sir now. The doors it could open. The money it could give me to realise my entrepreneur potential. The different path it could have made. The reason for me thinking this is because the Police will read this first and something tells me they cannot let me publish it, time to get the check book out boys, luckily for them I realise that had I went down the adulation road, it would of instantly propelled me to a "golf ball size boil on the Establishments collective arse" Luckily for the Establishment I am a proud Englishman and patriot at heart and love Queen and Country dearly and bloody well passionately too. Ergo, I felt I had a duty to come to you, the Establishment first, so let's be friends and see if I can open doors this way instead, as I really dislike boils. If you the reader can be classed as 'the general Joe' and you are reading this then the police didn't respond and I'm a very, very happy, well known and hopefully, rich man. Now bare with me here people.

I, as the author, want as many people to read this as possible and enjoy it as much as I did living and writing it and the realisation that that maybe won't happen kills me inside a little so I have a solution. I am assuming that you have academy schools that train the up and comers? Right good, so if you have a spare jail cell available, then, post haste, turn it into what Legend calls "The Room" said in a spooky and dramatic voice "The Room" would of course have a gate keeper, maybe an old maintenance guy or cleaner, whatever and each recruit is afforded 2 hours inside "The Room" with no electronics or clothes, only a government issued forensic suit and under the watchful eye of 4 cameras, defo promote the maintenance guy any serving or ex coppers could bribe him a tenner to have unofficial access, could be a good earner for the old bugger that could.

A few decades down the line "The recruit, since being a boy has listened in wonder, to his cop father talk about 'The Room' in hushed tones with his colleagues, about the most mystifying and curious of legends in cop folk law. He is almost foaming at the mouth in anticipation to his birth right and can finally fucking read it! The recruit is

permitted to inspect all the evidence and read what legend *calls "The Story, a Secret Manual to the Secret of how Not to be a Copper"* but only when or if they pass. The recruit is then sworn to secrecy to only discuss this with the people who have been patrons of "The Room"
Oh, if you could swing it, that I get access every couple of years I'd appreciate it, ta.

PC Tim, I hope you read this and take something away from it and learn a valuable lesson, I'm not hopeful but I forgive you, you could not anticipate what would happen next. I thank you, actually PC Tim, for you have provided me with hours of entertainment and inspired me. You helped me become a shit defence barrister and now an even shitter writer. I've had an absolute ball. I still have turrets when I ever I say your name but I'm getting control over it, I have, good days and bad. Thanks for the Good Times Tim. I'd like to thank the CPS for not letting me win and for only sending me my defence pack 2 days before the trial on a Saturday and containing a vital application to make PC Tim testify! Let's not forget that doozie of a witness statement. But of course had I won, it would have made nowhere

near as good a story. Imagine the tag lines "Good Sir Wins over Adversity"
"Justice Prevails for the Common Man" "Thoroughly Good Sir Beats the Establishment". Boring.

Instead you gave me,
"Oppression, Rule's Britannia's Justice System!"
"Burning Injustices for the Common Man in Our Courts!"
"Lies, Dammed lies & More Lies, A Story of Police Corruption!"
"Good Sir Sent to the Gallows from Dodgy Police Testimony!"
"Nice Guy Crushed by the Establishment" or my personal favourite
"The Big CPS Stitch Up - Time for a Rethink?" Skulduggery always makes for better headlines. I'd like to thank the Establishment in particular, for forcing PC Tim to see this through, got to protect the "Business" Guv! And not least Cleveland Police, firstly for employing PC Tim and secondly to thank you for pushing it this far, I could never of planned, anticipated, nor, could I ever, in a million months of Sunday's, made up what has transpired since I met PC Tim that

fateful day. Once the letter was received, I expected to have the tickets withdrawn and indeed, that would have nipped this in the bud straight away. I might have had a little fun with the letter but that would have been all. I'm so glad you didn't as I've been gifted a rich pot of an absolute fucking gem of a story, all the way from start to finish. You literally could not have made this shit up. I'm not against the Police or the Establishment and just remember it wasn't me who started all this, the only reason I wrote the letter, this book and represented myself so haphazardly was because I just *"BLOODY WELL KNEW HE DID NOT HAVE A GUN THAT DAY, THE LYING F..."* So I decided to have some fun with it and oh, fun with it I had. Thank you all because strangely, it feels like all of you, PC Tim, The Police, CPS and of course our 'Needs to get laid' (Me too NGL don't worry) really helped me along the way and I'm grateful to you all, sincerely I am, I'm sorry you picked on me that day Tim, as my friends and family would testify "This could only bloody happen to you Good Sir" Usually followed by head shaking disbelief or "You're an idiot" nodding, one of the two. I mostly thank you all because you have inspired me to become a writer, or typist as I like to call it, I'm going to write/type a book series on Good Sir and his Arseholes unique, insightful, heartbreaking and of course, funny life lessons and I think I can help people and I also need money to become the entrepreneur, I believe I can be and start my Bee charity maybe this is how I achieve that? Last but most definitely not least, of course the three lovely ladies Ma'm, Foxy and Sweetheart, you made it an absolute scream and I know you volunteered to usher, Sweetheart. Probably some strings pulled by the three pissed off magistrates, I can imagine it now.

Madge to NGL "WTF you mean, the district judge is hearing this, the fuck she is! NGL "Sorry but the decision has been made Madge, so you will just have to do as you are told won't you!"

Madge "FFS!!! Ok but Sweetheart is ushering, we want to know exactly what happens!" You could probably hear most of it Madge, as NGL walks away he turns to the other two magistrates "Bitch!! She really needs to get fucking laid" Again, I am positive that she is indeed lovely our NGL, I mean that too, no, really! My usher, she does look like she tells a good story, does our Sweetheart you can be my usher anytime! She was present at the preliminary hearing you see, big smiles and all. So was the Magistrate from the imagined conversation above though they have their own court rooms to usher/judge and that definitely wasn't Sweethearts usual court room. Ma'm, I hope, in my story I've not brought into question your integrity!? If so it's completely unintentional as I respect you greatly my dear and just as my integrity cannot be questioned, neither can yours, or can it?. Along with the other two lovely ladies you three are really the only blameless and innocent parties in this whole sorry but immensely enjoyable episode and I thank you all for your patience that day. Ah...The beautiful Foxy, an absolute pleasure and if you could sneak those court minutes to me I'd be extremely grateful...

Chapter Seven Just for Love
I have a girl, or nearly had that I love very dearly, who I let down, badly and I believe she has my heart lock, stock, she is the love of my life, she is just like me in so many ways and not like me in so many other awesome ways too a bit mad and daft

just like me and been through tragedy in her life just like me, I just need to convince her now, so I would like to add a 4th innocent and lovely strong lady to the story if I may girls and use this opportunity to tell her something.

Hello Beautiful, I'm so sorry I let you down, when it became clear the business was going under I really had no choice but to close and I realised I wasn't just walking away from the shop but you too. I went about it all wrong and could/should have handled it a lot better and I'm so sorry. I was also battling depression at the time and didn't really know it. What I've been through since that day has been profound and the hardest 5 months of my life and you helped save me, you beautiful being. I fell in love with you the first time I met you and just knew straightaway you were the girl for me. I was so reserved with you because I was your boss. Though I could not tell you this because of the boss thing and I was trying really hard to be professional when really I just wanted to do this...

He looks over at this most beautiful of girls, inside and out, she's unlike anybody he's ever met, to him a gift from a kind angel who sprinkled some magic dust on her way through and sent this sweet girl his way. She is devoid of any of the skulduggery traits of the human physique, a rose in a dark, brutal, dishonest and morally ashen world. She lights up any room she's in and people can't help but gravitate towards her. She is washing up after a busy service but not really concentrating on the task, her mind elsewhere, he notices the familiar subtle but heartbroken look on her face and knows instantly what she is feeling because he has had those same unbearable and heartbreaking pangs that come with the devastation at the loss of somebody who you loved dearly. His heart shatters at the sight of her grief, for he knows only too well, the bond she has lost and in that moment all he wants to do is run to her, grab her hand, pull her into his arms and whisper softly in her ear "It's going to be ok, I'm here now, you're not alone any more". At that moment still fighting the urge, watching her over the other side of the room still, he decided he would like the honourable task of making sure that this angel never feels sadness again. Indeed an impossible task but one he swore he would gave his fucking all. He knows she feels this connection too, but he's her boss and he is trying to be a good man so she has to come to him"

Stupid fucking morals! You unfortunately never got the chance because I had to close and lost my head maybe that was actually a good while before? Probably I don't know. You did nothing but support me, route for me, believe in me, you made me want to be a better person and I let you down. In all honesty the only reason the shop lasted as long as it did was because of you. The irony is I ended up making you, this beautiful creature, sad and upset and it kills me to think about it. The last 5 months of my life since then, I believe I have been on a profound journey of discovery and every time I hit rock bottom and thought I couldn't get any lower I just kept falling, until I hit the absolute bottom and complete hopelessness. Somehow I managed to find the mental strength to battle back, all because of you and the thought of "What if I sort myself out, become the man she needs me to be and maybe/what if/is there still hope?" I needed to find out and you, my girl, gave me the strength. If I can't win your heart and it's too late, I just want you to know I will always be so grateful to you and will love you until the day I die, which without you, my dear girl, would of come to pass by now, I fear. I thank you from the bottom to the top of my heart and I wish you all the happiness in the world, with me or sadly without me, you beautiful, sweet, funny, awesome girl. I owe you everything and I love you and I always will my Cheeky Blinder. xxx

Alas this might just be, the greatest story never told. Arsehole "PC Tim, I just want you to know I don't forgive you and also tell you something. Good Sir, the wet lettuce that he is, is so soft, there's a small part of him that was pleased you didn't break and you kept your job! Indeed, he has been trying to protect you from the beginning. Why? I've no fucking idea and neither does he. Reader, I hope you can see why I hate the Margaret by now but alas, PC Tim, I still think you're a c@&t, and a dirty fucking lying one at that and you always will be"

Good Sir "Good Times and well Played Arsehole, in fact, very well played indeed, old boy"

The Real End

The date was July and August 2019 I wrote the PC Tim story above. The story below is the considerable consequences of that fateful decision.

PRIXTURIOUS

PART 2

Michael Anthony Elwood

Witness Statement and Testimony.

I hereby swear that all information is correct and true and happened as told. I am of sound body and mind. Please release in the event of my death or unexplained disappearance/accidents etc.

Introduction

Imagine you created something that was truly ground breaking and would be the making of you, something nobody has done before and it was you, yes you that came up with it. Your creativity created this and only you deserve to profit. Fair comments you would say? Reasonable expectations you would think? Yeah me too, that is until you figure in human nature and its very selfish, greedy ways.

What you are about to hear is a story of betrayal, skulduggery, subterfuge, back stabbing, manipulations of epic proportions and a pretty clever plan to make a person think they are mentally ill. Family, friends, Cleveland Police, some very nasty underworld and business characters from Teesside, are all involved in this great tale of woe.

Why I hear you ask? Well we have to go back to the beginning for you to really understand. My name is Michael Elwood, by now my reputation and name are in ruins; my life is in danger and all because I came up with a new version, my version of the Teesside Chicken Parmo and stood up to my local corrupt police force. Now my recipe is ground breaking and for a few reasons of which I will go into more detail later. The problem is I am or was, a very trusting man. I had a vision of how people are and thought the majority of people of this world were kind, cared, were trustworthy and with integrity. Old School values. If I met you I would automatically assume you possessed these qualities. Oh what a stupid and silly twat I was, as you are about to hear...

Chapter One

The Parmo Recipe

What is a Teesside Parmo? Essentially, butter-flied chicken breast coated in breadcrumbs, deep fried, topped with a thick and creamy béchamel white sauce, topped with cheese and grilled to perfection. Sounds easy, doesn't it? It's not trust me. That's why so many takeaways and restaurants get it so wrong. They are stunning if done right, simply horrible if done wrong. The major majority are in the latter category.

May 2017

In May 2017, I had decided, after my father sadly passed, the year previously, that my future did not belong on the railways and I decided to accept the voluntary redundancy that was on offer. I knew what I wanted to do but I spent the first year, after accepting the redundancy, just enjoying myself, like most people stupidly tend to do when in receipt of a substantial pay off. My dream was to open a pizza shop and make beautiful food, delivered to your door. Being a big fan of the Teesside Parmo but always let down when ordering one, I thought I knew what the dish was missing. There are over 60 pizza shops in Stockton On Tees, each and everyone makes Parmo's using the same suppliers, ingredients and using the same methods. Absolute garbage and I would be enraged when I ordered one and the pitiful excuse for a Parmo that turned up. Eventually, I just stopped ordering them. Once in a while I would be feeling adventurous and after hearing of a new eatery that did a nice Parmo, I decided to order one but again they were just simply rubbish. Looking back it was getting on to 12 years since I'd had a good one delivered that I did not have to make myself. So after having fun for a year I realised I needed to sort myself out and get on with developing my recipe and develop a recipe I did!

August 2018 – September 2018

What was it that I thought a Parmo was missing? Well in the Pizza shops case, everything. Quality and flavour being the main ones. You see the art of making a Parmo was sadly being lost. Even restaurant versions weren't as satisfying as they should be. Why? For me it was the fact that the coating was always soggy and it seemed the bread crumbs were the same flavourless type in most cases. That was the main quest, to figure out how to keep that lovely contrast in texture, crispness right the way through, a crisp strong enough to withstand the white sauce and cheese from making the coating soggy. After experimenting with lots of different ingredients in the coating, I eventually found what I was looking for! Boom I was right! I had hit the proverbial nail on the head. What I did not anticipate was the realisation of what else was happening. This magic coating was doing something else to the Parmo's. What was happening with this coating, it was providing such an airtight seal around the chicken that the juices in the chicken breast were actually evaporating within the chicken and unable to escape, it just made it so bloody beautiful and tender! This meant the fat in the fryer could just get on with the job of making the coating crispy, add to that the spice mix I used, beautiful and creamy white sauce (the pizza shops generally use margarine instead of butter if the white sauce isn't out of a supplier made, absolute tosh and inedible, tub) and the best cheese mix you can buy in my opinion, made for probably one of the best Parmo recipes ever made. I realised very quickly that the recipe was good enough to make a Domino's style pizza shop chain and get Parmo's nationwide! I watched people eat them and just absolutely and positively salivate for the next bite, it was the best feeling ever! I was making people really happy with my food! I can't describe the pride that will encourage! Now to put the recipe to the test. I proceeded to make around 30 Parmo's over a week and made my lovely triple cooked chips with the skins still on, a tub of garlic sauce and salad and delivered them to local Parmo lovers in the area of Stockton that I live. The response? Unreal! Comments like "You will make millions with these" "The best Parmo's I've ever tasted" "Get your shop opened now!" "You have ruined every other Parmo for me now!" Overwhelmed but bloody well excited I looked at how quickly I could get trading. "This is it Little Mick you've made it!' Yeah, that hindsight again, mate you had a lot more work to do you naïve fool, I really needed a mentor with this type of business experience, looking back. I should have made a proper business plan and done this the right way but unfortunately for me my learning curve is fuck it all up spectacularly in many and varied ways then become really good at, whatever it is I am trying to get good at. I grew up believing I was useless and indeed my persona growing up was that of a simple idiot, though I think if you would of understood my learning curve it might of saved me a lot of trouble and a really wasted 36 years, nobody looked hard enough and told you are not the brightest enough times you tend to believe this narrative. I started to realise I was good at something when I was out with my father on the motorbikes back in 2008. Now my father Big Mick, is my hero and I spent most of my holidays, from the age 11 to 15 on the back of my old man's bikes bombing around most of Europe to various

European racecourses. We had some brilliant adventures and I have many funny stories to tell. It was awesome and that's when I got to know big Mick because up until that point I never really knew my dad as he wasn't big on home life and was building a pretty decent career and worked his socks off. I don't have many memories from my really younger years with my dad, say 4 to 9 years old, Xmas days and holidays are the most prevalent and thankfully too. Good memories and for the rest of the time, my later years with my hero, rock, inspiration, teacher, friend and coolest bike rider in the world, this more than made up for any thing, real or imagined. I have bug bears like any son but I will not hear a bad word said against him. He was the kindest man with a very big heart and I love you and miss you dearly Ol'man. I say old man but he was only 59 when he passed. My mother was 39. I am your son Dad and that's the truth. Anyway, I've kind of went off piste there so, Yeah, Na, Um, oh yeah, we went riding and Jan, my step mother told me that in the pub later he had told everyone how good of a rider I was! He said I was really talented at it but don't tell him I said that! I was stoked for weeks, still am. I then proceeded to have a really serious bike accident and was air lifted to hospital. It was in the script obviously. I started to wonder, though, what else might I be good at? Quite a lot it turns out. Who knew? Anyway back to Cheeky's.

November 2018

I have to point out, I had absolutely no business experience and had cooked for a maximum of 6 people at one time, though I am an excellent cook if what I was cooking was something I enjoyed myself. At this time I had to get myself back to work and I decided to do my HGV licence a year previously and was working as such at this time. I absolutely hated it and with a passion. I loved the driving but the not the industry. My experiences in the HGV industry would fill a book in and of itself. I enjoyed the actual driving aspect and was actually very talented at it but every other side of the industry just disgusted me and I had my business aspirations. This is where my old friend "Gary McCarten" came in. I was sat in my lorry cab for 5 hours waiting to be unloaded when I realised that Gary had recently taken on a pub in Teesside and had a free kitchen. Now Gary is a bit of a wrong-un. I met Gary a number of years ago and not one to judge someone for their choice of business, I had a good relationship with Gary and his "hardest in Stockton brother" John and classed them as friends. I was not interested in what they did to earn money and it was none of my business either. So I asked Gary if I could rent the pubs kitchen from him. He jumped at the chance. Brilliant! I then came up with the brand name and then got the brand designed. Cheeky Devils Parmo's was born. We opened, Friday, Saturday and Sundays for three weekends until I realised, the kitchen was not up to the standards of a commercial kitchen and knowing that environmental health were coming for an inspection soon that they would just shut us down. I also realised that the pub itself and its patrons was inhibiting anybody from actually coming to the restaurant. Though, it had served its purpose to prove the potential of the food. We did quite well and we gained a very big following in a very short space of time. I was very grateful to my "friend" right up until the point he stole my ingredients book out of the kitchen! Now I was not stupid enough to leave the book around unattended, usually but this day I stupidly forgot to take it with me, realising five minutes after leaving that I had forgotten the book I turned around and went straight back. Gone and so was Gary. Gary had been quite suspicious that day, looking back at it.

Yes Gary could see, as soon as he tried the Parmo's, the potential of the recipes too. Now I was only 85% sure it was him and was willing to give him the old benefit of the doubt until one day a couple of months later I ran into Gary's wife in my local shop and when she noticed me, she proceeded to completely shit herself, literally like she had seen a ghost and went very pale instantly. Now I was 150% sure it was Gary, thank you Gary's wife and I was very angry and might have been a bit vocal about it too, you fool. Just pissed off a well connected mid level Teesside Gangster there you have Michael. Oops.

Once I proved the potential of the recipes the first thing I did was go and see my Uncle Martin. Now Uncle Martin is a successful man, now retired, he was quite high up at not for profit company and was a well respected and connected man. Realising my inexperience I knew I needed a mentor and business partner but unfortunately I just could not get him interested or excited at all about Parmo's. He did lend me £1k though. I intended to prove the recipes at the pub and then hopefully get some proper support and guidance from my Uncle Martin. Something changed and he was not interested in helping me. Later he realised the potential and does Indeed, become a dishonest prick, though that fact will become clear later on. I realised I am on my own! I started to look for a new and better set up premises and through a friend I had found one sort of. The premises was previously used prior as a pizza shop and was called "La Pizza Bella" and was full of the equipment needed to run a conventional pizza shop. My friend set up a meeting with one of the owners. This is where we meet "Rasheed"

December 2018 to March 2019.

Rasheed is a successful Asian business man, very scruffy looking, short and portly with big bulging eyes, drives an old van, always wears a beanie hat and looks like a scruffy builder. It all belies the fact he is actually a very rich and ruthless man who with his other two partners owns a large percentage of Middlesbrough. I have to admit I quite liked Rasheed to begin with and upon meeting him, me being the idiot I was, I told him my goals with the recipes. He was very supportive. However I had huge reservations on the man and the premises. The problem with the premises was it was essentially just a room without a shop front and he wanted 6k for all the equipment in the shop. The equipment was worth the money and would at least get Cheeky's up and running again, though we really only needed the fridges and work tops. My gut was telling me this was a bad idea but unfortunately I had not learned to trust my gut feelings at this point in my life. Everybody around me was advising me to go for it and reluctantly I signed the lease on the 4th December 2018. With the benefit of hindsight I realise now that I needed to wait, go back on the lorries and get a proper shop in a much more suitable area.

Cheeky Devils Started Trading from La Pizza Bella on the 16th December 2018 to much success. We continued the great following we had started at Gary's pub. Brilliant reviews and we were very busy. Unfortunately the business ran me and due to my lack of experience I put far too much on myself. I would be going to multiple suppliers every morning, then preparing for service, then running the service. I was working 14hrs days and simply forgot about normal things like eating and ended up making myself very ill! Turns out I was passing a kidney stone, though when I went to hospital it was put down to an STD! Thanks, North Tees Hospital. I shut the day before New Year's Eve and did not reopen until the 4th. The stone passed on the 6th thankfully. We only did a five day service, Wednesday to Sunday, because nobody really bought takeaways on Monday or Tuesday. We were trucking quite well, on the last five days service we turned over 2.1k and that covered 5 kitchen hands, 7 delivery drivers, stock costs and left a couple of hundred for the shop! Excellent. This meant we would be profitable in the coming weeks! That was until the last night's service. At around 9pm the electricity suddenly went off. It took 30 minutes to come back on and ensured we were right up against it. Customers were now waiting 2 hours for food. Not good. Then at around 22.20 it went off again and this time stayed off, with our final six orders on the board. We unfortunately had to cancel them. Without hot water, lights etc, we had to abandon the shop. Until I got to the bottom of the problem I was also unable to reopen. The problem was that the shop was ran from a domestic 62 amp circuit and should have been ran from a minimum 100 amp commercial circuit, we had over heated the incoming 10mm cable which should have been a 16mm or somebody was playing silly buggers with the electricity box. The quotes I had to upgrade were absolutely ridiculous and predictably Rasheed said no. I could not afford it but I was planning to buy gas fryers anyway. We would just have to do with 62amp. At this time I was waiting for my business loan to drop and had applied for 13k which turns out was nowhere near enough. Two weeks after closing it landed but I was in such a mess financially that 4k got swallowed up with personal and business bills. I then had to hand over 6k to Rasheed for equipment I didn't need and needed restoring to be able to get the best price. This took too much time and with it being specialised equipment, I was unable to wait for top price. If I'd had the time, I would have been okay but I didn't and we needed our grills, fryers, hot cupboard etc. Basically I ran out of money before we could start making it again. Devastated is not the word. Yet I felt relieved to get out of the situation.

What else happened whist Cheeky's operated at La Pizza Bella? Now there is a very good question. The first being my next door neighbour, the delightfully fake "Jane" who it seems likes a bit of the brown as she is definitely shagging Rash! You know what they say, once you go brown you never come down. The saucy wench. I suspected very early on that she could possibly have a spare set of keys to the shop. I could just feel somebody had been in and after Janes very probing questions about my recipes, by this point she had obviously tried them, I was very suspicious of both Jane and Rasheed. So with me being quite paranoid at this point, due to Gary like, I went into Jane's pretentious gaff and quietly asked a staff member if they had "a spare set of keys as I have forgot mine" The Staff member dutifully went in the safe and produced the keys, I smiled made my excuses and walked out. I hope he didn't get too much of an arse kicking. Trust me she's that type of boss.

There were two occasions when one of the two locks on my door were left open, somebody left in a hurry after hearing my stupidly loud exhaust on my BMW (Yes I over compensate for something I'm 36, I do need to grow up) which always gives good warning of arrival. I was very OCD about security and always quadrupled the checks on locks and windows. I also realised when Rasheed took a hell of a lot of interest and watched what I was doing, intently whenever he was in the kitchen after obviously trying the recipe he instantly knew I was right too, not daft is our Rasheed. Rasheed is a multi millionaire and I'd told him how I planned to take it nationwide, after all they are that good and that different and really taste good and made with passion. Why? Because I care that's why, if your meal was not good enough, we messed it up somehow then I was bloody disgusted with myself and really actually beat myself up over it. That is what made them as good as they were, not just the recipe. I was forced to do the breadcrumbs at home to hide what goes in. Once mixed you really cannot tell what the ingredients are, thankfully. Jane would watch me intently through my very open windows, as this position was the smoking corner for Janes gaff. Also including people living in the flats or "the spies" as myself and my staff had come to call them! I also had it confirmed. Myself having always been trusting, I have inevitably been let down a lot in my life. It is a lesson I seem to subconsciously to be unable to learn, well until now at least. Now there is not anybody I trust, well maybe one. So a staff member from next door popped in to borrow some chicken which just happened to be Halal and they had some Asian customers and they wanted to sample next doors Parmo's. Oh, did I forget to mention Jane made Parmo's too? Or the fact Rasheed owns a restaurant which makes them too? Um. Anyway knowing the skulduggery being performed around me and realising it really is starting to become a recurring theme, I said to her "Ah, come on Donna just admit it you and Jane have been letting yourselves in trying to figure out the recipe and methods, haven't you Donna?" I said this in a jokey and mate like way, but her reaction was hilarious, Donna is a biggish girl, quite short, very fair and the sort of gal that cannot hide emotion because her rosy cheeks betray her feelings way too easily and guilt or embarrassment, especially. Donna proceeded to turn bright red and looked like she had just seen the ghost of Hitler carrying her own decapitated head in his arms. She proceeded to about turn and literally run out of the kitchen muttering something ineligible. I was gob smacked. Wow, Confirmed and spectacularly too.

She reappeared like a scared rabbit 10 minutes later. "Jane said its okay now, they've changed their mind" I bet they have Jane. Oh to be a fly on the wall in that pretentious gaff. Also, Jane told me Donna just so happens to have a husband that does leaflet delivery. He did not deliver the 5k leaflets like he was supposed to. I asked any new customers and nobody had received one. £60 and the cost of the leaflet menus. I hate you fake Jane. You and Rasheed are made for each other and I hope you are happy you filthy wench and dishonest businessman/gangster.

Next up is the electricity con and the scary flats basement theory...

So Rasheed decided that I didn't need to sign up with an energy company and all because the electricity metre was in the basement of the flats and no energy company has ever had access since Rasheed converted the old collage. I got told unknowingly to Rasheed by someone in the know that the reason the equipment is in the shop was because the owner of La Pizza Bella was a Turkish gentleman who through some monetary skulduggery pissed of some middle eastern gangster who had sent over two middle eastern gangsters to cut him up and retrieve money owed, knowing this the Turkish gentleman high tailed it to some place unknown and Rasheed told me he never actually paid his electricity bill and the estimation was a lot higher than the actual reading and I would get lots of free energy. I smelled a rat and I'd actually already spoken to a company and made a deal. Rasheed told me to tell the company I'd shut down and cancel the deal. I looked into this and if I had operated for any length of time, I and not Rash would have been liable for the full shebang! Upwards of forty grand I would say. The basement under the flats actually spooked the shit out of me especially after witnessing one of Rasheed's partners, who can only be described as the Asian version of Ving Rymes, 6ft 5in easily and with double tires in the back of his head and about 6ft wide and always in a smart suit. I once witnessed him direct two lads holding a dirty mattress down to the basements door. Of course my imagination played havoc with me, did the Turkish Gentleman really flee?? I'm scared! Seriously it freaked me the fuck out I'm not going to lie! Was that for me? My recipes and my methods planned to be gained by torture? My mind sometimes but honestly who knows, I bet that basement can tell a few stories, I'd say. I once got a bit shirty with Rash because he complained about the mess from the last night's service in the kitchen and I was pissed off because he had been in, surely on a lease he is prohibited without me there? Those eyes were a sight, quite unnerving. At the time I couldn't have gave less of a shit and let him have it totally forgetting who I'm actually talking too and it's highly likely I had just offended a rich and powerful local businessman. Oh dear. In my defence I could see the skulduggery performed around me at this point and can be forgiven for being a twat. Its right to say that my heart simply was not in it at this point, in fact it was just days before the business went under. I realised my mistake fairly quickly after signing the lease and was gutted really. I had royally fucked this up and there was nobody to blame but myself, though I am racking up powerful enemies at this point.

I need to mention the slight attempts at intimidation by the local pizza shop mafia. This included visits in the car park and abuse shouted at the shop, dickhead driving too. The car park is very dimly lit on a night and the shop is in a funny position and its pitch black outside Jane's gaff and at the other side of the shop too. You could easily be set upon from many angles. Then the Don turned up in his 8 series BMW with 3 heavies in toe in a separate BMW. Nothing says I'm a pizza shop gangster more than turning up in two 4 door cars and only four people and the king in the big expensive one on his own. I was really amused. They all do seem to be weary of me. He was friendly enough to begin with though he did try to insult me a couple of times but I was wise to his game and fronted him out. He stated he was here on behalf of the pizza shop owners in the area and wants two large Parmo's to take back to all the owners and dissect them, then figure out how I make them. I loved this, really? Good luck, for if you cannot tell in the raw mix you have not a hope in hell when cooked! He made me assure him it was Halal, which it was grudgingly. I'm not a fan of Halal. Nothing to do with Islam or race, I just simply don't like it. Sorry if that offends you, as none is intended to anybody native or otherwise. I dutifully made the Parmo's personally and made sure they were pukka. I hoped it was the nicest tasting food they had ever eaten and often wonder if they figured it out? I doubt it very much. Later on I did start to worry about this location and actually how badly set up on a night time it was. I realised I could not leave the girls alone really, unless it was absolutely necessary. I didn't realise straight away but there are easily 30 pizza shops in a 2 mile radius from my shops location and all ran by a certain section of society and when they started buying the shops, was the pin point of when the Parmo making skills started to go downhill. That is not racist but fact. It is more to do with the inexperienced moving in and the experienced moving out, along with the lack of will to learn or figure out how to make them well, it doesn't really make a difference where the inexperienced are from, the resulting loss in quality would always have happened. Those are my conclusions anyway. They were very worried about Cheeky's. When I say that they make the Parmo's all the same way and with the same ingredients I was not joking. It's like they all had a big meeting and decided "If we make them the same in every shop with the same cheap ingredients then they have no choice and nobody gets an edge". Then I come along and blow people away with my Parmo's, making a buzz in the area and online at the same time and start to take their business. In the end I have to admit I was glad the business went tits up and away from this situation, which my guts where telling me was a bad one to be in and only going to get worse, plus I needed to get away from that cellar, which I believe there was a special place down in the darkness for me and still is. I believe they sussed out my recipes and methods in the end.

Now I could do it properly and in the right location, after using the lessons painfully learned. I had a lot of internal and external issues to resolve before that could happen.

Chapter 2

The Court Case Aftermath and the Family and Friends Betrayal

In this chapter I am not going to tell the story of the actual court case, no that doozy has already been written and is still ongoing because I will be appealing, so it's not actually finished yet. Though if you are reading this then you have access to the book anyway so go read it and I hope you enjoy it as much as I did living and writing it. (Part one was a works all on its own at the time of writing and was only recently added) No, what I want to explain is the aftermath of that brilliant day, one of the best of my life and I've had some bloody good days, its not all doom and gloom. After Cheeky's went under at the end of March, I went through a period of depression and managed to come through it a few weeks before the trial. I felt brilliant. Inspired. Excited for the future and what might be possible. After Monday 15th July 2019, the trial date, something profound happened to me. Two days after the trial I was reliving in my head, the court case and its drama. Now at this point I was only planning to write a transcript and with the original letter post it on Facebook hoping for it to go viral and help me get my name out there and noticed. I had been gifted by Cleveland Police all the way through and because I was in the right I was going to take full advantage. Out of nowhere and whilst reliving the case, I got what I can only describe as a bolt of inspiration. Suddenly I knew what I had and in a split second I knew the start, middle and end to my book "Fuck You PC Tim" as I called it at the time. I furiously, in the notes of my Iphone 8 plus funnily enough, I spent hours hunched over that thing, I started writing the story. After two days it was my sister's graduation at Teesside University and for the first time, my family witnessed Mikey Elwood in full swing with members of the public. Now I will try to not sound too arrogant and remember my humility lesson that I'm really struggling to learn. I have an addiction, yes a serious addiction. Though this addiction is not drug related, no, no, I'm addicted to making people feel good about themselves and noticed some years ago that I am quite good at it.

A lad I met years ago, Hessy, he's a proper bona fide character is this lad, can hold an audience of some 100 people in a pub and have them eating out of his palm. Witty as hell. When I first witnessed Jamie in full swing, I was in awe of the man. I got to know Hess and pick his brain a bit over the years. This is what the mad little ball of pure muscle, I call him a badger, it's a complement Jamie don't worry, departed one Xmas night. This will have more meaning because Jamie spent Xmas evening around mine one year and was as quiet as a mouse, almost shy. Surprised and a little shocked, I asked him about this and he told me this peach of wisdom of a now very important lesson. What he said was...

"You can be who you need to be and when you need to be it, you just need to believe it, tonight I don't feel the need to be anybody so I'm just relaxed and taking it in"

You more than anybody, Jamie me lad, are responsible for the man I am today, what a insightful and awesome quote and really profound, I have gave that quote many a thought since that night. "Copy rights, Sir Jamie Heslop" And I guess I just started to compliment people more when ever when I was out, but the reactions I got were not one of offence, or unwanted attention just a little joy. From that developed the ability to actually walk into a room and own it. Just having a crack at it and see what happens. I could walk up to and talk to the toughest alpha male in the room and his lass and crack on with them and have them both laughing and smiling. Walk up to a table of 12 beautiful girls and all eyes would be on me, I could engage them as group and within 10mins knew every single one and be having a scream, all the while my scared mates are hiding in the bar down stairs. It's like there is an aura around me, people would be sat minding their own business and looking bored, then I would come in to their orbit and suddenly they're alive again smiling, in a minute I've got their names and they are happy, not quite sure what's happening, then as quick as I came, I'm gone and like a sudden release of a spell they are suddenly confused and a little stunned and are left thinking "What the fuck just happened?" I love it. The best one is seeing a person struggling with their confidence and a little sweet comment, said in the right way could make the day of that person and I have a sixth sense for it. For what took me 5secs has made somebody's day and made them feel good and that makes me feel good. One day whilst buying ingredients for the shop at ASDA in Darlo, I noticed a checkout girl, she was funky looking, blue hair, nose ring, eyebrow ring and looked like a cool little funky version of Harley Quinn. She was 17 or 18. She had a right face on her, did not look happy at all. As I approached her check out I saw her colleague who happened to face her in the next check out, scowling at her. I could taste the work place tension. A bit of a professor at work place tension, I surmised straight away that the other women was telling this young girl off about her appearance. I thought she looked cool as fuck. After she served me, she had perked up a little, I paid, looked ahead and not looking at her, I said, in a cool slightly American twang "Thank you funky checkout girl". I turned my head and was greeted with biggest smile I've ever witnessed, well more a surprised and shocked half smile, half silent scream, her eyes wide, I smiled as I looked at her and I seen her surprise and joy, I winked, she reverted to a normal and big smile. If she could have she would have jumped up and hugged me I think. I had called it spot on. With her looking so sullen I had not noticed how beautiful she actually was. I told her and bid her farewell. She was beaming. That is my favourite example out of many. I hit the nail on the head with my summation and the other middle aged women looked like her head would explode. If there was any justice it would have. I hate work place bullies. I hate bullies in general. The dour and sour cow. I have relived it over and over since that day and it still makes me smile every time. I know that bonny and funky lass will always remember me. I think it is in a way something I developed to cure depression, for sometimes those experiences would keep me happy and positive for days, weeks and even months. As addictions go I don't think it is a bad one really. Is that selfish? No I don't think so, okay I do it to make myself feel good, but I only feel good because they feel good now, I can't see any losers to be honest. It was this newly learned talent of being able to work a room and engage positively with pretty much everybody I meet that made me realise my potential. The graduation was eventful and I think my family had started to realise this potential too by then and see that I had more talent and intelligence than I had ever been given credit for. They had seen what a confident and happy Michael Elwood could be. For the next three weeks after the graduation I did nothing but write. Very quickly, I'd finished the start, middle and end but then the real work began. Endless hours of reading and changes and additions and corrections, it became an obsession, I loved it and hated it at the same time. I was so happy and inspired. I was planning to appeal the conviction so the story wasn't even finished. What I created was brilliant to me but ultimately it's anybody who reads it, they are the judges. All during this time I was sending out drafts for people to read and this is when the mental health

rumours started. My family seemed appalled at what I had wrote, my sister Carla, could not understand it, seemed to think I had wrote the book with her in mind?? Me either. She went to great lengths to try and convince me it was shit and "There are ghost writers out there, who can't get published what makes you think you could?"
"Why don't you just stick to lorry driving, it's what your good at!" or this beauty "My final thesis was 11000 words and took me 3 years to research, why is yours 14000?" I don't know sis, maybe the fact it's all true? The fact the source material was fucking gold? Most writers never get gifted such inspirational material to draw from, most wait at least a life time if they achieve it at all. My research was achieved in 45 minutes of living a court case, what else was she expecting? Study law for three years maybe? My niece Laurencia was supportive at first and told me it was brilliant and then suddenly she changed. Between them both they tried their very hardest to make me believe I was mentally ill and tell anybody who would listen the same too. The thing is I was really suffering for a couple of months after Cheeky's went under and nobody was anywhere to be seen and didn't want to know.

Now all of a sudden I am mentally ill? No, I was and needed help but I came through it without theirs and now they are worried? It all came to a head one day before I had finished the draft in its current state. Laurencia locked me in a room and I could not get out. Now my sister and niece are feisty lasses and we are a loud family that don't listen to each other in an argument ever. It's a pointless exercise for me, I once recently whilst arguing with my sister on the phone and completely on purpose spoke over my sister for a full ten minutes and she didn't notice once that I was speaking and talking and how she can't hear me and it's absolutely pointless. For ten whole fucking minutes. I even stopped talking at the same time as her. It was amusing. I've learnt to just walk away and talk to them later about it, when they can see other view points and the annoying high pitched wail of indignation has thankfully disappeared. I loved them dearly. This is why it was so heartbreaking.

Laurencia had been waiting for me at her Mums one day, knowing I was coming round to do some work on Carla's laptop and word to format the book. I'd noticed Laurencia's car outside and knowing she was going to be straight at me after we'd had an argument over something, I cannot remember now, I went to a friends for a couple of hours hoping she would leave as I did not want this aggro in my life any more, I ventured back and she was still there. Fuck. Ignoring my gut instinct I went in anyway, Bloody fool. Boom she was at me. I tried to get away but no, she removed the broken handle from the front room door and I was trapped with my tormentor. I had what can be only described as a panic attack and got extremely angry. Now I have never nor would I ever hurt a girl and indeed I did not hurt Laurencia, that day, I just tried to move her, after some moments my sister opened the door and I immediately calmed down, though I might of told Laurencia a home truth or two, one of the things I said was "You know Laurencia, I'm sick of these battles over everything I do, You always think you know best but I usually prove you wrong! Have you not realised yet that maybe, just fucking maybe, I know more than fucking you?! That maybe I have talents you do not, maybe I can see things you and your Mum cannot? You have got confused girl, somehow you think you are the Auntie and I am the Nephew. It is not that way Laurencia and telling me I'm just like Paul, well maybe I am. I know why Paul walks away from you in an argument, it's the same reason I walk away from your mother, it's a pointless fucking exercise, that's why" I could have said so much more and wish I had. She did not like this one bit and screamed that I was "Insane" "Mental" "Crazy" I have to point out that I was so angry and shocked that my family thought this about me when actually for the first time in my life I was okay. My mind was at peace for the very first time in my adult life, why would they do this to me? This was one reason I was so angry because I could see what they were doing. It did not make sense. Why would you try to bring somebody back down and back into depression like that? Somebody you love too? It dumbfounds me to this day and will forever. I guess only they know the answer to that question really. The thing is, I was in such a bad place from April until the end of June but nobody wanted to know then. That was when I needed help.

I walked out of my sisters and I never spoke to my niece again for 3 months. My sister went on holiday with Laurencia and her boyfriend Paul and he paid for Carla to go, this was around the time Carla changed tactics. I think from that day forth Laurencia decided to set out to prove she was cleverer than me, more devious, greedier, selfish, nasty, uncaring and more evil than me. I had basically scorned Laurencia and brought forth her natural spite and seemingly made enemies of the rest of my family in the process. Fuck me doesn't take much now does it? Now was the holiday where the scheming started? I would say so yes. However, with Carla's change, I was wise enough to play the game and pretend I knew she wasn't up to something. All of sudden when Carla returned the bitchiness stopped and she was full of fake concern and was extremely nice. Like a switch had been flicked. Operation "Make everybody believe Michael is crazy" had started. The problem with my sister is, yes she is very clever and congratulations on the first but she is not clever in the skulduggery stakes. Me either sis. You have to be a c**t to be good at that, isn't that right Laurencia and Paul? This marked the day I began to be subject to endless lies and manipulations from Carla and from afar Laurencia too. Carla is extremely inept at keeping secrets and when it comes to lies and subterfuge I can read her like a book. From August 2019 to Feb 2020 she was clearly playing a part, acting and a really fucking bad actor to boot too. She also left a good few clues. People contacting me at her behest and forbidden to tell me that but obvious nonetheless and just to gain information. It seems there is a big difference between academic ability and common sense! I've collared on straight away that she was suddenly really interested in what I was up too, my plans, anything really and after the holiday she was so fake in comparison from before she went with Laurencia and Paul. Where before she was hostile and always being snappy and rude to me, now she was my best friend and really sweet and nice but fake and so not naturally our Carla, it was actually really funny to witness and play along with. I did give her a certain benefit of the doubt, in a naïve hope that I was wrong but as time went by I realised she was at the centre of these rumours and later I realised Laurencia was in deep with this too.

My sisters ex boyfriend, has a big hand in this. Step-hen he is called and is an immoral scumbag of epic proportions and is much schooled in skulduggery. Very sleazy and shifty looking, been to prison a couple of times and is a right wrong-un. My sister loved him and stupidly thought she could change him. They split up and I was buzzing, but like a fly around shit he didn't want to let her go and neither did she. A fan of fucking lost causes and idiots is my sister. He moved out and proceeded to rent a flat from, you will never guess who, Rasheed! Only in a flat across from the shop and above that cellar! The plot thickens. I had stupidly allowed Step-hen to use my address for his correspondence and there were many attempts to make me extremely angry at him so I would go to Middlesbrough and do something stupid. Things like getting mobile phone contracts, blowing in a garages for fuel, the boss came to see me expecting me to pay, yeah, I don't think so mate, blowing in big hard pay weekly car dealers, he was really sound actually, a visit by Cleveland Police too and the big one. On this night I was at my local pub, the Rimswell in Fairfield, first time out in weeks, my sister was there and I was pissed off about the phone contracts, well never guess who turned up? I could see the trap immediately and went into the pub to stop me from chinning him. He went into the toilets. Now, I wanted to walk in and hurt him I am not ashamed to say as

Step-hen definitely fosters those feelings in people but I know better than that and could see the set up and my morals will not let me do something like that unless you come at me first. Knowing Cleveland Police are itching to have something over me I did the clever and right thing and stayed at my table. He was very pissed off and left. When Carla, stupidly told me how upset he was it really confirmed my suspicions. By now the mental health rumours were absolutely everywhere and told by people who had spent no time with me. I was back in depression over it, somewhere I didn't need to be again. I just could not understand why this was happening to me. This night in the pub my friends went too far and basically told me they think I am ill. My ex friend, Lee Russell actually set me up and got another friend to start on me just to see my reaction. I stood my ground. I fucked off home. When I awoke the next day, I spoke to my sister and she said that when she went home, Step-hen had turned up and they'd argued about the phone contracts as Step-hen had sold the phones apparently and in a rage Step-hen had thrown an ironing board at Carla and broke her nose and gave her a black eye. Only did he? I've had black eyes before and never have the bruises completely disappeared in 4 days, ever, the bruising goes through a process and turns different shades as it heals and this "healed" far too quickly, clearly her nose was not broken. I am of the opinion that this was a set up designed to enrage me and get me to Middlesbrough to sort Step-hen out, which would have been my pleasure, except he knows Rash and lives above that cellar. The other very suspicious thing is the fact she rang my "friend" Lee and he sat with her in North Tees Hospital apparently. It just doesn't add up. Usually I'd be the person she would ring. It helps that my niece is very talented at make up too I guess. The paper stitches just did not look right and nothing was visible when she removed them later. Around seven days there was nothing to show but it was the bruising that was the giveaway. I surprised Carla the next Saturday and she was very suspicious, like, shit I need to sort something quick before he sees me. She was in bed when I arrived to use her laptop and had been drinking the night before and stood at the top of the stairs trying to look at me whist twisting her head and upper body away from me, like she was guarding something. Suspicious as fuck, I shnortled and walked away. I need to state that a few weeks earlier Step-hen was pulled over by Cleveland police and swabbed and found with cannabis in his system. I was at my sisters when he set off. He rang my phone ten minutes later from the coppers phone to speak to Carla, why? Well it is known tactic from Cleveland since drug driving laws came in and the police basically target habitual cannabis smokers knowing they will fail a road side test and then get them to do little favours for them allowing the perp to keep their licence. Now he is living at a Rasheed owned property just over from the shop and above that cellar. Carla, also fucked up a good few times. The mental health rumours were everywhere by this point, stepped up because I purposely let my sister know my upcoming plans to see her reaction. I'm not ready to tell that part yet, it comes later don't worry. It seemed to me that whatever my plan was to get myself out of the shit, people were then one step ahead of me and pre-empting my plays and getting to the people concerned first with the mental health narrative.

This had even reached friends and family down south and could really have only come from two people, Carla and my Uncle Martin. How was my

Uncle getting the info? Who from? He had let slip some info on my life that he would simply not of known and was actually incorrect as had my Grandma, Big G. I have my suspicions that the answer lies in my Dads old friend Cleggy. You see Cleggy, knows people close to me and I believe has been feeding info on my life back to big Uncle Martin. What would Martins motivations be? Three reasons I can see. Firstly he has realised that I have the talent and potential to be one hundred times more successful than he will ever be. That scares the shit out of him. He was a big Director at a not for profit company and achieved a lot and was a star within that organisation. He has a train named after him. Now the thought that this little shit and black sheep of the family might possess the ability to knock him off the top spot of most successful Elwood ever? That will not sit well with a proud man like Uncle Martin, that won't. The mad thing is he is the jewel in the Elwood crown and I was proud of him and his achievements. I wrote him this letter

"Hello Uncle Tony, Sorry it took me so long to write this email and contrary to what grandma says, I'm not being a coward by doing it this way, more it's just easier to get all my points down that I want to say and a lot more

thought goes in to something like this than a conversation with which I always miss things out and forget to say everything I want. Firstly, I wanted to apologise for being a pain in the arse and the way I reacted when I visited last. I' sorry if I have been distant but I wanted the next time to see you to have a profitable business, but it wasn't to be this time. The £1000 I owe you will be paid back asap. As soon as I am working regularly or get up and running with the business again, I will set up a standing order. I really do appreciate you lending me that. If I've caused you any headaches, I'm sorry, that was never intended. Ultimately, I am not your problem and nor bloody should I be either. Ok I was disappointed to have failed to get you excited over Parmo's but that's life. Would I of had a better chance to succeed if I could have got your support? Yes of course I would have, there is no doubt in my mind... the catalogue of errors might not have been made with the right guidance and advice. But does that make it your fault? No of course not and not one single milli-percent Uncle Martin, if that's what anybody thinks I thought. Why would it? It was my failure to find what was needed, nobody's fault but my own. I can't fault you, if I were you I wouldn't of bet on me either, but I do believe in myself and think I'm capable given the right support. Yes, I thought when you lent me the money, I had indeed gained your backing, how could I fail with you behind me advising me! Let's be honest I could not afford to pay for your advice and support on the open market, but when it became apparent that actually it might not be there and I wasn't able to garner your interest in Cheeky

Devils, I'm not going to lie I was gutted. I would have loved having you in my corner! Dad was irreplaceable and the greatest man I knew but you are a man I look up to and respect greatly and since Spa before dad passed, we had become friends and I really liked that fact and hope that remains. With my dad I was always ok if he was there supporting me, guiding me and was proud of me and I guess with hindsight having somebody to not let down was what I was subconsciously looking for and missed the most, I didn't realise how much I needed it. I've failed miserably at life so far without him, but I have learned so much in the process, all hard life lessons but ones that needed to be made, I think. I know the sensible thing to do now would just be to give up, admit defeat and get a full-time job, the job bit I'm doing anyway but the giving up on the business I simply cannot. I believe whole heartedly in the potential of it and knowing how successful it could be, given the chance this time round when done right and, in this location, I must fight for it. I enclose my new business plan for you to look at, all I am hoping for is feedback on it and hopefully you know any investors who could possibly be interested in looking at it and helping me, I am sending it out to potential investors but it needs some feedback first and would be grateful for any help at all. You know looking around at all my cousins, Carla and Lauren, all of them are doing very well and I am proud of all of them and every single one is a credit to your generation of the family and Grandma obviously. I will make you all proud of me one day I just take longer to get there and hopefully when I do that's in

Big Gs lifetime. Anyway, have a read and give me a shout with any feedback.

Thank you,

Mike

Now the second reason, When I emailed the letter above I also sent a business plan for Cheeky Devils. During those months of battling my internal strife and 2 months before the trial I found the will to write my new Cheeky's business plan. When it was ready I sent out, to mainly family, the finished article. Now I was very proud of this and was expecting really good feedback and I would have sent it out straight away. I waited weeks, in fact not one of these people even acknowledged I had even sent anything, except two, my step mother Jan and my very good friend Katy, though I had to ask. This was around about 6 weeks before the trial. The others who did not comment included, Carla, Laurencia, her step mum Emma and of course Uncle Martin. Not one single word of encouragement or feedback. Nada. By now Martin and our relationship had become very strained but I still have no idea why. Towards the end of June I wrote Uncle Martin the heartfelt letter above and meant everything I said. I sent it all hoping for his advice and feedback or even if he might have known somebody who could help. Nada. I actually thought it was so bad that it needed a complete rewrite. I find this very strange to be honest with you. After around two months and having wrote the book and realised I could write, sort of, at this point, I re-read it. It was really good. I should have sent it to Duncan Bannatyne or someone like that. I started to re-read everything I could find from the past, my later years there were clues that maybe I had a little ability to write. Various business plans, complaining emails to companies, the letter I sent to Cleveland police, letter of support for colleagues at work facing the sack things like that, all really good, now I am suspicious about this. What's really going on? Why the silence and also why are my family telling everybody I am mentally ill all of a sudden? To anybody who would listen too? It seemed these assumptions of my mental health had reached everybody but not just that, something else but what else? I can only speculate but the telling thing for me was when I tried to contact my cousin Gareth. Now Gareth was the black sheep of the family originally, an ex heroin addict with a long rap sheet, he has been MIA from the family for neigh on twenty five years. He reached out recently and having turned his life around and it was really good to see him. However, I was in the middle of my re-birth and we did not speak again since that day about 8 months ago. I did however, speak to Big G about him and persuaded her he deserved another chance and I persuaded Big G it was the right thing to do. Now I tried to contact him and he is completely ignoring me. I can see Big G telling Uncle Martin about this and reaching out to Gareth and making it look like it was him whilst discrediting me. The rest of the family, have seemingly turned their collective back to me too. Not only family from that side but Laurencia's brother, my best friend and brother Steve Perkins son, god rest him, whoever god is, I don't know on that one. We were really good friends Jamie and I and are family. His other brother Martin, the spit of Ste in looks but sadly that is all. He has real mental health issues and stupidly I tried to help him and he returned that love and family bond I tried to provide him by robbing my house on a number of occasions. I once rented a room out to a lad called Michael and he proceeded to empty my loft of a pretty valuable train set and a family heirloom. I never go up there and did not notice for months. I'll find you one day Michael. Or was it a set up by my Uncle Martin? Now there's a thought? Of course I can see this will have got back to Uncle Martin and the family and will have been changed to, I sold it, probably or it was a set up by Martin? Just a thought...Yes I believe it was, the mad thing? All he had to do was ask for it and I would have happily gave him it.

Reason number three is the EU. I have been an out spoken and very effective persuader on Facebook and ruffled a few feathers. Now I did start to get noticed by the EU and of course my Uncle Martin could see my antics on Facebook because he was my friend on Facebook. Now my uncle knows a good few powerful people in the Big Smoke and with him being a big believer in the EU project, it's possible he is part of that powerful Remainer cabal in London and myself, being the complete opposite and out spoken Brexiteer, I now realise I might have made us natural enemies and turned my Uncle against me. I would not take it that personally but when you realise it has been a political war the last three years and how desperate Remainers are to remain, it's not an unrealistic possibility if I am honest with you. I have during this period since the business went under been financially fucked to say the least and have had to sell a lot of my possessions or stuff as I call it. I was unable to work for a few months while I sorted myself out. I also sold a lot of my dad's possessions to Cleggy. Now, if it belonged to my dad then Cleggy wants it. I obliged knowing that, when and not if, I become successful I will buy it all back. As much as I am weary and have a dislike of Cleggy, I at least trust they would be in good hands. We're talking three Motorcycles and his tools. I think they might really be for Uncle Martin. I don't think he is a good person is my Uncle and I could say a hell of a lot more, especially about the time I lived with him, but you know what? Those history lessons are just that, history and that's where they will stay and do not pertain to the current story and would only serve to be spiteful. I will say though Martin, I have apologised for my behaviour on multiple occasions from when I lived with you but have never received one in reply. You were an adult and do have more to apologise for than I. Curious. I was an emotionally fucked up ten year old who's

Mum was dying, what's your excuse? I am better than that and him. He made me promise that if I ever need help or want to sell the bungalow to come to him, especially on the bungalow. I was made to promise first refusal to him. The Bungalow was my fathers and I had helped him out by signing on to a remortgage when he divorced the Queen back in 06. I proceeded to forget until I went to buy a house and couldn't because I already owned one and needed a much bigger deposit. I have lived here on and off for the last 20 years. This used to be such a happy home when my dad lived here with Jan but since then the laughter has faded and in its place desperation, depression, anxiety, sadness, hopelessness and despair. This is what it represents to me now and is also my prison now too. I fucking hate this place. Sometime in between the business going under and the business plan, I went to see Uncle Tony to take him up on the promise he made me make. I just wanted to start again at this point and get away from these rumours, do Cheeky's down south instead, fuck Teesside. Yes, he said no, predictably. Now I am Indeed, in a mess financially and sussed the reason the help was denied. Why pay me x amount when he can just wait until it is repossessed and get it dirt cheap? He was very sheepish, with bright red cheeks, very un-Martin like. I got quietly angry and made my excuses and left. Looking back he looked very apprehensive and a little scared. Ironically it was me growing up that was scared of him. This confused me. Why would he be scared? This is a man who was the proper bona fide alpha male. Legend has it, he knocked the hardest in his school out whist in year eight and the other boy was much bigger and in year 11. He ruled that school for the rest of his time there. A man who was used to arguing his case in board rooms, with government ministers etc, why would he fear me? A guilty conscience maybe? Was he already planning skulduggery? Who knows, but I do wonder and he changed completely after that business plan and my Brexiteer antics online? Could it be he realised what I would have achieved with it and with the right guidance and support? Reasonable assumptions when you read between the lines, I would say. It is worth noting that Cleggy used to get belittled and bullied by Martin back in the day and even in adulthood. Yeah, he did the same to my dad too. My dad did not really like his brother until much later in life. I think he always felt in his shadow and being belittled and lauded over didn't help.

What about Carla and Laurencia's motives, well now that is a very good question? I'll deal with the latter first. You see, Laurencia was the first person to see I might be a lot more capable than meets the eye and consequently was, other than Jan, the first person to believe in me. This made me start to really believe in myself. I will always be grateful. Sometime, during this time Laurencia and our relationship changed. The roles were reversed, I had become the nephew and she the auntie it seemed. Everything to do with anything business or with Cheeky's was a battle and argument and I was always wrong about things. The problem was I would stick to my guns and fight my corner and the majority of times I was eventually proved right. I stopped engaging about the business so much after these battles became routine and really what could she say, I'd been running multiple busy services by that point. I was starting to realise why family and friends don't really mix in business. Never employ them directly. They think because of the family and friends connection they can undermine you with impunity. They quickly learn that is not so but in pointing this out, you end up falling out and tainting the relationship. Keep both separate is my advice. I think Laurencia woke up one day and she decided she was cleverer than everybody around her, intelligence wise and a few months ago I would have agreed, however, having reflected on the choices she has made since then, I have had to seriously review that erm, view point. Since the book and for many other reasons too she has realised that I might know a thing or two more than her and that's what I told her at my sisters that day. She has been in the background for three months and missing her I decided to reach out to her by sending her a friends request from my temporary Facebook (more on that later) She sent me a rather nice message that made me think and write back a lovely heartfelt reply. Unfortunately, I blocked Laurencia on Facebook and she did the same to me and the messages disappeared. However, I wrote my return message in my notes on my phone first and have a copy.

"Hiya Laurencia, the friends request, was me reaching out (She refused my friends request because we are not friends yet apparently...okay, then...) I will start by saying I love you dearly and am extremely sorry that I upset you. It's

been hard staying away from you and the kids, I'm not going to lie and I miss my niece greatly and Stevie and Ben so much. I think about you on a daily basis and well want you all back...except Paul of course lmao...now some explaining to do...When I said about Paul being an arsehole and you're the cause, you misunderstood what I was saying. You are not the cause for that, no that's in his genetic makeup as much as my arsehole-ness is too. What I was saying was, the reason he walks out during an argument was the same reason I walk away from your mother. Whether this is true only Paul will know that really. I was angry and things said in the heat of the moment should not taken too seriously. I apologise unreservedly for how angry I got. That was so out of character and I have gave this a great amount of thought since that day. Honestly? I think that being locked in that room I felt really claustrophobic and it had more in common with a panic attack, did you notice as soon as your mother opened the door I calmed down, that's quite telling to me...though I'm so glad sic sorry and I love you very fucking dearly Laurencia and don't forget that...Nothing will change that fact...Nothing! I'd die for you and those kids and that's the unbridled truth of it Loz. Mental state...I am not mentally ill. I suffer from depression and yes that is a form of mental illness but not in the greater sense of the word. I have suffered in silence with this all my life but this last couple of years it came to a much needed head. When I'd sorted my head out it was two weeks before the trial and after that I wrote the book, I was on top of the world for the first time in my life and so excited for the future, happy and content. Finally I was resolved in my mind and knew who the fuck I was for the very first time! Who the fuck knew I could write? I didn't...Then the mental health rumours started around about that time. I stayed away from you because you said I was "Mental" "Insane" and "Crazy" I was none of those things and you know what? I went home and cried. I couldn't believe you thought that about me. As time went on it became clear that these mental health rumours were really affecting people. Everyone's demeanour towards me changed. Funny looks and stares. "Friends" uncomfortable in my presence. People who would have been really happy to see me usually would just look at me at the other side of the pub.

Everyone showing concern to you, ya Ma, Jenny and Leeroy etc but never to me...now I can only speculate were these rumours originated from. Though if people were asking after me, just for the goss in my opinion and the people closest to me were then relaying their fears about my mental state to these people, well it's not hard to see where they maybe came from. (You think?) I found this soul destroying to realise this was happening to me. I went from being sorted in my mind to straight back into depression, a depression forced on me and really I never needed to be back there...these rumours followed me everywhere I went. They have destroyed my reputation and served to only discredit me. The funny thing is nobody spent any real time with me and I still find it fucking unreal that qualifies people to make these judgements. I suspect a lot of things but I generally keep these to myself now. I don't bother with anybody because I can't be around people who think that of me. Though they have not bothered with me either. The last time I was in the pub was absolutely horrible and I felt so judged and nobody was the same. Even Lee told me he thinks I'm mentally ill. I guess at least he said it to my face. Your Grandma did too and I worked it out, she'd spent 4 hours in my presence in the last year! She was really qualified to make that judgement. I only bothered to keep in touch with your Mam because she realised I would not bother with her if she kept this shit up. She at least faked she thought I was ok...There are so many things I could say, about my fears of what's really going on, my paranoia, yes I am very paranoid with good fucking reason too but that Mikey who lets everybody know what he's thinking or up to, to anybody who would listen is dead I am afraid. However, what is not dead is the person I am Laurencia. I'm still that person that cares way too fucking much and I've realised it's rather unnatural but that is who I am. I used to think the majority of people on this planet were the same as me, to realise that at 36 years of age that in fact it's the major minority is frankly soul destroying. What a shitty world it is. You know I went to the Stockton Arms a month ago on my own and within 30 minutes I had made three friends and we had a right laugh for the next three hours, I got told I should be a motivational speaker! They didn't once look at me like I was crazy. You know what that makes me so fucking sad. Later, still pissed, I took the dogs for a walk and realised I can only be myself around people who don't know me. These rumours have reached everybody really. My cousin Gareth used to be a right wrong un and wont even speak to me!!! Daz in New Milton, all the family in Great Yarmouth, fucking unreal...Yes I want to be successful but not at any cost. I'm scared I will get cancer or something and look back at my life and realise what it could have been, my whole adult life has been mental torture and I want my next (hopefully) 36 years to really count. Make every day a good day and try to make a difference. Oh to win that girls heart! Now I fear that's just a dream as she will have heard these rumours. I guess only time will tell on that one. Part of me doesn't want to find out. Please forgive me and let's put this shit behind us and can I have you three back please, STAT!...I really do love you all and need you in my life for the rest of it...I love you Loz and I am sorry xxxx"

I had a lot to say! As apology letters go it is honest and a heartfelt one at that, you would say. All would be forgiven you would say? She would

drop this bullshit surly for me and our relationship, you would say? Fair expectations, you would say? I thought so too. Not Laurencia no, no she came straight back at my jugular, like we were in her Mothers front room all over again.
"I don't mean to keep going on about it but"
"You don't want to admit the truth"
"All your friends think you are crazy, even Bev thinks it"
"These are peoples conclusions"
"Just look at your profile picture, you are clearly insane and crazy" (looking at the picture, desperately ill and suffering poisoning effects more like, more on later) "A sane person doesn't do that"
"Your books shit" (Massively Generalised and she said it was amazing book in her first message) "I don't want anything to do with you" Something about my Gift from an Angel. She is a better person than you will ever be Laurencia. All designed to provoke me. Nailed that one Laurencia but it was your biggest mistake too.

Wow, I couldn't believe it. The more I didn't reply to the first message the angrier she got in the preceding two and she said things she cannot ever

take back. My skulduggery metre is in over drive now. This paddy at the realisation that I was having none of her bullshit really messed it up for her and alerted me to her role in this. Up until then I just thought it was our Carla. Now seeing how shit Carla was at lying and skulduggery I realised she cannot be possibly driving this. I think I have just found the master manipulator in this story of great woe. All I replied after the first message back was "You need to leave this shit alone now Laurencia"
"By people who have spent no time with me"
"The Truth, Pffft..."
"I'll try again in a month, Laurencia"
"Oh, I will be getting a Psychological Evaluation and will post the results to the public" This seemed to upset her. I gave it until the next day and read the proceeding and angry next two messages and from them I wrote what was written above. I blocked Laurencia on Facebook straight away and now extremely upset I posted on Facebook explaining my fears, I have deleted the post which is a shame as I would have liked to print it and I did not make a copy. I have now not been around anybody negative for some time and I am thankfully back to my old self but this incident

made me scrutinise Laurencia's behaviour more closely and I have say she is right in the middle of the skulduggery and the major manipulator in this sorry tale of woe. That's what my gut tells me. She has definitely been directing my sister and I believe others too. The comments above after my essay, tell me she got very angry because she realised she could not manipulate me herself any longer and I was giving Carla Nada by now. What are Laurencia's motives? That business plan again and the fact she knows my methods and recipes maybe? Can I be forgiven for thinking this about her? All of this makes me sound like a paranoid schizophrenic. My Gut feelings are screaming at me that's been the bloody point all along. I think gut feelings are really your subconscious trying to get through to you? It's an interesting thought. My advice? Start listening to the fucker, it knows its shit...

I think this is a good time to introduce Paul to this story of skulduggery. I first met Paul some years ago now. He owns the barbers in the infamous old shop that people from a certain age have good old stories about, the Yard of Ale shops aka, The Yardie. You used to be able to buy single fags from the owner for 20p when we were kids, life saver it was and for many kids too. It was a public service, god dam it. Simpler times...Paul used to cut my hair but could never do my fringe right and always cut it too short and made it look like a comb over, so I switched to the girl who worked for him and when she left so did I. I used to bump into him at the gym and we would always be cordial and have a chat. I quite liked him. Then my niece sought him out and they got together. I then met the real Paul and I very quickly realised he was a Professional Dickhead of Epic Proportions. A 365 day a year steroid abuser. Bald and about my build. Until he stops the steroids then when the liquid leaves Paul, he turns into a hobbit. It's quite funny to watch, as if a pin was pushed into him he bursts and deflates and along with his size, goes his confidence and his ego. He is like-able when that happens. Self confessed arsehole too no less and more than aware of his own short comings. He is also a big sullen baby, stroppy and just a real Arsehole. Now, we are very different people, Paul and I but we do have something in common. I have that arsehole gene too, though not quite as chronic and acute as Paul's, I must say. We absolutely fucking despise each other now. We cannot even be in the same room. That is one person I would willingly fight any day of the week the complete prick and vice versa, I would think. His main problem is he works his socks off in the gym on the steroids and I am animal protein built and my size is not far off his (I was before the poisonings, more on later) and I hardly train. I used to be 15 stone and had no muscle so I decided to start training as I was fat as fuck and my health was suffering and I'd had enough. Seven years later and now 12st of pure muscle, no steroids except one course of Anavar, three years ago, which is very mild and my muscles are bigger and more defined now than then, I am 99% animal protein built and did it the hard way. It shows. He knows if I decided to take the crap he does I would be twice his size within weeks. Sticks in the craw that does doesn't it Paul? You do seem to get a lot more respect when people realise you did it the right way. When I do get back to it properly I will get some size on me for sure and naturally too. It transformed my looks and my presence. That decision to start to change was the pin point start of my growth to the man I am today. Food, milk and water are my steroids. His role in all this is obviously with Laurencia and he is in the middle of the skulduggery too. He has a lot of customers who know me and I bet I am a hot topic in his chairs. Other than that I think Laurencia is the intelligent one in that relationship and she would direct him. Although his shop is good little number he has also realised my potential too and won't like it one bit. He wants to be very successful does Paul but is devoid of the creativity needed to come up with something himself, I am afraid. Laurencia has the skill if she tried. Come up with your own shit and try to make a success of it, novel idea that is. My niece unfortunately has lived with this Dickhead of Epic Proportions for that long that sadly he has definitely rubbed off on this former, lovely lass. She is a symbol of a master manipulator to me now. Sinister. There is a photo on my phone of Laurencia and I from the graduation and it was a good one that I loved. Now she looks so evil to me in it, really sinister. I can now safely add Laurencia, Carla, The Dickhead of Epic Proportions, Uncle Martin and Step-hen to my list of enemies, not forgetting Cleveland Police Rasheed, Gary McCarten. Fuck me Little Mick, it's a talent.

I have to mention for the record my suspicions about a girl I had a short foray with recently a week before the trial. Sarah was her name 20 was her age and I met her at the Kings Arms at my good friends Big Den and Kayla's wedding. I chatted her up but didn't get the response I was after and moved on. The lass sent me a friends request and messaged me on the Monday. I was lonely and remembered I fancied her and we started talking. This was the Monday before the trial. We met up and had a really good bloody night together. The next time we met up she made me sleep in another room. Erm, why? Bit late for protecting your virtue now my love, stupid too, second time round is always ten times better than the first and the first was massively enjoyable for us both. I sensed a game but we had drunk 2 bottles of wine, I don't drink wine and with me in the spare bed I fell asleep within seconds. I awoke around 8 and asked to jump into bed with her. We nearly ended up making love, but I stopped it, I said if we could not do it last night and it would have been amazing for us both then why spoil it all by undoing all the hard work now? Stupid man, it turned out to be last chance with the lass. Why? Well I went from being the best man she had met, to Nada. Something changed. I got a message from her on the Thursday after the trial and she was really off. She was up and down a lot. I asked what was wrong. She said she "had just found something out and is gutted and I don't want to talk about it" Righto I thought, I'll see if she messages me again knowing she owes me £30 that I was relying on for dog food and not one for games I waited. Now I am a realist and know there is only one girl for me. With Sarah, I realised we did not have as much in common as it first seemed, she would get bored in conversations and always complain she was tired. I never heard from her again. She still owes me the money too, I did not think she would let my dogs down. It did serve me to realise my days with 20 year olds are over. My angel is 23 so that's ok. So did Sarah just stop liking me or was she told something about me? Laurencia was very interested in my time with Sarah. My gut tells me this is maybe another example of Laurencia's manipulations, you see Sarah added Laurencia on Facebook, I actually encouraged this because my niece has a real struggle striking and in particular, maintaining friendships. I always thought it was because Laurencia had the Kindness Curse, I now know it is definitely not that because I was clearly mistaken on that notion. I was just thankful for the company and it was needed. It reminded me what I've been missing and what is to come. I really believe I have a lot to offer and cannot wait to be taken advantage of.

Friends are involved up to their necks in this too, though other than the rumours I don't yet know the roles and motivations. Except one. Mark Davis, My oldest friend. When Cheeky's was in the pub in Thornaby he reached out and wanted to help along with his Mrs Clair. I was stoked and still am today. They both did a hell of a lot for me and only wanted to see me succeed. However, a few things happened. You see Mark is really crap at skulduggery too and guilt is written all over his face. Blatantly, Obviously and Bang to Fucking Rights. I was at home with Mark and had theses sticky white boards that well, stick to your wall and would use them to mastermind whatever business plan I was on with at the time. On this occasion it was the recipes. I completely trusted Mark at this point and didn't think anything of it. I went for a piss, while there he was intently keeping an eye on the board and with his phone in his hand, trying, I believe to get a picture. Now I kept leaning back to watch him and he looked guilty as fuck, those Rosie cheeks again and when I came back in to the kitchen you could just feel the skulduggery and tension. I don't think he got one. I was immediately buzzing with suspicions. By this point we were in the La Pizza Bella kitchen. He knew everything about the recipe except the spice mix measurements and what spices actually went in. My two main employees were my "Gift from an Angel" and her, cousin. Now you have to understand that Mark is a very talkative individual and never really shuts up, ever until I started measuring the spices in front of him and instantly he went as quiet as a mouse, watching intently, every time I looked up he would look away, you could not have been more obvious if you tried. I was stunned. Even the girls picked up on this and commented later when Mark went home, I didn't even bring it up with them. It is really funny when I think about it now. (I have to state Mark is not his real name. We are no longer friends as he delivered me spiked weed, though it was mild but unmistakable, because of our history I have decided to protect him)

Now this plan of mine to stop the skulduggery and save myself will be coming up later in much more detail. However, I decided to tell two people in particular about this plan. Carla and Mark. So needing a laptop and the benefit of word I asked my fake sister if I could borrow hers, now I have to say, my sister hated me using her laptop. Why I don't know, I suspect there was probably evidence of her skulduggery on the laptop if I looked hard enough, but usually when I ask to use it, it is like asking her to pull an eyeball out of her face with a pin and make her eat it, usually anyway but today she was my best friend and acting again so I got the use, I turned up and Carla was gardening. I hurriedly told her my plans and got the laptop out. Initially she was very supportive but within an hour something changed, she realised it would in fact stop the skulduggery in its tracks, Carla changed from helpful and friendly to agitated, worried, unsettled and was hovering around me like a fly around shit to the point I could not get fuck all done and gave up. Suspicions, Suspicions, Suspicions. This made me decide to go and see Mark and tell him to see his reaction. So I ordered a taxi. When I arrived Mark was sat there with his boss and close friend Matty. I like Matty, he is a good man, knows his industry inside and out and is a brilliant manager. I was happy to see him. I greeted them both and told them 'the plan" Mark proceeded to get, what can only be described as offended, like I had just insulted his personal hygiene. He spat at me with some venom that "I think it is a long shot and it depends if anybody would believe the story but that's up to you" Why wouldn't they believe it? I thought. All the while, saying this with visible disgust and irritation on his face. I looked at Matty, he had a slightly perplexed look mixed with amusement at the reaction. Matty knew Mark had fucked up spectacularly, just as I. Confirmed as with our Carla too. Now I am willing to give Mark and Clair the benefit of the doubt. I have to say his mother runs a takeaway in Hartlepool. I think Mark is driven by his brother Martin who is not a trustworthy individual and if there is any skulduggery afoot he will undoubtedly be at the centre. Mark and Clair I can forgive and don't want to know if I am right, though I think that is patently obvious don't you? Once I do what I am going to do, all is forgiven and I will still care and look after you and your family for all the help you gave me, if I make it. Your kids are my god kids and that means something. You have not tried to destroy me, like others have. Just be loyal from now on please. I will make it, I believe it.

Lastly in this chapter I want to explore my Sisters motivations. Unfortunately it took my sister a lot longer to realise and then accept I had talents. She'd grew up with me and been privy to my "thickness" or "misunderstood learning curve" I prefer to call it, she believed me to be nice but thick as shit. I believe now, she started to see I was more capable than she knew and started to realise this a couple of months before the graduation and had no choice but to believe it with the book. You see my sister had just worked her socks off at university for her well deserved first. She was understandably very proud, as was I, she was the highest achieving academic university student in the Elwood family and the Woods even, I would guess. When I wrote the book and business plan the realisation that I could achieve more potentially, pissed on her bonfire a lot, looking back. This cannot be, how? He was thick as fuck growing up? He must be fucking crazy?! Not hard to imagine that train of thought now is it? "Our Michael isn't clever for fuck sake, don't be daft, Pffft, I bet he can't beat me at Trivial Pursuit!" I can imagine the indignation and disgust when she says it, I know her that well. Sibling rivalry and all that. I remember recently, during writing my book, I could sense Laurencia was trying to convince her mother I was clever, when she made me play, you guessed it, Trivial Pursuit. A game she takes pride in being good at and always wins. Along with Step-hen, I reluctantly played along. She ran away with it and got her first 4 questions right. Even Step-hen was ahead of me, I came back and over took Step-hen, caught my sister and I was on sport, the couple of times I've played, I always leave sport to last, in the hope I get a motorcycle sport question and not football question and now being level with my sis, with just one colour to go each and both on sport, she'd just got her sport question wrong for the 4th time. My sport one was "How many lanes in an Olympic swimming pool?" Not having a scooby. I shut my eyes, pictured one in my head and counted. I got to six and realised it did not look right and that seven was odd so surmised in this picture it was eight. It looked right. I opened my eyes and said eight and I was right and I won. I was buzzing and she was devo'd, clearly. Just beat the Queen. Step-hen was still on four. My niece came back from where she had been, I was very amused when my sister, still fuming, pointedly and dejectedly told her I'd won and rolled her eyes, I smiled because I knew I had just proved a little point and the way Carla told Laurencia told me I was right and it was a light hearted test. We were still a family on this day and it was a nice day, for me at least.

Any other motivations? Money obviously. I could write a chapter alone on my fake sister's suspicious behaviour. Get drama lessons Sis. Carla essentially used to be a good person that sadly lost her way from the moment she started university and the fact she used to be a good person is the very reason she is so shit at skulduggery. I can pin point all the times she got information out of me and then something changed because of what I had told her. When I started a job at XPO I needed a lift to work as I fucked my knee and couldn't use the bike, she said she could but Step-hen would be in the car because she already agreed to drop him in Darlington to pick up a car from the big hard car tick man who had been to mine previously. I went fucking mad "What the fuck are you giving him the time of day for after what he did to you?" She said she had thrown an iron at him first. That's new. Oh fuck off I thought, it's all bullshit. I said not to worry as I would hurt him on sight and need money, not a prison stay. By this point I'm well aware of Carla's skulduggery. I got work to pick me up and it was funny listening to Carla try and glean the info of where I was working. I'd told her PD Ports at Teesport. I just did not want a single person to know who I was working for. Because I had messed up my knee I had no choice but to elicit to her the area that I worked, if I wanted her to pick me up because of my knee and avoid the resulting 3hrs walk home. I told her Middleton St George but not the company. Knowing how hard XPO is to find without local knowledge, I knew it would be a hard one. Big village is Middleton, home to Teesside's Airport. Thankfully back from near collapse and in public ownership where it should remain. In a friendly text from work she suggested I give her the company name and she will Google it and put it in her Sat Nav. She said she booted Stephen out on the way. You did what, I thought. I pulled over for my break and phoned her. Quick as a flash I asked her why she did that and where? She said "Middleton St George and because he needed to borrow £40 to get the car and he did not tell me so I couldn't get him to the centre or give him the money, I made him get out there" I smelt bullshit of the highest order. More like you agreed to lend him the money but only if he searched the village for lorry companies. I wouldn't have took too long really if you asked a local. I at least tried to make it hard for them. Indeed, after the phone call I sent Carla a pin point on Google maps through imessage and the pin point was the roundabout on the main road before the airport roundabout. I told her my ETA and set off to meet her. She was nowhere to be seen, I thought I heard her car a couple of times. Anyway I got to the pin and she's not there, my phone rings "Where are you!" she shouted. "I'm at the roundabout" I said

"I've been up and down this road twice now and around the village!" "Right why didn't you just pull over sis?"

"It's just a roundabout" she said

"Yes Carla, why did you not just pull over?"

"Because it's a roundabout" Jesus wept "Yes Carla but you would just pull over and somewhere safe and phone me, I don't understand why you would waste your petrol. You should have just stopped"..."But" For fuck sake "It doesn't matter just come get me" I snapped. I realise now she was expecting to pick me up at the company and when she realised it was just the roundabout, panicked and drove around trying to find it. Stressed, she looked when she arrived. Her boyfriend must have not come through. Maybe there was some truth to what she told me. Who knows? When we arrived outside my home we were talking about something when she stated to me in the reply "Because I am a good person you know Mikey" I looked at her. I did not say a word nor did she look in my direction. I swear we both thought "fucking bullshit" at exactly the same time. I wished her well but sadly I had reached the end of the road with my sister at this point and have not spoken since except the messages she has sent. The typing in the messages is so not Carla, like a bad actor has took her place. The fact I have ignored them and she is not angry or kicking off is frankly extremely telling, it is what would have happened at any time since we have been able to use phones. I did not hear from her for sometime after the Laurencia incident also strange as we left on good terms. I will print them...

Wednesday 16th October 1830 "Hiya is everything alright? You can talk to me you know! Xxx" *Just over an hour after the illness and braking my phone meltdown at XPO and the first in seven days...*

Saturday 19th October 10.28. After missed call. "Will you let me know you're ok bro? Xxx"

"I'm fine. I just need some time...I'll contact you when I'm ready. Xx" *I replied*

Monday 21st October. "Do you want to do anything to celebrate your birthday? Xx"

"No. x" *I replied.*

Thursday 24th October.
"Have you got your old Facebook back yet? Happy birthday bro xx"

The fuck has it got to do with you? Odd question...Shnortle

Thursday - later on "Ah just ignore me. I'm only your sister" Umm.

Monday 28th October. "How are you getting on? You talking to me yet?"

Nope.

Later "Would you like some courgette and cheddar soup?"

Tempting I do like it...

8. Thursday 31st October. It's the 2nd when I write this update. "How are you? Are you talking to me yet? Haven't seen you for ages and I do worry about you xxx"

Now Carla does not know why I am ignoring her. She can only but wonder. It's been 18 days since her first message from the XPO incident you would think she would ask me at least once "Ow dickhead, what the hell have I done like?" Curious, because she would have 100 times over by now, hell she would have been round mine kicking my door in any other time, if she was not guilty. These messages are a perfect example of an out of character and bad actor. They are starved of Intel. I'd be getting nervous by now. They have lost control of me and the situation. The tide is turning.

These messages seemed like hoped for ways in but with half arsed conviction and rather obviously forced.

I need to mention Nathan Graham. I bumped into Nathan, my friend Daniel's Gay brother. Having known him since a baby I stopped for a bit and we had a good chat. Weird relationship we have, I see him as my nephew and he wants to marry me. Now at this point I am still slowly and painfully trying to make sense of what is happening. I know Nathan is bestie's with Laurencia. Let's set a trap I thought. So I purposely made a big deal about trust "Nathan! Whatever I fucking tell you stays in this room" "You are probably the only person I can trust" shit like that. He promised he would, he lied. I told him that I believe Carla has been following me around and thwarting my employment efforts. Now I never put it so eloquently, obviously but I thought if that gets back to Carla and we get in an argument and she knows I said this to Nathan, she would be unable to keep it secret and blurt it out to me. She is a book. That is exactly what she did, the predictable cow. I also found out the real Nathan too. It was a slam dunk that one. He's always gutted because I am not gay and he wants to marry me. Thinks I would make the perfect husband. He tried to sell me the delights of anal, telling me "It's the only way for a man to achieve a full body orgasm" he professed "Um, thing is Nathan, I just would not let a man do that, though if somebody I really loved like my girl, wanted to do that with a strap on then I would be duty bound to perform a detailed risk assessment and consider it, but you my boy, have no fucking chance" I shnortled in amusement at his sadness and disappointment.

I wonder does this incident put me under the "master manipulator" category?

Where Carla's skulduggerability was so bad and clearly the weak link, her daughter on the other hand, she is devious, manipulative, thinks she is really clever and I frankly agree. What she has managed to do to me is quite impressive I would say and I would be proud of her talent if it was not used in the wrong way. Your mistake Laurencia was hitching up with such an Esteemed Prize Prick as Paul. I hope you are happy together. You deserve each other.

Chapter 3

Cleveland Police, Garry McCarten and Rasheed & Asian Community Tie In. What a Fucking Doozy, this one is...

Cleveland Police were alerted to my book "Fuck You Pc Tim" because I told them. Yes I rang them and told them they might want to get ahead of this and let's set up a meeting. Now when you read the book, I think it is very clear that my intentions are not to "bribe" the police, but remember I was wrongfully convicted under false testimony, they ignored me officially but have in fact been working to get something over me. They have found nothing they can use and it sticks in their craw I should imagine. It is quite hard to find something that does not exist, especially when you have not done anything wrong. That book is a very big embarrassment to an embarrassment of a Police force. Not forgetting it is one of the most corrupt and inept forces in the UK, in a class of one. I will start with my first and comically brilliant encounters with Cleveland Police after the trial. Around a month after, I was walking my dogs Brie & Bear over the local paths at the Sixfields across from my home. Now I only go so far because Bear bless him is scared of trains and won't go past a certain point which is always our marker to turn around and head back. So I did an about turn as quick as a flash and instantly into view came a bicycle helmet just peering over a bush about 100 yard further up and around the curve and slightly uphill, curious, I walked extremely quickly to the outer curve so I had a better view because then he was in my line of sight and I walked towards him double quickly, he dropped his bike and I shit you not, dropped on one knee and started to take a photo of a fucking daffodil! I was laughing and I knew straight away he was a copper or ex-copper, he was what I call "A Complete Fucking Norman". Normans usually work for the Police, Councils, VOSA, Speed Camera Van Operators etc.

Dictionary of Good Sir

A Complete Fucking Norman - Definition - "The sort of anal retentive person who needs rules and regulations to tell them what to do at any given time in life and are unable to deviate from said rules and have an innate inability to think for themselves, a "Complete Fucking Norman"

As I was passing him he suddenly stood up and I sorta shouted the "Now" and I said the now very sharp and short "Now Mate!" He jumped. "What ya doing? Taking pictures of nature?" I shnortled... "Ahh that's nice!" I said, greatly amused. I then proceed to watch him from a distance of 30 metres or so and put him under a little pressure, does wonders for guilt to come to the fore that does. He didn't know whether he was coming or going. He really was not expecting that about turn that's for sure, he eventually, after getting hold of himself, picked his bike up and rode off. I thought it was hilarious to be honest and often think what if I was wrong and it was just some poor member of the public? Yeah, Na fuck that, it was definitely a copper. There are just too many coincidences. Mainly why he was peering over the bush at me? The daffodil photo op? Come on who does that really? Not even a Complete Fucking Norman would do that.

Next up, the scumbag Step-hen from earlier brought Cleveland's finest to my door. When I opened the door I was confronted by a rather sexy lady Pc and what can only be described as a 6ft 9in, 3ft thick and 5ft wide, Police Gangster, Coz that's what he would of been had he not joined the force. Not actually intimidated and more amused and glad to see somebody new and to talk to, I immediately asked how they were. They asked after Step-hen and I told them my views on that particular man, they asked my name, "Michael Elwood" I proudly proclaimed, instantly the women Pc's face lit up into the biggest smile, while simultaneously, gangster cop stiffened up! I was smiling back at the women when I realised they knew or had heard exactly who I was! I'm not going to lie I was buzzing. I saw them off with "Enjoy the rest of your shift" and smiled all day long. Now Step-hen got pulled and swabbed if you remember? He rang my phone from the coppers phone. Yeah, I believe that was done on purpose to recruit a highly suitable target to become their CI and gain my number. They need something on me but I'm actually squeaky clean except my past occasional class A use, there is nothing on me they can use, so next best thing is to engineer it. I have no doubt I would have been in a cell by now if they had something on me. Start by isolating me and cut my options severely. Destroy my reputation, divide and conqueror. Well you all succeeded in the isolation stakes and definitely options, reputation, check, but you had a lot of help I believe.

Fizel

One day back in august I think, I was walking back from town with my dog Bear, Brie was on heat and he was passion drunk and wouldn't eat. I decided to take some dog food and Bear on his own and get him away from Brie so maybe he would eat. He wouldn't. Anyway when I reached the railway bridge between Bowesfield and Hartburn, I happen across a bald Middle Eastern looking man slumped against the fence and sat on the second step up. Turkish/Syrian/Libyan type.

As I take him in I see he is in some distress and holding a can of rice pudding. Curious, I walked past him and got to the top of the stairs. Looked back and in that time it took me to ascend the stairs I had decided to speak to him and ask him if he was ok. "Ow mate! You alright pal?" I said? He looked up at me "You want a cigarette?" I said "I don't smoke mate" he said in an accent.
"Maybe it's a good time to start by the looks of it Pal" I said as I started to descend the stairs with Bear in toe. I sat down next to the man on the step and introduced myself and Bear, I asked his name, he said "Fizel" I said nice to meet you "Fizel" he looked shocked for some reason, like he was surprised I had got his name right. I put my hand out to shake his hand. A firm hand shake was returned. Respectful. I asked again if he was alright. He replied "I'm drunk and have nothing and no money and don't know what to do"
"My mother has disowned me and my brother has died, I am alone" he said. Just as he said that a 60 something, smartly dressed women probably works in the offices around the corner, walked down the steps and she had to walk between us. I said "I'm so sorry my Dear" with a smile and moved Bear out of the way. She looked at me and

gave me a cheeky smile and said "No, not at all" the saucy wench. Of course my heart went out to him but smiling now, I said "Do not fear mate, get yourself down the social, get signed on, do a completely pointless Employment Eligibility course and get your security badge, highly employable you will be then. Look at ya big bold head, you look like a right nutter mate, get a job on the doors easy you would" Only after you complete a course that takes two weeks and is a complete waste of time that helps nobody. You see you have to do the stupid "Employment Eligibility" course for the course company to be able to get the money to pay for your security course. You see the government don't actually pay for the courses and it is paid by some obscure fucking EU fund which pays for the "Employment Eligibility" course and to then make enough from that to put you through the extra security course (another seven working days and then up to another ten working days for the badge to come through) and make a decent profit at the same time too. I shit you not. So we do pay for it really then? Yes we do, it's the EU giving back our own money but creating a profitable industry on the back of it in the process. It's a costly and needless process no less. You could not make it up. It's a curious set up don't you think? Anyway, I digress.

I then asked Fizel where he was from? I think he said "Syria" maybe. Anyway his accent and looks backed this up. That area at least. Though I remembered later in the conversation, he let slip he was born in Sheffield when telling me about his brothers sad demise, fucked up there Fizel I later realised. At the time I thought good old Fizel was genuine you see. I asked him "So why has your mother disowned you Fizel?" he looked ashamed and looked to the side "I'm Gay" he said. "Really?" I said? "Your mother disowned you because you're gay?" "Yeah" was the reply. "Well fuck your Mum then Fizel" He looked at me in alarm "Fuck my Mum?" he said "Yep, Fuck ya Mum!" he looked at me perplexed "A mothers love is unconditional and if your mother is willing to turn her back on the son she borne just because he takes it up the chuffer, then yes, Fizel, Fuck your Mum" He did not argue. I said my goodbyes, shook his hand and stood up. "Thank you my Good friend for stopping and trying to help me"

"Not at all Fizel, an absolute pleasure, if I see you again I will stop and talk to you. Remember be proud of who you are and Fuck ya Ma" I got to the top of the stairs and shouted back down "Is ya Ma, Muslim?" He did not say anything. I said "It's just they are quite conservative about the taking it up the arse and that would explain it" I said this without thinking as usual. I said goodbye again, wished him well and Bear and I left. When later giving this encounter a great amount of thought I realised "Fizel" was playing a character and after reviewing his mannerisms, his voice, his slip up, his sheer enjoyment at the role he was playing, I realised I had noticed slight slips in the accent just at the points maybe a Yorkshire accent would peek or bend maybe, is the best way I could explain it. I surmised that "Fizel" was probably CID. They are the coppers with the balls for a set up like that. Gathering Intel on the Perp? Maybe testing to see what kind of a person I am. See if I was racist? See if I was gay, maybe? Who knows? My Skulduggery metre never really kicked off at the time, probably self gloating that I was doing a good thing had overridden that mode, you self righteous mofo you, but I took everything in about that encounter and found it very curious later on. Life was ok then, this was just getting started and I was not aware of the skulduggery afoot and too come. I had no reason to be on guard. I was on guard though, my sub conscious again maybe? He's a complicated fucker.

The Local Asian Barber Encounter

On the day of my last hair cut about 6 weeks ago, I decided, after not being able to use my usual one, to try the Asian barbers next to Shawama on Prince Regent Street. Honestly, I just wanted to see what type of person the barber was and if there was any recognition and I really needed it cut. So I thought fuck it and went in. I was met by an early 30s northern Iraqi. Nice man it turns out. Broken English but well spoken, a pleasant man. He had trouble understanding my accent, time will not make that any better pal, I thought, so I do what I normally do and speak in broken English too so he can understand me. He did a bloody good job. After finding out why he moved here and his thoughts on the English and our culture, loves us, he said, a gentleman walked in. Now not really noticing any recognition in the Barber himself as such, I blatantly did with his Iraqi friend who walked in. He did a double take, looked surprised, said something very excitable in Arabic, was snapped at in reply and left pretty quickly, not taking his star struck look from me once. When he left I got a little worried. One, because I've realised by now I am getting recognised way too much by the Asian community and two, the cut throat razor bit was coming off next. I did get nervous at the jugular and was alert to any undue pressure or suddenly different technique, can't be too careful. He could tell I was skint and the barber tried to give me my money back. I was gobsmacked. I told him he was a good man and that he had earned this money and I could not take it back. He had done a spot on job too. I told him it was a pleasure to meet him. It was. I shook his hand and left. When I went over it I got to thinking, how could they know who I am? Was the refund attempt just a put on and he knew who I was? The only conclusions I can make is Rasheed and WhatsApp. Rasheed and Asians in general love using WhatsApp. They stick together and feuding factions will even team up if they are in need and have a common cause. I am of the opinion that I am rather infamous within the Asian community and my ugly mug has been plastered all over the "can only join if your Asian" WhatsApp groups. It would explain the recognitions and the sudden lack of Asian people willing to rip me off when I sell something. It seems if you take away the ability for any monetary skulduggery then you take away all your Asian customers. Curious, but I have been ripped off three times by two Asian Taxi drivers and an Asian Pizza delivery driver in the last three weeks. You do not help yourselves with my opinions of you. Though I am not racist, I do find the parts of the community I have dealt with very dishonest and without morals. They have tried very hard over the years to make me come to this conclusion but it is definitely from experience and not a natural dislike of the community. The Asian community has been in Teesside as long I have and are as much a part of Teesside's makeup as anybody native or otherwise. I have given many an opportunity for Asians to prove me wrong. I realise I maybe attracting the bad elements and remain hopeful that is so. The majority I have dealt with fail 98% of the time in the good person stakes and are really easy to read. Am I racist? No, I don't care about your pigmentation, where you are from or which god you love, no I care about the person you are. It is not my fault a particular section of society keeps coming up short and continually proves their skulduggerability. Maybe my standards are too high? I am simply being honest and telling it how I see it. If you think I am racist, you can suck eggs. I still give that same respect of assuming anybody I meet is good, no matter whom you are. I take every single person I meet on a person by person basis. I do not make judgements on people based on their colour or creed. Unless they are potentially, trying to kill me.

The Haircut, Before Last

I popped into Hair by David, on Oxbridge Avenue to get my hair cut by Rachael. Now Rachael has only recently started cutting my hair again. She is always happy to see me and we have known each other for years. Since my weight loss and muscle gain she has been a bit more pleased to see me. Not this time, this time she was so off and uncomfortable, she looked guilty straight away. She said could I come back in an hour please so she can finish a customer's hair. I said, yes sure Rach. I said I'd get some breakfast. She suggested I go to the Cafe next to Ropner Park as it's nice. I went to the Garage a bit puzzled by her reaction. I decided not to go to the one she suggested and went to the cafe next door to the garage instead. After 45 minutes I gave the obligatory review of my food..."Really nice and a massive improvement on the last owners and fat still on bacon but your eggs need cooking longer because they were still slimy on top" (Arsehole and food!)...I then went back. Rach, was very flustered to see me. I sat in the chair. She was extremely agitated, she was stressed. She looked guilty as fuck. Now my hair and beard takes around 25 minutes. I could feel my skulduggery metre kicking right off with good Ol'Rach. I just studied her. I started a conversation and could see she was not taking a single word in. I stopped mid sentence and she did not notice. I continued to watch. The more I watched the more nervous and guilty looking she became. Umm, curious. Somebody walked in and she jumped. Rach was so flustered and fake with them. Her eyes would meet mine and quickly hers would look away. What the fuck is going on here? I'm stunned. It was so out of character. She has never been like this before. I've known her years. I was glad to leave. When I replayed it in my head, I remembered when I walked back in and her surprise, she asked if I went to the cafe she recommended. I said no, I went to the one next to the garage. She looked worried at that. I then remembered I've seen Gary McCarten in here a few times in the past. Umm, I can't help but wonder what might of happened if I had taken Rach's advice and went to that quite a lot less public cafe next to Ropner Park? Pure speculation but with Rach's reactions it not hard to guess, is it? Gary McCarten and his brother John, these two boys are the biggest drug dealers in Stockton and have both recently in the last few years had a pinch each for said drug dealing and I believe under the thumb of Cleveland Police. It stands to reason when you read between the lines, it's obvious to me, Jonny did a really short stretch for the crime and they've just left Garry dangle with it and have not actually charged him. Now the Police do not let you dangle for 18 months to continue to ply your trade until they can be arsed to charge you, it does not happen, it is like giving a criminal an 18 month holiday, really? Come on now. Garry and Jonny work independently from each other, Jonny realises what a fucking idiot Garry is I think, though still close but I believe they made a CI deal with Good Ol'Cleveland Police. It's how it works, somebody has to sell the drugs, might well be somebody useful to the police and that they ultimately control. The fact I used Gary's pub and then pissed Cleveland police off is actually complete coincidence. Mad really but useful to all concerned nonetheless. I guess watch who you get mixed up with. Now I have not been quiet about the recipe book incident and let my anger be known, so yeah it stands to reason to all involved, I am a problem for a lot of people that needs sorting once and for all. Nice and neatly. About 18 months ago Gary came around mine for a few drinks, we were talking and I tried to convince him that legal business is the way to go, nice houses, flash cars, nice holidays, that's what successful legal business gives you. What does drug dealing give you? Endless supply of sub 10k cars and watches and the ability to rent nice houses, unlimited clothes and groceries, jewellery, fake tits and a new nose, plus potential loss of freedom? (Doesn't sound too bad actually) Fast forward to November last year at his pub and seeing the opportunity the recipes presented, he decided rather than try and help me, nurture me, see me as a way out of his drug dealing hell, he decided instead to rob his non judgemental friend and use them for his own gains, the treacherous c**t. I have to state I would not get involved in business with drug dealers, I have always known I would not do well in their world and maybe Gary realised this fact. It's one thing renting a kitchen and another thing using drug money to start a business. Thing is, this betrayal set something off in me. My faith in the human race was getting to the point of being irrevocably broken by now. When working in the pub, I met a guy who used to do the Sunday dinners and has a lot of food Industry experience. Now, he grabbed me and told me something, he said "I have never seen somebody unite the masses with something as subjective as the Parmo as yours have kid and with the Cheeky's brand you have something special, if done right, the branding is excellent and some of the best ever Parmo's, you just need to get the fuck away from Gary"

I should of recruited that guy there and then. Gary you blind fool and you Michael. So yes the McCarten's and corrupt elements within Cleveland

Police are working together and both have good reason to want me dealt with, one way or another. Has Rash got connections with Cleveland Police? I would say so yes. I would say a man like Rash has a lot of connections all over Teesside and it is safe and reasonable to assume that would include Cleveland Police. Plenty of powerful people will owe Rasheed favours. They are all connected my gut tells me. I'm really good at pissing people off. It's a talent. I believe Rasheed has tried to trick me into going to Boro a good few times now, his domain. That cellar. Yeah, Na, Fuck that Rash. I believe my dogs have kept any unwanted visitors at bay and kept me safe. Not liked by Asians are dogs. My dog's especially. They are big and loud and fool people into thinking they are mean. They are the loveliest and softest, most loving dogs in the world and would be no help in a fight, bless them. What they don't know and all that. Interesting fact, I also know Gary and Jonny's cousin Chris, he was my biker mate, now he never knew or engaged with Jonny or Gary growing up and only knew each other to nod at when I met Chris, though recently I'd seen them become great mates and know Chris and his Mrs are taking on a local pub, my old boozer and were absolutely blown away by my Parmo's just like Gary was, it's just a thought. I like Chris and his Mrs and hope they would be above that, but then profit and opportunity do funny things to people, I guess. Why have a slice when you can have the whole cake. They just need the nuisance to go away now. Other than that I don't know what other roles these boys are playing, obviously other than profit and trying to destroy me that is.

Chapter 4

The EU, Guy Verhofstad and Facebook and "The Play"

"The Play" was my way to stop all this skulduggery in its tracks and stop this madness. This is what I told Carla and Mark that day. My plan was to make awesome videos of the recipes and methods in full. My gift to Teesside. I believe it would garner a large interest and with the help of clever social media and bite size Facebook friendly videos, full YouTube versions, competitions and a good story for the local gazette. I hoped to raise 30k and reset and escape this nightmare I find myself in. if any more was raised then 20% would be recycled to the competition, 25% to charities and the rest to my business fund. I realised by me doing this I would garner the public's good will and be able to make or find the investment to become prep food suppliers to any interested pizza shops as well as our very own Cheeky's takeaways. I found that for the average pizza shop there is simply too much prep to really make nice food and is why the food is the way it is. They need to make things fast and with little fuss to get the orders out the door. They could use better ingredients though. Well what if we did all the prep for them and that's where I'll leave that as I don't want to give too much away as I've painfully learnt to my detriment. This would work and get traction and is what I should have done from the beginning. I was excited. Really excited. With hindsight it was a mistake to tell Carla and Mark my plans because around that time everything seemed to be stepped up 10 fold. I stupidly lost my phone around this time too. The very phone I had wrote so much on. I was pissed and took the dogs for a walk and lost it. The big, problem was I had 2 factor identification switched on but had lost use of the phone number but that was ok as long as you had the registered phone, which I'd lost, bugger. For the plan to work I needed access to my business page and as I didn't have the money to get my number back, I had no choice but to deal with Facebook. Who have blatantly ignored me and refused to help me regain access. All they have to do is turn off 2 factor identification and I'm in. I have sent a dozen emails in with the relevant documentation, which they have read. Now why would Facebook do this to me? Well that might be because I've been pissing off the EU and a certain Guy Verhofstad with posts on Facebook. Not abusive troll shit, no, not that, but with reason and sound arguments sticking up for Leavers. Now I am a staunch Brexiteer and have been for 20 years. I wrote an article you have access to and might of really pissed off the EU and Guy especially. I hit the nail on the fucking head with the case for leaving. You judge, I guess. I fear they may have lent on Facebook to deny me re-access and shut me up. People take notice when I post something you see, I seem to encourage debate in a good way and have a positive influence with my arguments, I make sense. They might not like that the EU, as shady an organisation as it is. It didn't shut me up though as I just created a new, temporary

Facebook and continued to make the case for Brexit and do my bit for the cause. I'm really quite good at it actually. I even regularly shame the abusive ones in a debate to apologise to me and quite meaningfully too. I was proud, that's an achievement that is. It's also worth mentioning my Uncle Martin is a staunch Remainer too. The plot thickens "Sir" (not quite sure what he has done to deserve to be knighted, seems they give these out way too easily) Nick Clegg now works for Facebook and is also a staunch Remainer. He is just the type of twat that my Uncle Martin would be friends with. They were both top of their games in the same era. Now if my Facebook is being withheld then that is shocking and proves Facebook is being used politically. I have been a member since 2008 and you can literally see the growth of me from insular and troubled 24 year old to the man I am today. I want it back and don't deserve this. I'm a good Facebook user and I am never abusive and have never been banned. Give me it back please I miss it. It's been part of my life for 12 years nearly but it also has a timeline for the Parmo recipe from conception through to Rasheed's gaff, I've even left Guy alone, not to mention that business page and the awesome reviews, plus the pages 1500 likes, all obtained in 3 months. Brilliant for the ad's function for use with the Go Fund Me. I proved you don't need Just Eat if you use social media right and the awesome video's I will make, I can't wait. Cheeky Devils Parmo's could be so big and will turn the takeaway industry on its head, while at the same time, converting the rest of the UK into Parmo lovers. That is the unbridled, un-denied and gods fucking honest truth of it, when you realise that everything wrote up to now makes perfect sense when you realise this fact. That is the prize people. Heartbreakingly everybody has decided that it is a really great idea, well done you but let's do it without you Michael, dead or alive but preferably dead. This is not the first time my ideas and business advice, have been used. No, it seems I have a talent for looking at an industry and can, within days see where they are going wrong and how to do it better. I once had really good idea on how to grow and make professional, the late night booze delivery service. Now, these companies are generally run by shady characters that need an easy way to launder money. I had a business plan and was very vocal about my ideas but only told the basics and left out the main ones, however these little snippets I gave to "friends" actually got adopted by the biggest one in our area. Things like card machines in the vans, going Ltd, special deals, cameras in the vans to identify customers and protect staff, things like that and had actually been adopted by Moonshine within a month of me saying it. I started to learn at that point, still a lot of learning to come, Mikey boy. Other examples, places I worked in the HGV industry. It would be easier to tell you who I have not worked for in the HGV industry in Teesside. I was a bit of a star in the industry when I was there. I pulled off some great feats, especially with my reversing talents and just a healthy knack for getting the job done. If the other drivers said it couldn't be done, they would give the job to me, (without me knowing anybody had said that) and I would get it done. I see why full-time drivers never really liked me for long. I seemed to make a splash where ever I went and lift that company's work rate. Yeah, nobody liked me in that industry! I wasn't trying to be a c**t like that, it's just how I work. I would look at how the company was operating and if I could see how it could be done better, safer and quicker I would tell them. Half the time my advice was adopted if I got a good manager to listen instead of one who takes offence. I was working as a consultant but not being paid as one. I really started to realise how talented I was and just could see things that most couldn't. Other people have obviously realised this and want to destroy me rather than use my talents and help me grow and help themselves at the same time. I'm a sharing is caring type of person, do they think I wouldn't of looked after them? Really? If that is the case, then you never ever knew me, that's for sure. Carla Wood and Laurencia Wood, you have broken my heart. Now suggesting that a large establishment like the EU and Facebook are in on this is frankly quite out there for even me, but honestly I'm not too sure any more. The EU is at war with UK Leavers, make no mistake, they are fighting for their very existence. The European Project does not work without the UK. I have come to realise, even appreciate their fears and struggle, though we still need to leave regardless. It's not a case of just creating a Super State without the UK because without the UK the EU fails before it can get to that point. A lot is at stake for the Europeans. They are willing to do anything they have to, to keep the dream alive. Who knows? They are in the background if they are connected and protected too. So what does my gut say? It says Guy, the EU, Uncle Martin, Nick Clegg and Facebook are all connected. Part of that Remainer Cabal in London. Martins last message to me, "I am going to London for the weekend, will contact you when I get back. T" What happened when he was in London?. Could they see if I became a success then I would naturally be a public gobshite of sound reason and argument? Maybe they could see with my style that I was winning most arguments and actually changing minds in debates on Facebook? There was always an obvious lack of Remainer replies with sound argument against what I said. The major majority, in fact, just abused me. I have a healthy knack for seeing any skulduggery afoot, I have been training for that all my life and on the daily, well I am still here after all, maybe they needed to censor me? Who knows but I would like to find out

Chapter No 5

The latest and most up to date skulduggery, poisoning and the spiking...

Now then, now then, now then, this is the game changer right here. This is the inspiration to give me the fight needed to succeed and realise it isn't in my head, it cannot be. I am an amateur experience writer, opinion writer, not fiction, it does not interest me. For the past two weeks I have been working at XPO in Middleton St George. I liked XPO because it's in Darlington and out of the jurisdiction of Cleveland Police, though that is the village Uncle Martin lives in. It was the perfect job because I could cycle there in 45 minutes and it would be perfect for getting me back on track with my bills, while I appealed my conviction and sent off the Cheeky's business plan. My plan was to put it on a business angel website but that costs money. I borrowed a push bike and started my daily routine. I'd get up at 5am and get sorted, then take the dogs. At 6.30am, I would ride 7 miles on the push bike, then do a high energy multi drop pallet round, around the Newcastle area, then ride 7 miles home. I did not stop. Now, I can get bad kidneys and have suffered from kidney stones. I have been operated on to remove them and I passed one back at New Year. I have for the last 6 weeks or so and very intermittently, been getting the symptoms of passing that stone. I would get the feeling of uncomfortable-ness in my Johnson and bladder and then for a very short piss, would come out what can only be described as extremely thick and black and muddy beck water. About 2/300ml, then within a couple of hours I would be tip top again. It was almost like passing the kidney stone, just without the actual slow passing. A super quick version. I was getting a lot worse the more I did this job and rode that bike. I had last weekend off and was tip fucking top on Saturday and Sunday, fine Monday then desperately ill at work by Tuesday. On Tuesday, I had felt so excruciatingly drained that I had to stop, piss the bloody sludge out, drink a litre of water and then slept for 45 minutes in the cab. I would slowly get better over a couple of hours. I was okay for the rest of the day. Wednesday I was the same in the morning and better by the afternoon. I rode home. When I arrived I sorted the dogs and ate something. Forced myself too because at around that time I felt an exhaustion that frankly I would not like to ever feel again. I could hardly walk, lift my head or do much of anything. I went to bed at 8pm and did not awake until 4.30am. I felt just like the night before, I tried as best I could to get ready for work but just collapsed back into bed. There I stayed flat out until 8pm. I then slept right through from 10pm until 7.30am the next day. I had to get myself up because I had to get to the town and to Lloyd's bank to transfer my weeks wages from my business account. By this point I had ran out of food for myself and the dogs and had broken my phone screen and couldn't use it. I was getting paid £400 from my 4 days work and needed to pay the mortgage too. I rode there in 10 minutes and went in to the bank. Holy fuck, I have never felt so ill in all my life and I've been really ill before, the mad thing? My piss colour and length and feelings down below had been fine for the last 18hrs or so. Why did I feel so ill? I spoke to the front clerk, a nice fellow who was a bit unsure of me at first but had warmed to me by the end. I told him I was ill because I knew that I looked like a clucking drug addict. He sorted me the mortgage advisor, a nice lady who invited me to sit down. I asked her if my house had been repossessed. I then proceeded to break down in tears as I explained that I can make a payment today and that I just wanted the chance to sell this "representation of sadness, anxiety, hopelessness and despair" I said this through the tears. Now, I'm not one to normally do that but I just could not help it. With feeling completely drained and ill it just came out. She looked at me with such kindness and said she would find out and picked up the phone. The lady spoke to the collections department who told her, it was just at the litigation stage and no they had not and of course I could make a payment. I felt better of sorts as that was a big weight off of my mind. Though, I still felt desperately ill. I thanked the lady and wished her well. I went back to the clerk and asked if I could phone my agency. I rang them and predictably I had messed up the invoice as usual, it has to be perfect apparently and I couldn't edit it on Quick Books because my phone is fucked. I nearly fainted. I put the phone down while I steadied myself. Suddenly, I remembered I have an account at the library around the corner and I should be able to log in to Quick Books. I said I'd be back to the clerk and walked to the library. I sat down and did what I needed to do then went back to the bank, phoned the agency and sat down to wait for them to transfer the money. Whilst waiting a dishevelled man came and sat next to me. I turned and said hello and we started chatting. He introduced himself as George and offered his hand. Now, I instantly looked at the most dirty and unwashed hands that generally only homeless people posses. I stupidly said, without thinking as usual "Fuck me mate you had a hard shift?"..."I'm homeless" was the reply. Shit. I apologised and then shook his hand dirty or no. We got chatting again and found out that he used to live in Redcar and his best friend had died in his flat and he refused to stay there. Finding the council the heartless bastards that they are, they refused to re-home him and basically said that is your decision and good luck on the streets. So I asked him if he can still claim benefits without an address and he said no, I cannot do anything. So, no charities to help you George? I asked? No was the reply. "So when you get on the streets you are essentially stuck forever with no hope and are fucked?" "Yes" he said. "Where do you sleep?" I asked. "Doorways or squats, I get spit on regularly and moved on from the good parts of the High Street. That big swallow hotel is just sat there empty" he added. I agreed and added I thought it was scandalous. I asked him why was he in the bank? "Oh", he said "my sister is transferring me

£50 and I'm just waiting for it." Fair enough I thought at the time. I went back to the phone and confirmed with the agency the money was transferred. As I ended the call, George appeared and said he was going and it was nice to meet you. I said the same and wished him all the best and apologised for his situation and shock his hand with a firm grip and looked him in the eyes too, I meant it and my heart went out to him. I then went about my business with the transfer and mortgage payment. Later, after the purchase of tobacco and a Costa (fuck how ill I was, nothing was stopping me enjoying those two delights together, nothing.) I did try to seek George out, to give him some backy. I couldn't find him though. Later when I reflected on the day's events I realised Lloyds had set up that encounter and paid George the money. Thank you Lloyds, that was a really good thing you did for me and George too. Nothing is a jolt to the system to people facing the loss of their homes and facing homelessness, than meeting poor old George. Though I already know I don't want nor deserve (who fucking does I ask you) homelessness. This served to just enrage me later on, enrage me because I could have been successful by now or at least on my way, had I just ignored everybody's silence and sent that Cheeky Devils bloody business plan out to every fucking potential investors in the country, instead of me believing it must be shit and needs rewriting then fighting these mental health rumours, I'd be sorted by now or well on my way. The shop that was available was guaranteed to be successful because Hartburn shops has never had a takeaway there before, it was perfect. I should have believed in myself more. I did not receive even one, "That's really good that is" or "Well done, get it sent out" no encouragement at all?? Is it me or does something not add up here?? My confidence needed that encouragement after the Rasheed decibel. So I got my coffee and went to seek out a new phone screen. I decided that "Kenny the Phone" would be a good choice. He knows people I know and always curious to see people's reaction, I decided it was worth the risk. I was walking towards Tommy Tuckers when I recognised someone, now this man can only be classed as a hairy gorilla, Caucasian still but some maybe Turkish decent in there somewhere. He is the type of man with hair thick from his head to his toes and all the way round. He is 6ft and broad; he has also since birth hit every ugly stick on the way up. Unmistakably it was him. I looked at him as I walked past I waited for the recognition, now I have to say that this man is friends with my sister. I've decided not to name him so ill just give you his first name, Nigel, he was dressed as a homeless man but it was unmistakably him. He looked at me quickly twice. Nada. My skulduggery metre is kicking right off now. I continued walking. I stopped 15 metres after passing him and did the old about turn and I just looked at him. Nigel, just like Norman, he was flustered by that and especially because he had already started to walk in my direction you see. He stopped and walked left, then walked right then back left, I shnortled and started giggling and walked off. I'm not really suggesting anything really, make your own conclusions but I actually find it hilarious. Though, again I cannot help but wonder. Is it just designed to make me paranoid? The thing is I have always been paranoid because I've always been fucked over, you see. All my life, since I was really young. I used to give all my sweets away to the other kids and then they would all leave me on my own. You foolish child you might think? Not to me, no to me I was happy I had made them happy. I never really had friends until I reached age 11, up until that point I was always an outcast and with a, I am fast realising, an unnatural kindness, or the "Kindness Curse" as I call it. An expectation that the rest of the world was like that, I believed that up until very recently. It's a curse but I use it as a weapon now and to my benefit, also. Though, I am angry because of that realisation. When somebody would do something to me that I would be unable to do to a fellow human being I would take it so personally and to heart. It gets broken into pieces every time it happens. Believe me that is an unquantifiable amount of times now. Told you, it's unnatural

From all those years of varied let downs and constant work battles, I grew the ability to sniff out skulduggery, I should be a detective really. I can read people, their mannerisms and gesture changes, the looks to the side before a lie, it is almost like I'm looking into your soul and why people find it hard to hide guilt around me and when I suspect it, can feel it, when I really look someone in the eyes they tend to fold, it is intense scrutiny, I just watch and see the change. If I know you well, I will notice this subtle change and tells instantly and can feel the guilt and skulduggery in my guts. If I don't know you, it just takes a little longer. I'm good at it. It is a skill that I have had an unconscious amount of training in that you simply cannot buy. I have battled many a varied enemy since a child. I have seen guilt and foul play in many forms. I have witnessed the varied reactions of the guilty many, many times. I am a thinker by accidental design and process likely motives and plays rather diligently and quickly. These skills have been useful and maybe explain why I am still alive. That and how much water I drink.

Now Kenny used to be a bit of a lad back in the day but is a fossil from those days now. He was friends with Ste Perkins, my best friend and Bruv and Laurencia's Dad and with a man called Stevie Sexton, also Ste Perkins best friend and I looked up to both. These two larger than life monsters of men to a star struck eleven year old, they were scary but my friends, I was in awe. They were hard and dangerous but charming and funny men. There were a good few in that era in Stockton I would say, hard men I mean. I have to say Steven Perkins could also have a very big heart and took me under his wing from the very first time I met him and my life was punctuated with Steve's wisdom and guidance and not forgetting Jane, his wise, wise sister. Not good at following her own advice sometimes though. It did not matter how bad it got, you went to see Jane and she sat you down with a spliff and a cuppa and would listen and break it all down and put it into perspective, with solutions and good advice plus positivity. I ended up looking forward to my next drama, she was awesome and the same to a lot of people in that respect, including my family. I think, Jane, Ste and I have essentially been suffering the same emotional shit all our lives and were very similar in that respect and we all subconsciously knew it too. I loved them both fucking dearly and think of them both often as sadly neither are with us any longer and you know what the world is a worse off place without them and that's the truth. You make up my ancestors that I look up to for answers when in need. Give me the strength along with my Mum and Dad. You all taught me so much and tried to help me too. I miss those four diamonds immensely and oh, what a different tale this would be if they were all still here, or maybe I would never of happened upon this recipe, or poison chalice, it might have been much different and who knows? Maybe it is the loss we suffer that ultimately gives us human's real strength? You remember the lessons because in mulling over past memories, which you do a million fold more when you lose somebody you loved, you are acutely more aware of the lessons that they departed. Some intentional but most not and can sometimes only become apparent years later. A good thought, that is.

Now Ste had always warned me that, under any circumstances do not trust Kenny the phone and that was 20 years ago! You see, I have always remembered it and why I was only introducing myself now. So I went into the shop and introduced myself. There was recognition there I swear it, like he was expecting me. I explained who I was and the connection we had, he told me Stevie Sexton was in yesterday too, was he now? I nodded and then I asked "How much for a phone screen?"..."£55" was the reply. Brilliant I thought, knowing the screen would be utter shite, I asked how long? He said 1.5 hrs. He asked for the code to unlock it and I gave him it. I went to the bank and doubled back and went back into the shop and asked him if he minded me waiting. He said no. I could not see my phone. Um curious. I watched Kenny on his phone for while, studying him and I was offered one of the rollie's he was furiously making whilst at his desk. Like a habit. He had a big pile of backy on the table and Kenny was making one after the other. He handed me one "Pre made for you mate" he said. At this point I feel like I am going to collapse again. Holding it together, I smoked this very thick and very tightly rolled rollie. When I make them they don't last 2 seconds but this one lasted longer than 2 tailor made would. Being polite I smoked 2 thirds, it took a while, and put the other third out. Kenny whilst on the phone, noted this with interest. A couple of minutes later two lads walked in. I had a craic with them and they were there waiting for their phones Kenny told me. Um, were they? Worried are we Kenny, I thought. Why? These boys were thuggish looking and there for a reason. The lads seemed quite weary of me. I felt too ill to give a shit to be honest. I had already eyed up the three closest, potential make shift weapons and was in quite a good position. I was confident I could still handle them both if I needed too, ill or not. The telling thing was he then ordered them to go to the phone shop around the corner and retrieve my phone, Kenny half asking them and half ordering them. Ah that's where the phone is, you see Kenny told me he had suffered a stroke some time ago and I could see he would be unable to fix my phone. Fair enough I thought at the time. While waiting for the lads to come back we were talking about his stroke when he produced multiple boxes of the pain killer OraMorph out of a draw, explaining they were for his stroke. Also fair enough, I again thought. They came back with the phone and I paid, said my thanks and left. Picked my bike up and rode home. The entire bike ride I felt like I was floating. I dismounted the bike at the bottom of my drive. I nearly collapsed. I made it to the step outside my door, breathing heavily but still with this floating feeling, I calmed down and that's when it hit me. Disclaimer, I am a working class boy and consequently I have led a working class boys life and we generally have dabbled in the old days, though a bit more sensible nowadays. Plus I don't like the 3 day hangover which sometime extends much further than that even but yes I have dabbled in the past. What I experienced whilst slumped on the step, I received a sudden taste of what can only be described as the taste you get by smoking a white pharmaceutical powder. I have smoked normal cocaine on a cigarette before and am familiar with the taste. It doesn't matter the substance as long as it is processed and white it basically tastes the same. Unmistakable, I grinned, the feelings of floating are consistent with opiate based medicine too. Holy Fuck I've been spiked. Knowing the likely substance, I wasn't worried and started giggling because of how ill I was and what that sort of drug would do for me and low and behold I felt fucking awesome for around 6 hours after that and was thankful to the old man in a way. Thank you, Kenny. I walked to the shop to get dog food and really found myself enjoying the buzz, I've had that much morphine in hospital I do have an appreciation of medical opiates. If I'm going for an op I will positively look forward to that part. I got back and reflected on my life the last two years and started writing. That was Friday 18th October 2019. My health has returned properly since Saturday morning too. I have to say I draw the line at my fear I've been getting poisoned, it even sounds far-fetched to my paranoid addled brain because I do have kidney problems, so pinch of salt there, though I do believe there are keys out there to the bungalow and have had the feeling people have been in. My symptoms are so up and down and punctuated with feeling completely normal. Such little bloody urine and then the black sludge, for such little volume I can't help but wonder because it is completely different to my usual symptoms than anything in the past. Because now I'm back in my prison and it leaves not much opportunity to gain access to the bungalow and I am fine again. I make precautions now too.

***Update as of Sunday 3rd November @ 0703
I have by now had a lot of time to review everything and I am afraid to say I am of the opinion that I was indeed being poisoned. My health is the best it's been since August, my muscle mass has returned, my healthy look too. I feel fit and strong again. I have not trained once. My pisses are normal, healthy in length and colour. Many times more frequent too. When I think back at how gaunt and exhausted I was during these last six weeks compared to now and the lack of access to the bungalow then yes I do believe it. I am certain in fact. When I thought about the symptoms and how on and off and unlike anything experienced before. That sludge was my body getting rid of whatever the substance used. If I did not drink as much water as I do and have a chronic tolerance of infections, I've

suffered many after all, I think I would quite possibly be dead by now.***

By spiking me, Kenny had ignited a spark in me that had first started to ignite during my recent 24hrs in bed. I had a Tony Soprano moment, for the fans of the show, it's where Tony gets food poisoning and hallucinates, Tony pieces everything together and he figures out Big Pussy is a rat, my subconscious connected the dots and the same sort of thing happened to me as Tony, I knew what I had to do. Unfortunately Kenny only compounded this. Thinking back over the last couple of days they knew quickly I had fucked my phone. My sister sent me a message within an hour of me finishing work, I had departed to the lady at XPO that my life was messed up. Then bang, out of nowhere and for the first time in more than a week, Carla sent me a message. She was all friendly and concerned "Are you ok? Is everything alright? You can talk to me you know! xxx"

I'd just had a really bad fall out with her daughter. It just didn't add up. They are getting very sloppy now, confident of upcoming victory, I should imagine. How did she know I was in strife because of the loss of my phone screen and how ill I was?? It was too obvious. I also think they had predicted I would go to Kenny's knowing my current mistrust of the Asian community. I have to say that whenever I went to town, there were many occasions, I noticed double takes and recognition from the Asian community, I still do. I had not seen any of them before. I had noticed that whenever I would put catering equipment up for sale I was inundated with pathetic offers by the Asian community, then one day not one. Not one single call or message. That remains true to this day. Nada. If you turned up at my home to view something and showed me disrespect by trying to rip me off and spoke in your native tongue while clearly saying derogatory things about me to the nice person you arrived with, then yes you would be made aware of my distaste. Rightly so too. Anybody, and I mean anybody, would be given the respect to be assumed to be a good person upon meeting them and it would be your actions from then on in that would form my opinion of you. No matter your creed or pigmentation, fake god etc. I don't care about all that, just what type of person you are. I have met some absolute diamonds within the immigrant community, though it seems to me the majority I have met unfortunately are just not good people and I have dealt with a good few by now. I state again I am not racist. I am not an enemy of immigrants either. I think the play was, knowing I would go to Kenny's and knowing I was ill, I would eventually go to hospital, like I was planning to do and when they checked my bloods, it would have been full of opiates. The hospital would have had a duty of care to the DVLA and public in general and had to inform the DVLA, bang goes my HGV entitlements. Boxed in completely then, I would be. Or maybe he took pity on me being ill and thought fuck it, I will help him feel better? Who knows really? But who does that though? I would also like a hair sample checked for all substances ASAP too, I was definitely spiked that day and why the handmade cigarette was so thick and tight. I hope to be proved wrong on the poisoning theory too, I really do, if I had a lorry crash it would have been nice, neat and tidy and I was that ill until the sludge came out, it could very easily of happened and nearly did in fact, if I did not stop on both the Tuesday and the Wednesday, I dread to think what would of happened, I'm so glad I did. The amount of water I naturally drink really helped me. I guess all will be exposed with the hair sample test.

Tuesday 21st October 2019

I rode to XPO in Middleton to sort my time sheet. Every time I leave the house now it is like a scene from a really crap smoggy version of Jason Bourne and without the expensive training too. I'm super alert and can actually scan quite a number of people quickly and pick out potential threats. Now I am not going to lie, I do racially profile. I know that some Eastern Europeans, Turkish, Libyan etc, they are half way between Arab and Caucasian and blend in easily with the latter too. Unless your Extremely Paranoid and on guard like me, then you stick out. I will of clocked them in a nano second and be risk assessing all the time. I also realise that people of African descent have hard to remember features unless you know them. A good few hours after I got back from XPO, I walked to the shop. Now this is the level of my paranoia, in these three next instances and especially after that eventful Friday, the paranoia is off the fucking chart by now. I am a realist but I am going on my gut feelings, not just now, but at the time too.

Incident No 1

I left the house after doing my lock checks and backing this up, and wiping the note book I'm using. I get half way to the shop, 150 yards and cross over. I notice straight away a Turkish decent looking man walking around 50 metres behind me. He had a short beard, more stubble, my height and weight and I didn't like it. Not the type of gentleman to usually walk down the most well to do street in Stockton on tees. Full of upper working class and lower middle, it's as good as Stockton town gets. I have never belonged on this road and amongst its residents. Having been on Darlington Road, 20 years on and off, you get to know a thing or two about it. I hate living here. Just like me, he did not fit and was unusual. It's was around 19.30 ish. Now my gut started to scream at me that this is suspicious. I reach his side of the road. I have massively short 29in inside leg, I'm 5ft 7in and it seems the only bodily thing I inherited from my dad was his back length and his good looks, obviously, everything else was from me Mum! A fast walker I am not, though weirdly I am a decent runner and since I have lost the fat I am much more nimble and fit now! Who knew? I also noticed very quickly how quiet it was, no traffic and nobody around. Monday night around that time it does get quieter. I kept looking to the side and getting him in my peripheral and trying to keep an eye on the gap. He was closing fast every time I looked. When he hit 15 metres and closing, I quick as a flash and instinctively did a 90 degree turn and walked over the other side of the road. Once on the other side I studied him and he had no choice but to continue walking. Giving away little. He stared straight ahead but he did have a little tell, he wanted to look at me so badly his head twitched slightly in my direction half a dozen times. By this point he was 15 metres in front of me on the other side of the road and I just watched him, he was clearly fighting the urge to look at me and I have to say if somebody had done what I had done in front of me, I would have been pissing myself laughing and looking at you asking "What the fuck was all that about mate?" He steamed past the shop not looking back once and disappeared around the corner. My gut tells me he does not know anybody in those big and massive, beautiful houses down the rest of Darlington road. The middle class end of lovely opulence and privacy. I did what I needed to do and on guard I walked home. Once I am in my home and with my dogs I am safe. You are in my domain then boys and you need surprise because if I see it coming, expect the fight of and for your life. I will give it my fucking all. I am primed for it. I am expecting it, I have accepted it. I am ready for it. I will want it more than you. If I have to fight for my life I am more than willing. I am willing to die for what is right and the truth of this. It makes all of this right and worth the fight and my life. I will do everything I have to, to survive. They know this. Plus it is too messy to murder me in my home. Though a stabbing on a quiet street or in the town centre by assailants unknown would be perfect, don't you think? The next best thing to crashing my lorry, it would give the opportunity for Cleveland police to control the investigation and tidy up their considerable mess. Was the man an assassin? Or was he an innocent member of the public? Honestly who knows, I cannot help but wonder.

Incident No 2. Tuesday

Not a bad one really and nothing bad happened.
The next night I went to the shop at around the same time and on the way back, around one hundred yards up and on my side of the road, I notice a black man with a Del Boy coat on. So, being cautious, I calmly and sensibly walked across to the path opposite and watched in my peripheral. He was looking at me a lot. Could he of just been walking that day? Maybe, positively likely even. Sorry if I offended you Del. Non ever intended, now or then, just precautions old boy.

Incident No 3. Wednesday

I had run out of backy and money and asked my lovely friend, Nikki if I could borrow £20 until Friday. She said yes bless her and said she's out and can meet me at the garage in Oxbridge in 5 minutes. This was worth the risk to me and I was there in 5 minutes flat. Me and this mountain bike are really starting to gel. I've got to know her intently and just like you have to get to know a motorcycle. Bikers will understand that comment. I'm a demon on the bloody thing now. I was that intent at looking at everybody on the forecourt, I didn't realise Nikki was blatantly right in front of me! Sat in her car, not two metres away and with the window down! For about 30 seconds too! She was just smiling at me shaking her head and suddenly came into focus. I shnortled (I feel I must explain "Shnortle" it is a term I made up for the noise one makes when he "shnorts" through his, or hers nose in amusement. I would like it if anybody "Shnortles" they then have to proceed this by saying the actual word "Shnortle" Its amusing, to me anyway. Copy Rights - Dictionary of Good Sir) Anyway I trust this lady in my gut, she is a good egg. I told her I cannot explain what is going on and you will just have read it but I promise you, my life is in danger. She was immediately concerned and tried to get me to tell her. Now have you seen the word count up to now? Yeah and I would sounded fucking nuts too no, a garage forecourt is not the right arena for that conversation Nikki my love. You will have to read it and all the other written works too. I said. I thanked her and said goodbye and went into the garage. Two things happened; I clocked recognition in three people I did not recognise. All by the time I got some coffee and joined the queue. After a minute or so I turn around and looked behind me a women was looking suspiciously at me whist on the phone, immediately suspicious I looked her in the eyes for a good 10 seconds. She suddenly walked to join the queue herself and loudly started talking in to her phone. Very Strange. Recognition? Undoubtedly. In the queue in front of me I see Kenny the mechanic from Tilstons motorcycles in Stockton, usually happy to see me, not this time though he was stiff and focused on not letting me know he had seen me. Eyes centre front, even as I joined the queue and making it painfully obvious he had seen me and recognised me but did not want me to know. I have a lot of history with Tillos and recently reached out for a job. It would have been awesome and I believed I could turn it around for them. Yamaha have just binned them and I know why. The majority of Teesside's bikers get their Yamaha's from elsewhere and Yamaha can see lots of registered bikes in the north east from other dealers in the country and have realised that, yes they hit their targets but they should be exceeding them by this many registered bikes in the area that they cover. Why? Because they piss people off that's why. I know so many people who buy the Japanese big 4 manufacturers from other dealers because of their experiences with them or hearing the horror stories. I have a couple myself. I would have got them back no problem and had a vision to make it the bike stop of the North East. It is the perfect location for it. It's in a little square you see. They own most of the buildings. I would have opened a cafe, a textile custom leathers shop and introduced a bike night. Also put a rolling road in. Also the Facebook page has barely 500 likes and is years old. It would have been something I would be excellent at because I would have loved it. Something I am passionate about and get my teeth stuck into and help revive this clearly failing and stale business while I take my time with Cheeky's. When the fossils that run it go extinct boys, get in touch. Until I told my sister that is and whoever, Uncle Martin, Cleggy, Carla, Laurencia? Who knows take your pick, got there first and ruined any chance of that. I sent Peter the owner a brilliant letter and pleaded for a job at least. Nada. That story though, does not explain Kenny's reaction in the garage. He looked quite uncomfortable. I was amused actually. Why was he being like this? We were both served at the same time and left with me behind him, I was enjoying his uncomfortable-ness and then jumped on my bike and rode home. I felt intensely watched. Why?

Today (Thursday) I went to town. It is actually my birthday today, 24th October. I was born in 1982.
I am 37 years good, fuck. *I am now older than my dad, when my Mum passed.* You realise when you get older, that your parents were just winging it, just like the rest of us. I used to think they knew what it was all about, like some wise super hero's. Nope, not a clue and learning on the job as you go too, it's called the reality of life, I guess. There is just billions of us clueless folk, wandering around, dazed and confused bumping into each other. Some lucky ones figure it out and realise you cannot, erm, figure it out and think fuck it and stop trying and embrace life. Now I am painfully isolated and looking over my shoulder, by design and by choice, for I simply do not know who I can trust. I worry about getting anybody else involved; I will only do that when I have too. I purposely fell out with my neighbours so they wouldn't try to help me. They may be the only two of three people my gut says I can trust but it's too risky. (Silly boy) Jan bless her, she sent me a message on the morning of the 24th and said "I've put £30

in your bank, happy bday xxx" God, I love that women. The closest thing to a mother I've had since my Mum. She is also my Friend and my Rock, the latter especially since my dad passed. I was buzzing knowing I didn't get paid until the next day. "Fuck it" I thought, I am going to town to buy some green, it's my birthday and I have not smoked any since Sunday. Now, where I got it from and who from, does not matter and I will deny ever knowing him as I like him and his little companion, (Fuck him his name is Tony Carter) good judge of character he is and the green is always spot on. I knew the risk I was taking but something else compelled me to take this very risky move and it seems right now, all over £20 worth of green. Yeah and Na, Fuck Yeah, Err, Sort of Half Right. What was really compelling me was the thought that if I exit through the patio door instead of the front door and leave the latch on the front door, if I could block the conservatory door with the broken key stuck in it but lock the patio door inside the conservatory then I might stop them and at least make it hard for them to get in. Martin my nephew had found a way into my back garden without anybody seeing, the crafty little fucker and how he was able to burgle me with ease. He had a key for the French doors you see. So knowing this I put my plan into effect. I left the key in the French doors only halfway, knowing you cannot unlock it from the outside, even with the key (Or so I thought). I put gaffer tape over the front door and in three places, my thinking was if they tried to open the front door then it would hit the latch and break the tape seals without giving any way to put them back. I locked the patio door. Now to block the conservatory door that I will be unable to lock because the key is snapped in the inside lock and has been that way for some time. I used a chair against the handle, it did not quite reach but it did not matter. I then turned my pub style bench on its side and against the chair. Next I put an old table top against that and then a heavy chiminea. After ten minutes of fucking around I found a good hold of all of it all with the mini ratchet strap I have. Now it was nice and tight and done properly and neatly, with the ratchet over the top of the upper seat of the pub bench and to get it so neat, that can be hard to do sometimes. Both hooks, hooked on the handle of the conservatory door. There is a technique with them. I knew it would be hard to put back exactly the same, especially when under pressure and if they don't have much experience with ratchet straps, then it's guaranteed. Maybe they will think I have blocked the door because I can't lock the inside patio door. Can I get them to make any mistakes? Only time will tell I thought. Satisfied with my work but pissed off because my phone had run out of battery and died just as I went to take a picture, you fucking wally, I jumped over my now ratchet strapped up gate at the side of my house and jumped on my bike and rode through Ropner Park and to a cash machine near Oxbridge garage, I was disguised as best I could. Wearing a cap and my Valentino Rossi jacket I'd found again recently. I then went into town to see the person I don't know (Tony Carter). On my way up the start of the high street I get shouted at by these two ruff looking lads, who shouted at me with some urgency *"Ow!, come here kid"* I ignored them and rode on, I took a route that passes Kenny's, I stopped and stared, as soon as he'd seen me, I smiled and rode off. I got to where I was going and got told to come back in 15 minutes. I am immediately suspicious and ever since I set off too. My guts feelings have been kicking right off. Firstly as I set off and I travelled 100 metres down the road from the bungalow down towards the "brickie" pond and back up the road somebody beeped twice, I stopped and had a good look. Seemed suspicious, a coast is clear, beep, beep maybe? I couldn't see anything unusual just Darren's car, Katies bother. I also noticed Katies's Mum in her upstairs window, that is not unusual anyway. I walked my bike over and around Skinner Street doubled back on myself and jumped back on the bike and rode off down Dovecot Street. I dismounted in the pedestrian part as I know you're not allowed to ride in those bits and thought maybe that is why those lads had shouted at me? I chained my bike up across from the car park to the new style lamp post down the side of Lloyds around twenty yards away. I'm a mixture of nervousness and excitement, I am super alert. The adrenalin and a bit of testosterone effects, maybe? I am under pressure that's for sure. I walked towards the library and walking in Fatso's direction I clocked a big lad straight away, 20 I would say, heavy build, big shoulders, dressed like a chav in matching tracksuit and the obligatory Nike trainers and walking towards me with the timing to be behind me on my current heading, the sort of hard as nails ruff up and coming, council estate top dog and eager to prove himself hard man, I know the type well because I grew up with a few and I was friends with a couple of the fuckers. I slowed my pace, so as to meet him at the same time and three metres away suddenly stopped, looked at him and swept my hand out in a Good Sir gesture of politeness and good intentions. Well he had no choice but accept my gracious invitation and I matched his pace keeping at a constant 5m gap. Whatdoyaknow, he takes the exact route to the library as me, past the war memorial, down the cut through and to the crossing outside the library, I'd be surprised if he could even read never mind a member of a library. There were lots of people around thankfully. As I catch him up at the roadside, I see an opportunity to cross the road quick as a flash and time only just for that as a car goes past a second later and then I slip into the library. Safety! I could breath. I have to say the entire journey behind this young fellow, matching his pace, which did slow a couple of times, to maintain the gap was a very primed moment, I am expecting an attack. To reach that safety and quite skilfully too, it was exciting to me. I'm a little nut's but not mentally ill in that sense. I think you can understand my caution and over active imagination by now. Was it just a coincidence? I cannot help but wonder. I went straight upstairs and chose the least busy table. I took my coat off and went and ordered a glass of much needed water. Water and a large cappuccino. Yes please but more thirsty for the water at this point. I downed the water from the pretty server at the small cafe up there. She made the coffee and I went to sit back down. Bloody lovely. I then, after realising my phone was dead, realised that I might be able to access my Gmail with my other Hotmail email, turns out I was wrong. It was Apple, I set that up with, realising now. So I logged off and drank my coffee and set off to where I never went and see the guy I don't know and have never met and his little companion who likes me as much as is possible for him too, anyway, I would say more tolerates. Brilliant judge of character is his companion. Always greets me and we have a certain ritual with each other, in that brief and meaningful encounter, I have been judged and accepted, greeted and wished well, even goodbye. He will not pay me any more heed for the rest of my brief stay but I believe him to judge everybody who comes to visit and is right more than he is wrong, and quite a few don't get accepted, I truly believe it and I got accepted and that's it. His boss always says he doesn't like anybody even him, he proclaims it. I say, he might be aware that you can be a c**t but he sees your good side too and because you're the boss in his world and are his god really, in his own way he looks out for you, even if he doesn't quite like, what he sees. I get to 20 yards from NatWest and notice a busker playing a song, I decide to go over and give him 50p. I then walk towards NatWest again on a diagonal trajectory and notice a black man out of nowhere, watching me and walking diagonally in my direction, fucking primed I am now, every sinew and nerve in my body is tingling, he's closing fast, I reach a bench and phone box and suddenly move behind what can be only described as a silver metal box with an ashtray on top putting that between him and me. I stared at the man. Looked him right in the eyes. It was returned with a half menacing and half surprised look, the look on my face dared him to attack. He continued walking and went to the phone box and whilst looking at me he slipped in the door. Quickly and with purpose whist not taking my eyes from the man and his eyes from me, I walked in the direction I needed to be. I gained ground quickly, turned into a cut between the buildings and then I was gone. If this was another coincidence then a very high fucking tension one. My whole body was screaming that this was a very dangerous situation I find myself in this day. I at least, cannot help but wonder. I get to the place I have never been and see the guy I don't know, I do my ritual with his companion, relieved and pleased to see him and accepted, I look at the boss. Surprise mixed with a little adulation and respect. Quite a dour man usually, he was noticeably more animated than I had ever seen him and he was also nervous and jittery. My gut tells me he might not have been expecting me back that day or any other, I fear. With telling me to come back in 15 minutes when I got there I realised later that he was leaned on and knew what was happening that day. I cannot blame him. Though, I cannot help but wonder. I thanked him and left. I took a good route back to the bike and all was good until Yorkshire bank. I spot an Asian/Turkish man walking behind me some 20 metres back. They realise they need to surprise me because if I see it coming they know they will be in a fight for their very lives. I have to say I have never been to the town with a weapon before, ever. He was quite trendy and smart, I am suspicious of everyone and everything by now and straight away I did the old quick as a flash 90 degree turn and I crossed the road at Lloyds and just past the building and on the opposite side of the road I stopped and just watched. There were lots of people around but not one where I am stood. I didn't move and the man continued walking, paying me no mind, except a few twitches in my direction. Fighting the urge to look maybe? Why? He walked to a double parked white car on the road outside the car park not 20 yards from my bike, got in the passenger seat and sat there, only pulling away after I had unlocked my bike. I kept looking at the car. It did not help my suspicions I can tell you. Coincidence? I really cannot help but fucking wonder. I, as quickly as I could, unlocked the bike and set off. On the bike I feel disguised and safe. I rode home in good spirits and as fast as I could. I felt like I had dodged a death sentence. I was elated. I reached my drive and dismounted at my front door and climbed over the gate to the back door, instantly noticing the change in the furniture, my god, I studied it and then checked the ratchet strap. Loose! I looked at the actual ratchet and the strap twisted and caught in the mechanism and under the top seat too, the completely wrong way to how I'd left it. Gone was the neat and tidiness and it had obviously been tampered with. The furniture had obviously moved. Excited and gob smacked my plan had worked, I started swearing "The Bastards!" I proclaimed repeatedly, I cannot help but wonder. Yeah, Na, Fuck That. Confirmed and spectacularly but who? Why? Well now take your pick. You Michael, have managed to unintentionally make the biggest enemies and with the most powerful and varied factions in Teesside to boot. It's a very fucking dodgy make up is Old Teesside, motivated them in the process, you have too. Not to mention the EU, Guy Verhofstad and their Remainer cabal. Of your own making? I'd say so yes. Accidentally or not. Yes I am an opinionated Arsehole. I stand up for what is right. My big lesson from all this is "Making a stand for what is right, will undoubtedly make you enemies but ultimately it is worth the fight, nonetheless" Copy Rights Dictionary of Good Sir, there is a bit of Winston Wisdom in the quote. I don't think the perpetrators got in but they obviously had to see if the patio was left open and maybe not realising the ratchet problems they would undoubtedly have. I'd of loved to have filmed it. I dismantled the blockage and entered the house and checked the front door. All good. However a card was on the floor from Katy. I can trust nobody now, that tactic is good for not leaving many ways to use people against me. I realised I am alone and an army of one, especially after coming up with my plan to relocate to Swindon and earn some really good money working for royal mail over Xmas. Job sorted and place sorted too. Then Carla found out and within a week my friend who kindly offered his spare room and my dogs a home in Swindon, suddenly his son was scared of dogs. Every avenue of help was unceremoniously denied and every door was slammed in my face. Thinking back it was a brilliant plan. Get down there, get myself back again, get my Facebook back, make videos and then do go fund me. I told Carla this plan. In fact, I gave her a running commentary come to think about it. Couldn't have that now could they? Can you see this cannot be in my head? You could not make this shit up. My birthday was an eventful and memorable one to say the least. Real life Jason Bourne shit and in Stockton on Tees too. It is unbelievable, I know. I have to say I have written every single word of this as it happened to me. It's almost a live journal because I am writing this at the same time too. Everything I have wrote in other documents you have read are from the heart and what I call "experience writing". I am coming from a place of truth. I just cannot make this shit up, I promise you. This is my witness statement and not a book people.

Friday 25th October - Pay Day

I was stunned all night long and quite apprehensive about having to go back to town to do my banking. Until it started pissing down. I smiled, At around 14.30 and in the pissing rain, I set off to town. Today felt different. The town on market day was near deserted in the rain and was sparsely populated. Most stalls were being dismantled and it could not have been more different to yesterday. I felt quite safe on the way in and my gut was okay too. I then noticed a GM (Gary McCarten) liveried van next to one of the stalls. I smiled. On my way back from XPO on Tuesday, I went past the Parkwood Pub near my home and another Gary McCarten, GM fencing, liveried car was in the pub car park. I immediately skidded to a stop and rode into the car park and faced the pub windows and just looked, willing him to come out, after 30s or so I rode off. It probably wasn't him. I also knew it was not likely to be him in the town either. I walked past thrice times and brazenly not giving a fuck. I was obviously recognised although I do not know these people. At a guess it was his father in law maybe. Not finding myself feeling any of the skulduggery of yesterday I pretty much went about my business with no issues. I was a little disappointed strangely. Just as I was leaving I noticed two lads walking towards me, its only Gary's cousin and one of his employees. They see me and quickly ducked around the corner. Had it been a sunny market day then it might have been a very different situation I think. It was certainly perfect timing in the rain that's for sure. Thank fuck for English weather. I did not bother with blocking the door but still left via the patio with the latch on the front door. The confirmation of the day before meaning I didn't really have too. I walked with the dogs to the vet's appointment and made good time. The employees in the vets were quite weary of me though. I am now back in my safe zone and prison. Though I feel, on Thursday somebody was Indeed looking over me and have been for some time. I hope it is my ancestors, displeased at all the skulduggery performed on the up against it but still in the fight and beloved brethren, friend and son, it's a nice thought. Maybe it is these thoughts themselves that give me the strength, so by association and at the minimum, it is Indeed, my ancestors doing. I do find it interesting that the potential assassins were, a council estate Caucasian, a skulduggery laden black man and a playboy Asian. Nice to know that gangsters, dodgy businessmen and corrupt police officers subscribe to the equal opportunity employment ethos and do not discriminate. Kudos boys. I cannot sufficiently depart to you how real that day was and how dangerous a situation I felt I was in. Even if it is all in my head, it was very real to me I can confirm. I did not have time to feel scared. My only focus was on what was around me and potentially any danger. I focused on my objectives. I could not have foreseen what would happen. Why would you put yourself in danger like that? More sane people would have hid. I can only say, I was driven to go, I needed an excuse to go, I was itching to go. I needed it to be confirmed. I needed to know it was not in my head. I needed to see how far they were willing to go. I needed to see if they would try to enter my home. I was also very fucking angry. It does help. After Fridays uneventful foray into town I then had the weekend to process and write down what had happened. Though, something strange happened to me. My mind struggled with the facts. The adrenalin had worn off and was replaced with shock. Writing helped greatly. My emotions are in check when needed to be but all over the place when I am safe. I keep expecting all the family to jump out and say "Surprise! It was all about giving you the inspiration to write a kickass book" If only. I cannot shake the utter disbelief and heartbreak of my families actions. I do not understand how anybody could do this to somebody they love. I get gangsters, greedy businessmen's and corrupt coppers motives, my families on the other hand are much, much harder to fathom.

Chapter No 6

Everything wrote down below was written until the next Star before Thursday 24th*

The Conclusions

Where do I start? Honestly where? I don't know really. It seems after the trial things just went mental. It was like I was being suppressed purposely to stop me writing and shut me up and also so I did not send out the business plan or do the go fund me. It's all been a carefully orchestrated plan to keep me down and from succeeding. Ruin me basically. Now if I had told you my fears and suspicions face to face, you would think I am indeed "Nuts" "Crazy" "Insane" because I do too when I hear it. Now though, they went too far and forced me in to doing one of the very things they've been trying to censor me from doing all this time. What do I hope to achieve with this? Prove my sanity and save my life more importantly. I am not scared as such but more apprehensive and anxious and truly believe my life to be in danger. If they suspect I'm writing this then I think they will panic and do something stupid. Actually they might already know! I got a very unusual phone call from Jan, my step mum, the other night. Now just the fact she rang me was strange enough in and of itself, she never rings me. It's always me who rings her. I answered and proceeded to blurt out my fears. I did indeed sound crazy. She did not take me seriously, obviously. One thing I did say was that "I bloody well hope I can still trust you women!" She told me "Don't worry I don't speak to anybody" Oh Jan, I know that to be a fib, now. You speak to Carla all the time because she told me you do. She's shit at secrets remember. Laurencia, in those disgusting messages she sent me also said Jan believes me to be mentally ill. Umm. Definitely does not sound like you do not speak to anybody now does it? So as I looked at the clues a theory popped up that I choose to believe. I owe Jan an considerable amount of money, 20K she told Carla, who she doesn't speak to. Now I had not realised it had got that high but was not bothered because I know I will be successful and will pay her back 10 fold. Knowing they will be panicking, not knowing what I am doing, I hope. It was a phone call that was very suspicious when I replayed it in my head. Now whether they are worried about this document I can only guess, but I do believe the main worry is the go fund me but possibly this too now. I hope they are all shitting themselves that I've figured it all out. I can forgive Jan because I believe she is being manipulated from afar by my family and the thought of Jan getting any money from Uncle Martin and then when, not if, I am successful, her getting 20k one hundred fold if I can, makes me fucking smile as she will get that whether she wants it or not and she knows it. I love that kind and sweet women dearly and I might have unintentionally taken advantage of her. For that I am truly sorry. Of course Jan putting a post on Facebook within 30mins of the call, proclaiming she is going to Australia at Xmas didn't help! You fucking enjoy it Jan and I hope you took Uncle Martin for every penny you could! Even, if it was just the holiday. If I've called it right, then actually, I am really proud of you Jan!

Having realised the Kenny play, that's when it really hit me how much my life is in danger and that I have not a clue how far this goes and all the actual players involved. Remember the Prize. A potential multi million pound takeaway company, that is what ultimately, my recipes represent. That's the truth of it. My dogs, my carefulness and my willingness to fight are keeping me safe, for now. I am really a prisoner in this hell that is the bungalow and now I need help. I have nowhere to turn, nobody to believe me. How far does this travel? Are all the players, playing together or are they working independently? There are so many unanswered questions still. I never wanted to write this in this way, it's more like a final insurance policy and will and testament than my attempt at getting published. I don't want it to be published, not in this guise. Compare this with me writing "Fuck You Pc Tim" and gone is the excitement, gone is the inspiration, gone is the happiness of it all, the magic. It shows in the writing I would say. No, I have to force myself on a morning to start. Sometimes it takes me a couple of hours before I get the encouragement. It's heartbreaking it really is. The point of the books was to help people. My original plan was to tell my life story over three books and I have had to condense it down into this, missing many a great story and lesson in the process. I think one of the fears was that I would drag the Elwood name through the mud. That is simply not true. I would have protected it and anybody in them. My aim could never be spite or revenge. No, one thing I have learnt is leave the past where it is and let that shit go. I forgive each and every player involved. I have to because if Michael Elwood did revenge, well it would be biblical. If you read this and you are in a position too, then please help me. I need to get out of here and for me to do the go fund me. It's the only answer. It kills their plans dead and saves me too. I cannot explain what it has been like living this hell, the last 6 months, always chasing your tail and playing catch up, two steps behind every time.

My Local Shop

Watching everybody around you completely change, even the girls at my local shop and is an experience I would not wish on anybody. Now these girls have been my only contact with other human beings for weeks sometimes and I noticed this change painfully. I have to say that they probably have noticed my changes from happy to depressed, over the last couple of years. I would look forward to seeing them and having a chat. It was nice to be around people, even for as short a time as being served. Ironically, I am a very social person but I have a chronic tolerance of loneliness it seems. They were always nice to me and interested in what I was up to. I especially looked forward to seeing Hanna and Kelsey. Kelsey was always good as I used to drink with her many moons ago and the fact her parents hate my guts, I was always pleasantly surprised she was nice to me. Now my local shop is very badly run. Its pap and with no real leadership it seems. Full of young and old women, there is lack of any male presence. At around August, I noticed a lot of out of area and dodgy looking people start using the shop. Around about this time the girl's demeanour changed. I thought I might be making them feel uncomfortable, maybe I was showing them too much attention? So I decided to be a little less friendly because I could not bare that thought. By doing this I was a lot more aware of what was happening in the shop and around this time, I lost the use of my car and have walked to the shop since. I had noticed a lot more shop lifters for example. Not even trying to hide it. Now not one to stop such a thing as petty theft I just went about my business. Not my problem is petty theft. That's the shops problem that is. Now I got caught shoplifting when I was 13. I was marched to an office and treated like the little shit I was. I got screamed at then sent home. They rang my home phone at 6pm as promised and I sat there as my Dad got told what his son had done. Getting angry looks, that got perpetually more angry as the call progressed. Eventually the call came to its natural end, apologies made and arrangements agreed and I knew what was coming next. It was not a cuddle and do you wanna talk about it, no not like parents of today, the bomb that was my Dad went off. It was not funny at the time, but with the benefit of hindsight it's hilarious to me now. My dad went so mad that I had to defend myself. I don't mean fight back just, dodge and weave and put feet in the air to block him, shit like that. I did really well and never suffered a direct hit in a good 5 minutes of trying, in fact my poor suffering Ol'man hit my feet and trainers so hard he bust his wrist and was in a bandage for a week! Anyway he marched me back around the shop, pushing me the whole way in disgust at this despicable thief of a son. We got in the office and met the scary women and the butcher who had so effectively scorned me earlier. It was not nice, I felt nothing but shame. The women even started crying. So did I. My dad clipped me a few times too when I didn't answer her quickly enough. They did not hurt and I had a certain tolerance to clips around the ear by then. I had deserved a few and I felt I deserved them then and even now too. I will tell you this experience had a profound effect on me and I never stole anything from anyone ever again. I, with love and tough love, by people who truly cared was shamed by it, made to face up to it but with a care and underlying kindness by all nevertheless. Because what I had done was wrong. They taught me a valuable and well remembered lesson. Can you imagine that scenario happening in this day and age? No me either. Shop lifting is seen as beneath the police to even investigate, it is effectively decriminalised and now it's not even cared about or acknowledged. That's sad. What is to say if my Dad and the women in the shop did not care enough about it, that I would of gone on to a life as a criminal? My Dad even got the local copper to come around and lambaste me for 20 minutes and threaten me with arrest, though they were friends and drank in the same pub. Lessons like that are important. Interesting thought, how many lessons are not being passed on by generations and are being lost to time? Something very important is being lost.

Robbery however, I would have a duty to the girls in the shop to do something and make sure they are safe. Knowing that rumours of my mental health perpetrated by my family no less, had obviously reached them was a horrible experience especially noticing peoples demeanour towards me change, that was so hard to take. The girls reminded me they care. Especially, Hanna and Kelsey. I only ever see concern in their eyes when they see me. Especially when slowly everyone around me disappeared, they were my link to normality in a way. I think they know something else is going on. I cannot say anything, I cannot risk people's safety. Anyway, around 4 months ago, I had seen Hanna in the shop and it was just her and I and we started chatting. We don't often get the chance because she is always serving and it is a busy little shop. The rumours were just getting started at this point. We got on to shoplifting and she told me they had been getting targeted by shop lifters all the time in fact 60k worth of stock in three months, personally I had only noticed the wrong-uns for the last few weeks. Over a grand in cheese in one go she told me! Now this made me suspicious, £1000 of cheese is a hell of a lot, around 400 blocks and 160 odd KG, yeah you would need a pallet and pallet truck to nick that in one go! I asked what the police are doing about it? "We don't bother they won't do anything" I was flabbergasted. Sounds to me this isn't petty theft, no this is robbery plain and simple. A week went by and I was okay, happy, eating, training I looked good, fit, strong and with the Alfa male look I get when happy, eating and training. I went to the shop one day, I don't remember exactly when and had a tight t-shirt on and looked good. I walked in the shop, I did what I needed, got served by Hanna and we had a little chit chat, said goodbye and turned and started to walk out. As I approached the doors, I was immediately faced with two very ruff looking gentlemen, the one closest to me he was weathered, tattoo on his neck short hair, tracksuit bottoms, trainers and the other pretty much the same. Not of this area, that's for sure. Both clocked me walking towards them at the door and instantly did an about turn and walked back out of the shop. I, walking that way anyway, I was naturally suspicions and bemused. As I walked outside I noticed they both carried good size sport bags with them each and were on bikes. I took in the two boy's profile and realised they were just about to rob the place. Fill their bags up and do one, knowing that it would be full of girls working and nobody has been or would be there to stop them. Except the boyo's clearly did not bargain on me. I turned around and walked back in the shop. I walked up to Hanna who was

serving this old Gypsy type looking man with old jail tats, you know, done with a compass by hand and with ink. I paid him no mind after assessing him, he was paying, after all. I said to Hanna "Hanna you know you're getting done over!?" she looked at me perplexed. Just as I said that a man bolted from the fridge aisle, ran out of the shop and up the road. I shnortled, turned to Hanna and shouted excitedly "See!!"…"Ring the police!" I went back outside and the two boys had moved over the road to the cut, it is at a diagonal from the shop and 30 yards away, peering around every few seconds, obviously waiting for me to leave. I stood on the wall and added two foot to my short stature and stood tall and proud. Chest puffed out. Worrier mode enabled. I just stared at them. Every time they peered they just saw the Worrier, waiting. The manager, 2ft shorter than the wolf now, the Warrior turned to the manager and said "Have you phoned the police?"
"No they would not do anything" I just looked down at her. Angry, for one that Cleveland Police are that shit that they would not even investigate and two, that the silly women cannot tell the difference between petty theft and organised robbery. Shop lifters generally do not work in

threes. I told Hanna this fact a couple of days later and not the manager. Why? Because I can see how badly run of a shop it is and just did not want to waste my time. After a time the gaps between looks from the boys had eventually got longer and longer until not at all. I was satisfied the boys had left and were not coming back so knowing Hanna was safe I went home. I must have looked a sight to the public at those shops that day who were oblivious to what was happening, and me stood proud on that wall, in all of my Worrier glory, for around 10 minutes. You couldn't make this up! It is so funny, looking back at it. Do I deserve any credit? No I don't think so. I did not really do anything except look fit and strong. Not like I heroically put my life in danger, though I think the robberies stopped after that but it has become a hot bed of petty theft as word has spread about this softest of targets. Especially kids nicking sweets. It near enough advertises to people with the inclination that it is fair game. I see it all the time. This shit is what a half decent police force would do something about. No not Cleveland Police. I believe there are many good people that work for them but they are ruled and lead by corrupt, inept and criminal elements (you think?).

This has been the case for some time. Nobody gives a shit about Teesside and its whole scale corruption is unchecked, unseen and always has been. It could be so much better. Teesside's, miseries are then compounded and encourage by the most inept and corrupt of police forces that seriously is hampered from doing the very thing it's task and responsibility to the council tax payers of this area has a duty to do, protect and fucking serve. Simply how can it be for the people if it is ran to the benefit of its corrupt core? People in the know, know who the real gangsters of Teesside are and it not the criminals, no half of them obviously work for good old Cleveland Police. If the leadership is bad then the force has to be bad. Even if full of good people. They don't have the power. This needs to change because Teesside is fast becoming the lawless east without an effective and properly run police force. The public of Teesside in general are very fearful and weary I can see. I don't think people feel safe. Time for a clear out and get the good people in charge again. Nobody had been able to get at Cleveland Police's corrupt elements in the past, maybe this is how? Maybe they have fucked with the wrong Stockton on Tees citizen? Nice thought that is. The Smoggies version of a diabolically shit Jason Bourne "He seeks nothing but the truth in his fight back to the girl he loves." I could walk there, it's only down the road, only take a couple of hours, 45min on the bike it would. Yeah I know it's more a mental fight to her, getting there though. I see many a strange character up that shop still too. A few were there to try and intimidate me by following me around the shop, one exactly the same size as Carl McCarten, I just fronted it out like I have learnt to do, its strange, I actually was not intimidated by him, its like the bigger you are the more game I am. I am not suggesting that these robberies had anything to do with me, say to fit me up? I like to think so when I muse it over, be ironic that would if you think about it. The very man being fit up as a shop lifting gang boss is the very man who puts a stop to the very thing they are trying to fit him up for. My mind sometimes is an amusing place. This is just a musing but it would be poetic justice if I am right. My gut does smell something off with what happened. It is pure speculation and until I can freely speak to people about this I do not know. Still I thought it needs mentioning as it is curious and an amusing experience and makes for a good story too that should be on the record, it might have more significance in the future. I can just imagine the top guy at Cleveland police running the show against me and how fucking frustrated he must be by now, it makes me smile...

I absolutely hate going anywhere people know me now. It is in people's eyes, a mixture of sadness, pity and unease at being around a supposed mental patient and god knows what else too. It's got to the point that if you give me that look I can't look you in the eyes any longer because it's so painful to see. I ignore everybody if I see that look, which won't help with the rumours, I know but I simply cannot bare it. I'm screaming inside "I'm ok, I promise you, I'm the same I always was. I promise you, please believe me" It's been heartbreaking. I am not going to lie. Then when the realisation and emotions hit when I've slowly been piecing it all together, anger, disbelief, torment, sickly feelings in my stomach, knots in my stomach. The feeling of Betrayal especially, now I am not depressed any longer. Everyone of those other feelings is much better, even collectively and at the same time. I feel sad that people can do this to one another. What did I do to these people? Why? I could not do this to a fellow human being, never mind my family. There are many more situations and suspicions I could include and I think you can see that you cannot make this shit up. Just too many coincidences for it to be the ravings of a paranoid schizophrenic and like I say, that is exactly what it makes me sound like. They very nearly had me fooled for a time. I fear they banked on me either, topping myself by now, crashing my lorry or doing something daft to get banged up at the least. I spend far too much time on my own and hope to change that. I know when I am out of this situation I will be back to my old self again, instantly. I cannot wait for that day. This dream is what keeps me going, the thought of much, much better days to come. That and Love...

Chapter 7

The truth, the whole truth, so help me god

Now to dispel the biggest subject that I believe to be in the process of being used against me, this will be hard reading but please don't judge me until you have read it all. I have to be totally honest. It is definitely the hardest thing I have put down on paper. It has taken at lot of motivation. I guess what is happening is enough. This subject is actually not that interesting to me now it is resolved. It might explain these recognitions and looks, the change in people. This means I have to be honest. It's not hard really is it? I've written thousands of words of truth up to now so a bit more is no mind, even as hard as it will undoubtedly be. I was always intending to write this in the third book of my trilogy, I thought I had years until then. It's a funny old world.

The Cheeky Devils Aftermath

After Cheeky's went under I essentially had a break down over a period of three months and for a few reasons. I have suffered with depression and anxiety without really knowing it, on and off my whole adult life. What I am about to explain to you does not deserve any sympathy for me nor is it needed, nor is it warranted. Yes Cheeky's was the catalyst but not the biggest reason. When I was 9 my mother, Sharon was diagnosed with cancer and started her two year battle with this fucking horrible disease. My dad had a very stressful job and really struggled with my mother being ill, I ended up moving to Great Yarmouth with Grandma Margaret and Granddad Tony, Auntie Joey, Uncle Cliffy and my cousins Katie and Ruth. My Mum moved back to Stockton with Nana Nora and my dad stayed in Grimsby where we had lived for the last year. I, after 9 months in Hemsby just outside Yarmouth, I was moved to my Uncle Martin's in Stockton to be closer to my Mum. It's safe to say it was a very strange and lonely two years without your family. I could only see my Mum once every two weeks when I lived in Stockton and not at all when in Yarmouth and Martin only lived a 25 min walk away too. My dad came to Yarmouth a couple of times and then every other weekend when I went to Uncle Martins. With hindsight and I'm not judging anybody for the decisions made, I would of preferred to live with my Mum and Nana. I completely get that my Mum did not want me to see her in pain, see her deteriorate but I realise now that she had good days and bad so how many good days did I miss in Yarmouth and Uncle Martins? As much as I loved living with Big G and I did, I really thrived in Hemsby or the times I missed while I was at my Uncle Martin's? Those good days would have been worth the bad and when it was bad I could have stayed over Martins, just how many precious days could we have had? I get angry when I think about it and subconsciously I have been a little angry at my Mum over this I am ashamed to say. I felt forgotten about, disregarded, an inconvenience. My new stepmother Dianne could never understand why I was an emotionally messed up kid. No really.

I have battled internal strife all my adult life due to abuse I suffered by the local paedophile back when I was twelve. This fucked me up for many reasons, I was already second base active at that age and not long after actually lost my virginity so it's not like I didn't know what he was doing and the fact I laughed and giggled while he did it completely fucked my mind up. I also experimented with other children of around the same age way too young. These stories will remain with me because I would like to protect the people involved and no one needs to know really. I've learned it's not uncommon for kids to experiment like that. Just know that the PTSD I was suffering is a consequence of abuse and I am a victim. This fucked me up and stopped me from having a normal life. He chose to do that to me for his own sexual needs and messed up any chance of a proper life for my first 18 years of adulthood as well as a messed up childhood in general. I had silently battled these demons all on my own and all my adult life. You see suicide is the biggest killer in men, bigger than cancer, the top one and many, many times higher than women. I was going to write about my experiences to try and help people because I wonder how many men have struggled in this way and not found the strength? Thought they had nowhere to turn? Can you imagine living with the thought that you are maybe the most hated and shamed things you could possibly be in western society? To be something you would pay anything not to be, any price, any price at all, Please God help give me the strength, not hard to see why some troubled soles turn to the understanding and forgiving nature of the church now is it? Now I say no actual Paedophiles have had this torment, no they accepted it and embraced it, encourage it and helped it grow, learned to live with it, even love it. They choose to be bad and wrong. They decided to put their sexual needs above the well being of children. They made that choice, to basically sponsor the robbing of children's precious lives. Or the very people they could or should have been. In a way it is a type of life robbery and murder of a better future or at the very least making it extra hard to get one, if they find their way at all. I have been lucky to find that strength to see this through to its bitter end and the beginning of a much, more happy chapter in my life or so I thought. That will happen at some point, I just could not let anybody in. My teenage years were quite good by and large, after my mother passed. I was successful with the girls and went on some brilliant adventures and have fantastic memories and looking back was worth all the trouble I always accidentally seemed to find myself in but I could not adjust to adult life until around the beginning of 2007 when I decided to quit smoking cannabis and start drinking, I had smoked too much cannabis from a young age and it did not help as my brain was not ready. I felt I had no one to turn too. No one could understand. When it comes to that man and what he did, I often think about his three kids. You see, Tony Hill the Paedophile had a daughter my age and one a few years younger and a six year old son. Now at the time of the attack I was being sweetly serenaded by the eldest daughter. She was lovely and looking back, so quiet and an overwhelming sadness and kindness in her. The middle child was quiet and sullen at all times and the son was very troubled. What worries me greatly is if he messed me up in one hour of me being alone with him then what was it like for those poor kids? I often wonder if they have had to endure their own silent torment and had to deal with what he did to them too. How damaged they are now, especially the boy as Tony didn't seem into girls looking back. Did anybody save them? Do they have normal lives? Did they find peace? What could they have been without that burden? I cannot help but wonder. I found out after he had been arrested, that locals used to see him run around naked after the son with his front room curtains open. Now I am going to try and remember the era here but if that is true then all you residents who knew this and did nothing to save those kids is a fucking shame on you in my book. He was also known to the police as a prolific Paedophile. You would think that, even in those days of the early 90s somebody would of said "Hey maybe it's not such a good idea to have this man around children fucking ever, especially his own" His wife was just as bad. They even let him and the wife have a teddy bear shop, if they had done something then maybe they could have saved his kids and a good few fucking others too from this torment. I have stopped hating him now. I don't want to kill him any longer. Though I think if I met his kids now and really spoke to them I would shamefully seek him out and kill the man dead and with my bear hands too, if he is still alive, that is. He lived 200 yards from two schools in a council house. What the fuck? Who thought that was a good idea to re-home him there? This man was pure twisted sickness and evil and frankly needed to be put down like the rabid dog and oxygen thief he was and still is if alive. That man has never felt shame. He has never experienced torment over his choice to be that monster, to be a Paedophile. He never feels guilt, nor his wife. Just as sick in my opinion. How many little lives did he selfishly and inextricably alter and help destroy for his own sick needs?

It all got too much and eventually after years and years of silent torment and constantly having to pick myself up again and again my mind eventually burst and kicked back and I let out what was happening to me, to family and friends and I started to confront my mind. It was liberating. It helped me so much. After seeing a psychologist and talking about it for the first time in my life my mind was at peace and I knew who I was, I wasn't bad! I wasnt "THAT" I was definitely good like people have always told me. Things were good for the next 6 months until a month after Cheeky's went under and it was a friends wife's birthday and I had been invited, not really wanting to go, I reluctantly made myself attend, I walked in and my friend Leeroy was there on the first seat of the table and the chair opposite was free so I sat in it without thinking as you do, not seeing anybody to sit next to further up. I sit down. I then noticed Jonny's kid is sat next to me. Everybody else turned up. Carrie, the birthday girl is also Jonny's kid's mother and Jonny's wife and was sat a few chairs down from me. Now I'm not being big headed but Carrie will usually give me admiring glances when I'm out, at my roguish good looks, smug twat, it's true but this time it was in absolute concern for her child sat next to me. I felt intensely watched, studied, then pissed off and upset at this development I went for a smoke outside. When I returned Jonny had swapped seats with his kid. This is when I realised that what I had told to a very select few people had gone main stream and Chinese whispers prevailed, I'd heard later that apparently I'd been raped for example. She felt she had to be worried about me sat next to her child. Holy fuck, this devastated me. She actually thought I was a Paedophile and sexually attracted to pre-pubescent children! My world fell apart because that could not be further from the truth. My very worst nightmare had happened and I descended into complete hopelessness and I'm not going to lie, I very nearly took the everlasting sleep, again, recurring theme looking back. I have faced my own morality many times now. Ultimately I found the strength to battle back knowing I was ok and I had found the strength to say Fuck It, Fuck them if that's what they think and if that's what you think, then Fuck You too. It was a revelation and because I genuinely did not care for the first time ever what people thought and it liberated my mind! With that my depression evaporated. My positivity was off the chart, my newly found zest for life was formed. My self belief was unlimited and I had the unshakable mental strength of 10 men! Simply, a fantastic feeling, I felt I could take on the world and win. Just know I am not nor was I ever a Paedophile as you will find out.

If a man is tormented by his confusion about what is happening to him, his fears and desperately wants it to stop and would never ever do a bad thing, then does that not make him the very antithesis of a Paedophile? That man needs love and understanding, help most of all. Not ever judgement. No, for he seeks help and guidance and desperately wants it to end and be somebody else. Herein lies the problem. The subject and peoples natural reaction to the word Paedophile ensures a man has nowhere to turn because the subject and name turn people off instantly. No place he will not be judged, nowhere to hide if someone is told and mistakes them for a Paedophile. He is now painted from this day and forth as the lowest vermin in society. How many innocent men have lost their mental fight and overcome by the torment because of having nowhere to turn. We need to change this attitude to people in need. A proper active and clinical Paedophile is a lost cause and should be dealt with, very severely but an innocent and tormented soul needs saving, it needs Help, Guidance, Acceptance. No matter what that souls torment.

My hand has been forced much sooner than I would have of liked on this but here goes. By telling the world about my experience I hope to provoke a sensible debate on this subject.

After my misspent childhood and the local paedophile encounter, I had a good time whist I was at school but when I left, I quickly realised that I could not connect with adults and their world. In work situations, I just rub people up the wrong way and in every single job I have had I've battled colleagues working to make my life hell and fuck me over. Every single job I have had. I need to be the boss, then I notice something else happens, people want me to succeed because I want them to succeed and I inspire and lead by example, people know if I succeed then so would they. To a young and very troubled 17 year old, I did not like this world. I was introvert and snappy. I was deeply unhappy. Why? What was it that was making me different? At 17, I left my father's home after my Dads new wife found cannabis paraphernalia in my room. What were you doing in my wardrobe anyway? My dad would of seen it, would not of had a scooby what he was looking at, asked what it was, I'd say it was an experiment of some kind and my Dad would have just shnortled, accepted it and ultimately knowing I am full of shit but not really caring. Now add a pretentious Queen to that scenario and my Dad would have been duty bound to pass on the shit from the top, like any good mid level boss would. Rather than take shit from this women I didn't like and not wanting the chew with my dad, I packed a bag and moved out, before my angry Dad got home. Seems my dad did not learn his lesson from his last relationship and had rushed into yet another ill advised pairing and quicker than a drunken wedding in Vegas, he put a ring on it. Fuck this I thought, you're on your own with this precious Queen Dad. She taught him good this time. Quite brutally, if not skilfully too. Then he re-meets Jan, so it's all good from that point. I moved out and lost my job and was staying at my friend Peely's old flat. Well squatting really. I had lost my job and was heading nowhere fast. Luckily to my rescue came Sir Steven Perkins, having came to Stockton to visit Laurencia from Swindon, where he was living he came to the flat, seen the state I was in and talked me into moving to Swindon with him. It wasn't hard. I jumped at it and Sir Steven Perkins probably saved my life that day. This was a Saturday and in 2000. So on Sunday we packed up his Vauxhall Calibra and I moved to Swindon with Ste and by Tuesday I had a job. I was never out of work from that day until one day in May 2017. This was Exciting. Steve was a ball of excitement and danger and my Brother. What an adventure to a 17 year old. He would be around 48 now. He would have been a character-full old geezer, would Steve, wasn't much he had not experienced in his life time. He had brilliant adventures and was a ex army medic and proper alpha male, lady killing, hard man. He had faced his morality on more occasions than he would have liked and in circumstances he would have wanted to avoid. These profoundly affected Ste's mental state. He suffered PTSD before there was such a thing and any help for it too. His story, harrowing in places, are stories that will stay with me. As extremely interesting as though the stories are, the stories would not serve anybody and are between myself and my very good friend and fallen brother Sir Steven James Perkins. Still, despite Steve and Jane's efforts, I was unable to adapt to adult life. I did not know how to act or be confident or friendly. The more people were off with me at work the more introvert and private I became. If I sensed this dislike of me in them then I would just ignore those people. It eventually became that I ran out of people to talk to and I would just do my job, completely isolated and talked about. Unless you made me angry. I've always been an opinionated twat. I noticed a pattern that was sadly repeated to this day in every company I've ever worked at longer than a week. Even at XPO recently. Everybody just ends up hating me. Always comments on my sexuality from my first job at Samsung right until I got bigger muscles. Even going as far as manipulating situations to trip me up. Make up rumours. Do anything to make my life hell. I've always been confused for a gay man unless I am in the gym and eating properly, then I look scary and not gay. Looking scary is always shattered when I start being me and people are at ease within seconds. Though, it is more my mannerisms and use of words that can make me sound posh and slightly effeminate. I am emotional so must be some girl in there somewhere and a little eccentric. Most of what I say is lost on a lot of people unless I write it down. I'm good at explaining with written words but unlike Sir Jamie I have not learnt the art of how to tell a good story. I would rather teach Sir Jamie the stories and listen to him tell them, as if he was there. Really funny that would be. This all had a profound effect on me between the ages of 17 and 24 years of age. The strange thing was that if you knew me outside of work you generally ended up liking me and could see I liked girls. These rumours by the time I was 18 had got me questioning my sexuality. Never even a question at school, it followed me everywhere now. At around about the time I moved to Swindon, I started having what can only be described as flashbacks or visions, unknowingly connected to my experiences as a child and with the local paedophile. I didn't know that was what they were. They would happen out of nowhere and with no context of what I was thinking about at the time. I did not know why they were happening. I must be "THAT" if they keep happening I thought. They did. For years I would be in absolute despair every single time. I kept thinking A. I might be Gay. B. Definitely Heterosexual. C. Quite possibly "THAT" and D. All at the same time, that, I can tell you, was a lot to deal with. My mind could not cope. My work situations tormented me by day and my mind tormented me by night. My only escape was sleep, that gratefully my body and my mind readily accepts and looks forward too. I say, I am always at my happiest when I am asleep. I rarely remember any dreams. It's a bliss of nothingness. I honestly do not know how I am still here. I guess I have been in mental training all my life, always picking myself up and soldering on. Over and over again, multiple times a year or month sometimes. I would have very good periods of months, it would be bliss. Then bang out of nowhere, now comfortable again, they would come. The visions and flash backs. Boom, I back was in absolute despair. I cannot tell you the anguish I would find myself in. Absolute grief, at this complete and utter torture. Then after the worst, reason and calmness would come and I would start the process of rebuilding myself back up again, and again, and again, and again, and again. Every time it was like a bomb going off in my head, the payload was anxiety, depression, despair and hopelessness. From 1999 right to 2018. I could not hazard a guess at a number. Countless times, it got better and less frequent at 24 years old when I rightly quit ganga. I then swapped it for the "taste" or lager, as it is otherwise known. This started the growth of a more confident Mikey Elwood, valiantly still trying to grow as a person despite his burden. Outside of work I was quite liked. None of the shit from work happened to me in my social circles. These flashbacks were always there, just biding its time to strike. It would, like a skilled assassin of hurt, know the best times to attack. It would be simply the most opportune and tactically brilliant times. Usually following, bouts of happiness or contentedness especially. It couldn't have that now could it? I have to say if counselling was a thing when I was a kid then I think from the age of eleven I maybe should have received a lot of it, definitely later too. I had so many issues with so many different things and never ever spoke about it. As I had learnt with two years away from my family, it had taught me to suffer in silence. I suffered silently and alone, just me and my thoughts. Never was there anybody close enough or anybody who might understand what I was going through. People around me who care and love me but this curse makes you even more isolated no matter who loves you. You have nowhere to turn. Deal with it or die and do the honourable thing. Those are your choices with that particular subject. If anybody mentioned that subject I would freeze up and wonder if they had sussed I had problems? I used to stare at children without realising, I have to say never, undressing them, no never that, but in fascination at the state their minds are at, at this point in their little lives and if they have good people around them and dodge tragedy, such as some sick fuck inextricably decides to alter the little ones life to satisfy their sick fucking perversions, then yes that child could fly. I would then start to wonder about what I would have been like had I dodged tragedy, all the while I have not realised I'm still looking at this child and people noticed. When I noticed they'd noticed, from then on I would not look at children unless they engaged me first. Questions of why a good looking lad would have such little girlfriend action. Simply because how could I let anybody in? Though I was still more successful than most of my friends, I must say and at least I got some, seems it was only me that got wondered about. Why? They could tell I was troubled that's why. The question always remained…But why was Michael so troubled?

I sorted my sexuality issue out around about the time of quitting the ganga, I realised that I never fantasised about men and squirmed if I happened upon men's porn. I just don't fancy being fucked up the arse by a man. Nor does it excite me at the thought of me doing the same to another man's sweaty arse. No thank you. I have enough problems with mine as it is. I realised I have a healthy love of the opposite sex and enjoy the art of making a girl come. Which I was absolutely shit at, at the age 24 until I found the clitoris at the age of 28 or 29, it's a fucker that one, I believe some men never find it but when you do you fly. Congratulations my Good Sir, for you have unlocked the key to a life of great sex. I care about my partners experience and can be classed as a "Giving" or "Unselfish" lover. I make an effort and enjoy doing so. I get great satisfaction from her satisfaction. Again I cannot see any losers. Still these flashbacks persisted. Contentedness and then Hopelessness over and over and over, how long could I fight this? Turns out not to shabby in the silent torment stakes, I've earned a chronic tolerance to it, I guess I am a professor in this very subject by now. It would always be there under

the skin and when these unwanted and devastating thoughts hit they made me scream inside
"No not this, NO! Not the very thing I hate! The very thing I despise, No, No, No! Oh god please, No..." My father would notice this, monthly, quarterly or six monthly change. He was always bewildered and never knew what to say to me in those periods, neither did Jan, bless her, though she knew a lot more than most, but the subject was never raised. What could they say? They had just witnessed a man go from happy and outgoing to despair and hopelessness for the umpteenth time. They could see the pattern. He was there for me as best as he knew how. He was there, always, until one day he sadly and heartbreakingly wasn't. I was like a lost puppy. I have to say in my heart I knew I could not be this. How could I be the very thing I hated? I could never touch a child in that way, it would break my heart, to know what you would be robbing them of. I could never look at child porn either, I would not be able to stop crying for the child being abused, I could not condone or endorse those pictures or video's of children being destroyed emotionally. Never mind achieve a fucking orgasm. I feel physically sick at the thought. I simply could not. I believe you should

serve a life sentence for molesting or looking at or making or downloading child porn. Every child I see, I silently hope they don't suffer tragedy. I feel it deeply. I am an emotional guy and can be a little girl about some things. Injustice, tragedy and cruelty, especially. You have to understand I did not know these were flashbacks, I thought it was my desperately unwanted thoughts that I had to fight against, developed from very young age and a by-product of doing things and experiencing things no child should be doing at that age and Indeed, not doing for years to come, they just kept coming back for another fight, I feared the worst. Then I would think about it, look at the facts and realise there is something wrong with me but I am not that but why do they keep happening then? Then the re-build started. Slowly I would put the pieces back and life would return to normal. That was until my head popped. Some months before the Parmo's, my mentally ill nephew Martin was living with me and it happened again. I give up this time, I was tired. Very tired. Mentally exhausted. I decided that an everlasting sleep was what I felt was needed and not for the first time, the perfect antidote or remedy. The honourable thing. The decision calmed me. This silent hell must come to an end one way or another and right then, it was running away with the point card scores. Then I decided if I am dead already, fuck it, why not let people in and try and explain what is happening to me? You have nothing to lose; if it doesn't work then the eternal sleep abounds anyway. So I did. Carla, Laurencia, Martin Jon Jones, Laura Calvert, Lee Russell and Chris to be precise. My family did not take it as well as I had hoped. My sister was ok because she knew my history. My friends were supportive for a time. It was a revelation to get it off of my chest for the first time ever. Wow a problem shared looking back, it was Laurencia that struggled with it the most. She has been secretly probing my life and trying to figure me out since that day. I will explain later. In the past few months I've had my suspicions that Laurencia has been manipulating my life. Very cleverly in the back ground and in devious ways. You will find out in more detail later, not quite ready for that yet. Yes there is more. I still did not understand what was happening to me though, so how could they? After talking to Laurencia she gave me a card for a Psychologist and told me she was good, "She managed to get Paul to stop being a dick when he was seeing her" She must be good, I thought. Appreciative of this, I phoned Amanda and made an appointment. On a Saturday afternoon I went to see her. It was the hardest Journey I've ever made. What if she tells you, you are in fact a Paedophile? I contemplated. She greeted me with respect. We went up stairs and into a box room. After a brief explanation she said she "Wasn't that bothered about the mother and father aspect and we will deal with that later"

It fucking bothers me my love, I can tell you and is, in fact inextricably linked. I found this a funny thing to say. I told her what's been happening. Condensed it down to 40 minutes, its 40 quid a pop and I wanted my monies worth, I didn't want to be left with a cliff hanger, until next week. No, I wanted to hear her initial summations. These were fucking awesome. She said that it sounds to me like you are suffering PTSD and what you are experiencing is your mind kicking back and telling you, that you need to resolve it. It's an effect of PTSD. She said the fact you are in my chair is testament to that. Generally Paedophiles, who are actually sexually aroused by prepubescent children, would just accept it or have ended their life, if not. (Or found god and joined the church, I remember thinking) It is my experience that Paedophiles never seek help. Wow I started crying. She found this curious. Why? Stupid women, you just told me I am not a Paedophile and have just dispelled my deepest, darkest fear, the source of much anguish and you are, erm, surprised I'm crying? Really?

"Well, do you find children attractive Michael?" She asked. I thought about this and thought about all the times I reasoned with myself in my darkest hours. I said "Well, let's look at this properly. I do not have dreams about children. I do not fantasise about children. I do not feel the need to touch a child when I am around them. I could never gain sexual pleasure from the fantasy of abusing a child or by abusing one myself. The thought does not make me stir; no it repulses me and sickens me. I don't watch or look at child porn nor have I been tempted. It is everything I hate. I added that I am very uncomfortable around children and can freeze up. Like I feel they maybe in some danger just being around me. That seems fucking ridiculous to me now. She said, well you have answered your own question in a way. That was the first time I'd said all that out loud. I realised I am not and never was a Paedophile. I asked her if

I was just suffering a "fear of being a Paedophile?" she agreed that was very possible. We came to the end, she said, please come back so I can use some dodgy device on your brain and make you relive the moment as if you were actually there. Yeah, na, fuck that I thought. I didn't like the sound of that one bit, I can tell you or her for that matter. I binned her off as I had what I needed. It was as easy as that. Once I understood why it was happening I could stop it and mull it over and over many an hour too. I was finally fixed. I don't get them any longer. I have never been more comfortable and happy at the realisation that my only interest in children is their safety and well being. That is the truth of the matter too. I can hold my head up high. If you believe me to be a nonce then fuck you. Simple. Though, I would advise you not to say this to my face to avoid an unintentional and impulsive, spontaneous and yet satisfying reaction of fist hitting jaw. Girls you have free rain. However, I caution that I can zero in on your insecurities and I am good at it too, you have been warned. I still had many more trips into hopelessness to come yet, it wasn't over by a long shot, there were just different reasons and the beginning of all this really. I just could not help the feeling that I was ultimately, more qualified than Amanda in any benefits that I could gain from her from here on in, until you have been through what I have love and the lessons and conclusions learned from it you always be my understudy in the mind stakes, Amanda my dear. Arrogant? Probably, a fine line between arrogance and confidence, I think. I contacted Amanda recently to see if she knew any psychiatrists for a psychological evaluation. She replied and said she would help but I have heard nothing back since.

Eventually I would notice little set ups from people I know with kids. I was conscious of the unease feeling that they gave off. For example my friend Chris used to live with me and his kids would stay over regularly and I looked to them as nieces, I had near enough seen them grow since babies. I have an interest in their growth because I care about them both. Tends to happen when you see them grow and spend quality time with them throughout their lives. After he moved out, a few times he has brought the kids around mine unannounced. I would be happy to see them but I could feel it was just to study my reactions with them there. I felt this because of Chris's unusual behaviour. He was always watching me and assessing me. It was quite obvious and quite comical really. He was not being natural and my skulduggery metre kicked right off. Especially amused because he thinks I might see his daughters as what, a target? An object of desire? No mate my desire is for them both to not grow up too quickly. Be kids for as long as they can be. What did you expect mate, for me to slip your 13 year old daughter my number on the sly? Promise them chocolate if I met them in the Park? What exactly? I actually giggled more than once at your reaction whist talking to you and you were that engrossed in me you never wondered why. I would purposely move around the room and you would subconsciously move in front of your kids in a fatherly protective way, still totally oblivious to what I am doing or my visible amusement and disbelief. What a horrible feeling and so obvious. I was glad when you left, though still always appreciative to see him and the girls nonetheless. I cannot just switch off feelings and love for people just because they have turned into Arseholes. The kids are innocent too. Good kids they are and have been brought up right and thankfully no real tragedy. Fingers and toes crossed.

Next one is at Allison and Andy. Now I am a massive Andy fan he is a man with integrity and I like him and always loved Allison too. I'm an infrequent visitor but when I do, once a year or so, I always get warmly greeted. I popped in around a year ago and the daughter popped out as I was leaving. Allison had told me she was 15 now and I had only seen her in passing once or twice for the last 18 months. She was the annoying and uncomfortable 12/13 year old the last time I remembered. Now, it seems I noticed instantly, the most adult body and shapely and womanly everything on a 15 year old I had ever seen and she knew exactly what to wear to accentuate her newly found womanly figure, which was dispelled the moment you looked at her 15 year old face. It looks, pretty but pretty erm, 15. Show any man a headless photo and he would say 20 to 25 year old model, fitness one at that. I'd say so. My first thoughts? "Holy Fuck! She's gunna be a man eater in a couple of years, look out the male population of Stockton, you ain't going to know what's hit ya" She, the knowingly smart girl for her age that she is, clearly read my reaction and double take, spot on but may have unfortunately confused my surprise with me actually fancying her, I can't blame her but you are wrong young-en. Her dad, well he's in for few sleepless ones, she's feisty. My interest in her could never be as an object of desire, she is simply too young. Her dad is also held in too much high esteem by me, even if she was much older. Though I did, in a non sexual way, appreciate her newly found female form. Fast forward to my second visit in as many weeks a couple of months ago and Allison had changed. Her daughter was there, she was clearly trying to garner my attention and it was obvious. Later when she was stood above me in the living room she, with a very tight top on, she performed the most obvious and put on yawn, she stretched up, her hand pointed for the ceiling and trying to do as sexy a pose as a now 16 year old could do. I looked up and looked for a split second, seen ample under boob and crinkled my face, turned to Andy, nodded back in her direction, shnortled and we started laughing, then carried on with our conversation. Even Andy knew what she was doing. She huffed and stormed off. Too, obvious my dear. You are not an object of desire to me.

You are a student of life but nice try. The next time I went round Allisons she treated me as the Taxman and I've not been back since. It was clear all the rumours had now reached them. I told Carla I had been around to see them you see. I don't mention them often to her, they were like my secret friends. I remember her taking a mental note, Carla did that a lot by now. They were almost animations of her logging the fact and thinking about the information gained. Talking to Andy, it turns out, he's met and knows Rasheed and in the not too distant past too. Something to do with his security company. Coincidence I believe. After we realised the connection? Who knows?

The dinner with Jonny's wife, case in point too. Set up, intensely watched. Especially Lee and Trev. Trev actually hid from me in Jonny's profile and I never even knew he was at the table for 10 minutes. I believe, so I would not go and sit with him. Um. Plenty of other instances too. I'm good in myself by this point in this regard and was a bit dumbfounded that one of the side effects of me being ok and coming to an understanding with it, is now people believe me to like kids. Oh the fucking Irony. He giveth with one hand and teketh with the other. I believe Laurencia to have a big hand in this "belief" too. You see she did change towards me and was always studying me, with her kids and some conversations that were had. Once, during the book writing, I was in Carla's back garden and out of nowhere Laurencia started talking about how men liking 14 year old girls wasn't that bad and how you should not be classed as a Paedo and men shouldn't be ashamed, it is not that bad etc. It felt forced, rehearsed. A bit confused about what the she is talking about and what it pertains to in the current conversation. I did not engage and continued to mind my business on this occasion. Not the next time though. We were alone, same location, strangely, here we go again, I thought, I snapped back, "Here's what I think Laurencia, I think at 14 years old you are essentially just a child. Make no mistake, they might be getting to start to do adult things and even getting the bumps but that does not change the fact that they are more child than fucking adult at that age. Though you have some 14 year old's, who have lived a ruff fucking life and they are more adult than adults. Nevertheless still children, Laurencia. Whether a man is fucking lonely or not is not an excuse to give in to your wants. You are indeed a Paedophile if you take up with a 14 year old and cross that line, the ages you are suggesting with your muddled thinking on the subject are really around 16 and 17, there is a moral line there where people can get away with that and by then the kids are more in the middle of kid and adult and the clock swings the other way. A 16 or 17 year old is capable of making sound decisions for themselves" I started to give Laurencia's behaviour a considerable amount of thought, after our little debate. I realised something else too. Her old friend Lauren, she was Laurencia's best friend when they were both 14 and I lived across the road and on the same road as them both. This girl had quite recently departed to me that she thought I fancied her when she was 14, I was 30ish, she used to purposely hang around my front garden and stick her fingers up at me, things like that and I would do the same back. "Erm, Excuse me?" I said, "That's not how I remember that like. I remember at that age you being an annoying little twat who I only engaged with because you were our Laurencia's Bff and any other kid, I would have just ignored them and shut the blinds. The most of a thought you got from me was, she has potential when she is older." That transpired actually. By the time Lauren was seventeen I happened to be living with Laurencia and Carla at the time and she had indeed blossomed to a beautiful girl. She is a cheeky tom boy is Lauren. She would come into my room and flirt with me, I lapped it up and gave it back obviously and honestly I just had to reach out for her and she would have been mine. I pointed this out to her. I choose not to give in to temptation. I really wanted too, I'm ashamed to say. But I did not. Why? Because it did not feel right that she was seventeen that's why. I felt I would be taking advantage of her. There was exciting sexual tension between us. Undoubtedly we would have had a good experience together. Yet still, I could not. If I could not do that to you at seventeen Lauren, then fourteen year old you had no chance my dear. I also pointed this out to her. I have tried many a time to get the now 23 year old out with me, she always agrees but it never comes off in the end. So I put that together with what Laurencia was saying and I could see I was trying to be painted as a man who liked 14 year old girls. My niece thinks I like 14 year old girls? What the fuck? Why? Was it to spread unfounded and untrue roamers about me? Who knows...Only she does I guess

Sammy

I was 22 in around 2005 sometime. I was living at my sisters in Brookfield Road, she had gone to live in Spain with Ste, Jane and their Mum, Jenny. I just moved back from Swindon and landed a job straight away. Good timing. Dad was still with the precious Queen by then, though on it's last legs. Don't worry Dad, ten years of love and contented laughter coming right up, Ol'man. Hang in there. It'll get tough but you will get through it. It did. He did. He re-met Jan and realised it was all worth it in the end. I agree my Ol'man. Here, here. So around this time I lived around the corner from Daniel, one of my oldest friends. He is one very selfish person. I have my issues with Daniel but he has been a friend all my life and is family really that it seems, after various let downs, he is a friend that always seems to stick. I can't get rid of the fucker. The local coke dealer for years he was the king of Fairfield was our Daniel. He truthfully nicked 80 odd cars by the time he was 12. He was a one boy crime wave. Bullied when younger he lauded it over his former bullies now, the Boyo. Anyway, by then he had settled into steady drug dealing and had calmed a little. Erm, that means he only went missing for 4 days now and not three weeks. Due to developing a suffering with panic attacks, whenever he left his manor! He was a constant visitor. Every now and then his 14 year old cousin, Sammy would accompany him and I got to know this absolutely lovely and sweet lass. She would always have a big smile for me and we would always be happy to see each other. It was attention I'd been starved of, for some time and I really connected with this girl. I remember joking that I was gutted she wasn't 18. Not really joking and she looked sad and readily agreed. What did I like about Sam? It was not the fact she was 14, no it was because she was Sam. She was me in so many ways and a sufferer of "The Kindness Curse" She was kind and really sweet. Good hearted with the biggest beautiful smile. I was an insular, tortured soul at that time and she brought light into my life. I felt I had more in common with Sam than I ever did with an adult, up to that point in my life. It was unfortunate that she happened to be 14. Very beautiful and well developed. She was already sexually active. Now I have to state nothing ever happened between us until a few years later. She would come over mine but always with her adult cousin and we would just chat and watch TV. It was nice. Then we realised that it was not good to see each other any longer and we would not make any effort to. I said get back in touch when you are 18, if it is meant to be it's meant to be. She did just that when she was nearly 18. Not minding the age because of, well, its Sam and I wanted to be with her forever. I jumped to her. Unfortunately for me, well that's a strange one actually, Sam had gotten pregnant at 16 with twins and at this time was really still recovering and her mind and body had taken the battering that only twins and child birth will do to a lass. This was the completely wrong time for her and for me too, unfortunately it did not work. She was not ready. I know she would not change the past for the world now and has two fantastic kids and is a brilliant mother, but I will always wonder what if? She is my friend and on my Facebook, she has read a couple of drafts of Prixturious too, no matter how bad I would feel or how low I felt, if Sammy put a new picture on her profile of her big beautiful smile and I happened on it in my news feed it would always make me smile and lift my spirits and see a little light again. She has constantly over the years been doing this for me since I met her. I will always have a soft spot for her and care for her. So let's review. I had the apple in front of me and could have given into temptation but I did not. Can we see a pattern here please people? Why didn't I? Because it would have been wrong that's why. I also think it was not that I wanted Sam to be 18 but rather I wanted to be 14 again with Sam when life was good and I was happy. Judge me all you want but these facts remain. I have actually never done anything wrong and proved that faced with the temptation I still stayed strong. Again I can hold my head up high. If this does not make you understand then maybe you are not meant to. I am not nor ever was I, a Paedophile. That is all I have to say on the subject really. If rumours have been floating around about me which I believe that to be so and is the reason I have wrote this chapter and by my own evil niece no less, then this document should dispel those notions as of now. I will not waste a second more on that subject unless it is to help somebody. I've had enough. That was a hard write and the only thing they could try to use against me. Everything is the truth and happened. I could not make this up. I simply could not have done. Or if it is then put me in hospital and I will willingly go. Then again if I can come up with shit like this in my mind and it is fiction, do I really want to be cured? No, I'm not crazy. I know it. Boxed in and under extreme pressure, yes definitely, I have just survived multiple attempts on my life. I am running out of options and fast. Debtors are moving in and I need to get this out to people. On its own it's a good yarn but with all the documentation and the time lines it has its gravitas. It is undeniably compelling reading. I need help. Even the courts are chasing me for money and are threatening my arrest. I do not know how much longer I can hold out and keep myself safe. If you are not in a position to help and then know I will know that. Please keep safe and share only with people you trust but still share it. I want it out there. I had a visit from the council yesterday and it really unsettled me. He wanted the engine number from my car. Yeah fuck off. Why now? He could be connected with Cleveland police. I had to go to bed because I did not know what to do. I was shaking uncontrollably. It seems I'm okay with murderous Gangsters/Business men and Bent Coppers but evil and uncaring "Fuck

You Pay Me" council workers dressed as coppers I'm fucking terrified of. I think it is because they can really fuck me over and are demanding 2k from me. I lose the house I'm dead within days. I worked it out the most I owe them is £800. Strange one.

Sleep

Sleep helps greatly with stress. I can sleep no matter what and is a coping mechanism I developed as a child. I don't ever remember my dreams. Except one. In this dream, always stars Cara Delevingne. She is very busy is our Cara and only visits once or twice a year for about the last 5. It is always the most vivid of dreams, truly like I am there. Every single time it gets to the actual intercourse bit I always wake up. After that moment of who the fuck I am, everybody gets when you awake, I suddenly get hit with the reality and am fuming because it felt so real and I never fucked her. I just want to go back to sleep and I am always gutted. I have realised that it is strange that I always remember in great detail that dream and never remember any other time. I believe it is to do with my subconscious. He steers my dreams, processes the day's events, plans and then leaves me with no clue when I wake as to what to do, but I just know. He is always one step ahead but cannot tell me, only try and guide me with feelings, gut feelings and such. He lets Cara through because he knows she is busy and I think he likes Cara too, though he needs me to entertain her shall we say and I believe the only time he is sober. Hence why I never know what he's been up to usually. I'd say the c**t also finds it hilarious I spend 8 hours in the build up and foreplay and never actually get to nail the beautiful Cara, she always enjoys her stay nevertheless and I think probably looks forward to it. She doesn't really have to do anything for her odd socks and children's screams, that I imagine she usually gets paid with. Maybe I am a freebie and why I see her so infrequently. Maybe she just likes being the one pampered once in a while. Maybe we are both getting paid just not in the monetary sense. I've realised I have just characterised Cara Delevingne as a Dream Whore; something tells me this would amuse Mrs Delevingne if she read this.

Erm, so yeah, moving on, sleep is good for me and I awoke feeling calm and with a plan. I realised I have uncovered a conspiracy of epic proportions that could at the least bring down the corrupt elements at Cleveland police. I need to approach honest coppers. I need to get out of the jurisdiction of Cleveland Police before I do. The end game is coming, tactics, tactics, moves, moves and counter moves. This really could only happen to me. Exciting? Yes very and because the end of this sorry and skulduggery laden saga is coming and one way or another the truth will air and I get the girl, hopefully. Nerve racking? Yes, definitely. Determined and driven? You fucking bet I am. I'm fighting for something bigger than justice, truth and righteousness, I am fighting for love and a love that I don't even know is reciprocated or wanted. I am scared of being rejected most of all. Petrified. Though, if I have my Tom Hanks and Helen Hunt moment from Cast Away I, like the brilliant Tom H, would accept it, thank her, wish her well and then walk away. For she did for me what Mrs Hunt did for Tom and if you truly love somebody then you have no choice but to let them go if your love is ultimately rejected. That is the hardest choice by far; ergo it proves your love in bounds. This Journey that started with me leaving her and Cheeky's behind and will end with the longest, greatest, hardest, exciting, heartbreaking and interesting roads travelled a to get back to her. It truly is a story of love. She only lives five miles away. She might of well have been in Timbucktoo, on another planet even. I have to be sure I am sorted in every way to reach out to her. Know we can *be*, without all of this fucking drama, that she is safe. If I had reached out before now and been rejected I don't think I would have had the strength to fight or worse still, they try to use her against me, I simply could not take that risk. You know living with the thought and knowledge that everybody who you love has turned their back on you and physically worked with the aim of my demise is the hardest thing to come to terms with. It is the very definition of Irony. I, for the first time in my life, free my mind, able to let in any and all into my sphere for the first time. The cost of that epiphany? Only everybody I love and hold dear, thus making the giant strides of my mind a rather empty and useless gift or another way to look at it is, it is the cost of my journey to reach her. These people have had a massive fucking advantage and control for so long. I was always following my tail. I have for months been isolated and starved of information, I was not even sure I was in a war. That was the mistake they made. That is the pin point of the tidal change. You see once I knew for definite I was in a fight and for my life no less, once I put everything together, that was advantage lost for them. Now they are the ones in the dark. Now they are the ones guessing what I am up to, what my plays are and more importantly, what I know. Chasing their tails now they are. Now I have put this on paper, spent hours thinking and remembering, analysing and surmising. It's been interesting. No wonder I could not effectively tell anybody what my fears were without sounding like a lunatic. It is simply too big and complicated, until I put it down on paper. Now it is the last thing I sound. Everything makes sense. Since Wednesday 16th of October until now, Sunday 3rd November, I have had many hours to reflect and I am pretty certain I was in fact poisoned and over sometime too. Around six weeks I would say. My body since the 16th is in the condition it was before in August. I am fit and strong and healthy looking. I have gained weight and muscle mass. I have suffered not one symptom since that of the 18th after I recovered. For weeks I have been so ill and gaunt, weight loss and massive feelings of exhaustion. Funny heartbeat patterns. I would have days of being totally fine then, desperately ill. I just put it down to my kidney problems. After all, I would never expect poisoning. I can only conclude that the time line of my health returning fits with people not being able to access the bungalow because of my precautions. The symptoms themselves were consistent with a foreign substance being ejected from my body. I was so desperately ill. Then the short sludge piss, then the water I would drink and over the next couple of hours I would then get better. I did not suffer any symptoms at all at the weekend prior. Though, I was bad Thursday and Friday at work, much less than that on Tuesday 15th and Wednesday 16th October nobody had access to the bungalow over the weekend because I was in. I was perfectly fine on Monday. Desperately ill by Tuesday, fucking thought I was dying by Wednesday. Monday, being the first time away from the bungalow. Umm, it's all curious. Hair test asap.

I will know when the right time will come to reach out to my Angel. It won't be long now. She gives me a need I have never felt before, my world is her. My desires and wants, my dreams and my happiest thoughts are her. To be the man to experience and share her smell, her embrace, her kiss, her love, her happiness, her satisfaction and her wants, her affections, her fears. To be her cure and for she to be mine. She is my Juliet and I her Romeo. (Hopefully) This is my drive. This is what Michael Elwood fights for. This is what is at stake. Not Fucking Parmo's. Though as nice as they are, like. I can never be arsed to make them at home. The go fund me also means I won't have too. Where's my dad's old video camera? I'm sure it's in the loft somewhere. Probably nicked with that train set. Fuck it, C'est la vie...

To be continued.

Stay tuned, for the resolution to Elwood vs Regina and The Dark Forces of Teesside...and find out if I get the girl...

Yours Truthfully and Sincerely

Michael Elwood

PRIXTURIOUS

PART THREE

Chapter 8 – The Calm
Monday 13th January 2020

The last update above was 3rd November 2019. A lot has happened since. This chapter is going to cover the time period of 03-11-2019 to the 01/03/2020. I'd decided, after a good think that I needed to get out of Teesside. I was in touch with an old school friend called Amber. Amber was a good old friend and we'd reconnected on Facebook and she'd come up and visited me around 18 months prior. There was nothing in it other than friendship. She lived in a village called Hordle in the New Forest where I lived for a coupe of years in my teens. She said the dogs and I could stay with her and she will look after the dogs while I went out to work. I was buzzing and could see safety and a way out. I sold all the other possessions that I could and borrowed £200 from Jan for a deposit for a hire car. I sorted one for the following Monday. I sorted the garage at home out and as quickly as I could I moved the car in. It only just went in. I ended up denting the bumper and washing machine but I got it in. I wanted everybody to think I had taken my car. It must have been a funny sight for the neighbours. I was so excited when I set off and was hooping because I thought I was finally safe. I got there and had a sinking feeling from the moment I walked into Ambers that this might not be a good idea. For one she has cats, two, both hated dogs and my dogs hate cats. Amber also smoke's pure weed joints like rollies and once consumed she loses the ability to be able to hold and concentrate on any task or conversation. She also, strangely, stubbed out the pure weed joint with a centimetre, if not more, still full of pure weed above the roach? You what? There were about 100 in the ashtray. I'd say a decent amount of money in that ashtray and the most expensive bingers I had ever seen. Bemused, I fought these niggly feelings and went to sleep on the settee. I awoke around 06.30, had a coffee or three, I walked to the hire car and as I walked out, I noticed a van driving past slowly and instantly recognized the silhouette behind the steamed up van window. It was him I was 95% sure, my old school friend (I've decided not to name him) Our eyes met and locked for a few seconds and then he went out of view. Fuck, now my sister will know where I am. Then I started thinking? What would he be doing three miles from home on this very quiet, non main road street at 07.30 in the morning? Looking for my car perhaps? Why would he not stop? I then realised if anybody wanted to hurt me or disappear me it would be a lot easier down here than at home unless nobody knew I was here, which now they did. I was confident that Amber wasn't involved. The hire car was due to go back on the Wednesday in Christchurch and I would be stuck down there with the dogs. I now had a decision to make. Do I stay and risk it or do I go home where at least in the bungalow I am safe and it is harder for them? I mulled it over. After an hour I decided this would not work and running is not the answer. Amber got up and I told her my decision and thanked her. I asked Amber if I could borrow £20 for fuel. She agreed. I took the £20 from Amber and opened my wallet, expecting to see the £35 in there from last night to find there was only £15 and I still had £35 in my wallet when I counted it after adding the £20. Erm, she just gave me back my own £20! I just looked at her. I could not believe it. I didn't say anything as I didn't want to shame her though she looked sheepish. I left and put fuel in and travelled the 320 miles at 56mph to make sure I got home. The strange thing is I was relieved going back. I had definitely felt vulnerable down there even if there was a very small chance that was not my old friend. I got the car back to the rental company and started thinking about my next move but pissed off that essentially, I had just wasted precious resources on a day trip to see Amber. When I got back home, I decided I needed to make a complaint to Cleveland police. I found out that to make a complaint against the Police there is part of every force called the "Standard and Ethics Department" set up to investigate claims of in-proper conduct and corruption. However a week prior to contacting them I sent a copy of this document amongst all the others and started a case with the IOPC, The Independent Office for Police Conduct and sent a copy to Durham Police. The IOPC told me I have to give Cleveland Police 15 working days to respond and either log it as a complaint or not. I could then lodge an appeal with the IOPC, though the IOPC cannot investigate the original claims still but only enquire what they are doing about it. I learned quickly that there is not a lot either can do and in fact the only people who can investigate Cleveland Police is, you guessed it, Cleveland Police. Unless the force themselves refer, erm themselves to the IOPC. I decided it was good to have a record of the documents with other institutions. I knew this whole endeavour to be a waste of time but I tried anyway, in some naïve and stupid hope that the Standards department, were independent of the main force and contained good people.

On the 12th November 2019 - I spoke to the Standards and Ethics Department and said I would be sending an email and can they please read the files and then contact me. I sent the email. I waited a week then contacted the department again. I was told that the files on the original email would not work and could not be accessed. I resent them. I was faced with Victoria Finnegan, she is the office manager and two weeks in she still has not read it. I lose my temper but finally get her to look at it. An hour later I get a phone call proclaiming "Mr Elwood I am 23 pages in and it's all about Parmo's and I just don't know where this is going"

"Best read the other 150 odd pages then hadn't you Mrs Finnegan"

"I cannot justify the time" Was the reply.

I was given the complete run around and the thing is if she had took me seriously and started an investigation then the likely evidence under my sink would have been found during those 15 working days before it was cleaned up. Not to mention all the people to interview and public CCTV footage to scroll through, my tachograph card, the staff at XPO...etc

After the 15 working days, on the 2nd of December 2019, I got a confirmation letter from the Standards Department of the complete run around and wrote one back to them on the 3rd whilst at the same time filling in the online appeal form for the

IOPC. All the three weeks had done was give Cleveland Police a road map and the time needed to clean their mess up.

CLEVELAND POLICE

Postal Reply to: DIRECTORATE OF STANDARDS AND ETHICS
Shared Service Centre
Ash House
III Acres
Princeton Drive
Thornaby
Stockton on Tees
TS17 6AJ
Website: www.cleveland.police.uk

Our Ref: IX/01968/19

28 November 2019

Telephone: 101

Dear Mr Elwood

I received a large amount of documents from you, these included a 173 page witness statement and a Cheeky Devil Parmos menu. On 28 November 2019, you called the department to ask if I had looked into your complaint, I asked specifically what you would like to make a Police complaint about. You advise the only document you wanted me to read was the 173 page witness statement.

I called you back after reading through the document to ask what matters you would like to raise, this is usual practise to establish what complaints you would like to make, you refused to answer the questions and hung up the line. For this reason I am unable to make a decision on your compliant, I feel I have made efforts to establish these details.

If you are able to be more specific about your Police complaint, what matters are you dissatisfied with regarding Cleveland Police. If you can put these in writing to me within 7 days I am more than happy to look into those matters.

Yours sincerely

Victoria Finnegan
Office Manager
Directorate of Standards & Ethics

Mr M Elwood
Emailed to : mikeyelwood@gmail.com

CRIMESTOPPERS
0800 555 111

We are an equal opportunities employer

Dear Victoria Finnegan,

Thank you for your reply dated 28/11/2019, though I do have some questions that you may be able to help me with.

- * Why in your letter have you stated that you have read the whole 173 page document when in fact you stated to me, not once but on multiple occasions, including 02/12/2019, that you only read 23 pages of my witness statement?

- * You asked me what it was that I would like to complain about. Well if you had read the full 173 page document you would have known that with some clarity and much certainty.

- * Why did you ring me back after starting to read the 173 page witness statement a mere 30 minutes later, proclaiming "Mr Elwood, I am 23 pages in and I just don't know where this is going" Yet in your letter you have stated you read the full document? Why lie? A competent person in your position would surly realise that with 150 pages left to review, that in fact you were not expected to be any the wiser at that point. Stating to me that it's all about "Parmo's" and what the actual complaint was about, after only reading 23 pages, you can understand my frustration with your blatant incompetence and lack of empathy. Why have you focused on the "Cheeky Devils Parmo's Menu" when let's be honest it is the least important part of any document that I sent you?

- * Why did you ask me why I didn't report being poisoned? If you had done your job and been able to concentrate for more than a 5 minute Facebook post you would have known very clearly and you would not have needed to ask such a silly question.

* After pleading with you that my life is in the balance and I am expecting you to do your job and "just bloody read it you evil woman" why would you state to me that "I'm sorry Mr Elwood but I cannot justify the time it would take to read this!" I beg to differ, I would say that is a big prerequisite of your bloody job description. I have to ask Victoria have you really read it all and are being strong armed by the corrupt elements within the "even more than you, incompetent and lying police force?" that you unfortunately work for? I hope so for your sake Miss Finnegan.

* Why, is the letter dated the 28/11/2019?

* Can you please explain to me why your department would not be able to investigate the blatant persecution by Cleveland police against myself as you stated to me in our last call? 02/12/2019. Is that not the very reason the standards and ethics department was created for?

* Why would your return address on the letter be your traffic division? That is not where you are located, could it be that the corrupt elements that are persecuting me and possibly pressuring you, are stationed there? Curious.

You have stated I need to launch an appeal. I cannot in all good conscience do that as my confidence in your ability to do what is right or even give a flying F*** about a fellow human beings life, means I am forced to go beyond Cleveland Police and their/your continued incompetence, lack of empathy and humanity. You are all just bad people to deal with. I am unable to waste any more time with you or Cleveland's Police Force. Please do not think it is the last you will hear of this Miss Finnegan. I hope for your sake as well as mine, that I don't get murdered or disappear without a trace. That would bring national attention and not a good outcome for you or the force.

Yours Sincerely

Michael Elwood

President and Founder and Chairman of "The Party of Perpetual Annoyance Against ~~Plonker~~ Persecuting Policing" The Four P's for short.

On Wednesday the 4th I get aloud bang at the door. I ignore it, again, 30 minutes later, another bang on the door. I did not answer these aggressive knocks. 15 minutes later a letter comes through the door from the NHS Mental Health Crises Team asking me to contact them. I called straight away and tried to explain what has been happening. I then sent an email with all the files and asked them to read it.

This is the email I wrote the Crises Team…

"To whom it may concern...

Concentrate on my witness statement and give it all to a keen reader in your team, that is very important. It is also very important you read it fully to understand. I am of sound body and mind. My family are part of this. Yes they are very worried and so they should be but I assure you the worry is not concerning myself and my mental state but for the consequences of their considerably bad decisions and equally terrible actions. Every word I have wrote is the truth and in the case of the witness statement I could add 100 more pages since then!

Do not trust them. This is a tactic. I am more than willing to have a psychiatrist assess me. Please do not come to my home unannounced and make an appointment next time.

It will be nice to see someone and talk...so please do. I am no danger to anybody except in self defence as with most people.

Don't judge me until you have read it all and in its entirety. I also highly recommend "Fuck you Pc Tim" blinding read and not one word of a lie in any document I have sent you. That is the truth too. Please keep confidential, the documents will be used in an upcoming civil case against the police and name names. It's sensitive stuff.

I look forward to meeting you, 'To whom it may concern'...

Kind Regards

Michael Elwood"

By 1800 on the 6th of December 2019, 3 days after my email and appeal to the IOPC the police had forced their way into my home without a warrant and I was forcibly cuffed and committed to a mental health institution under section two of the mental health act. Let that sink in a moment, I start an appeal with the IOPC after butting heads with the Standards Department and within 3 days I am committed to a mental health facility because my estranged family are "worried" Umm. I contacted the IOPC whilst in Roseberry Park and the appeal that I have the email

confirmation for, there was no trace of it ever being received. It's all curious. This was clearly planned in advance and I was always being sectioned no matter what I said that day.

Here is a status update from Facebook that I posted about what happened to me the day I was unlawfully and without a warrant, sectioned...

"Hello, I've decided to tell the story of what happened on Friday the 6th December 2019. I just want to put the story out there and on record.

On Wednesday 4th December 2019 I got very hard a knock at the door. I did not answer. A letter came through explaining it was the mental health crises team and to get in touch. I rang them straight away. I explained what had been happening to me and said I'll send you the files. Read them and you will understand. I have not told one word of a lie in anything I have ever written. I then went about my business until Friday the 6th. I had one missed call from the crises team but 12 missed calls from a withheld number which I would never answer. I was busy doing something or another and had a knock at the door, the time was around 17.30. I, stupidly without looking through the peep hole first, opened the door. I was confronted by 2 Cleveland Police officers and three crises team members. I immediately tried to shut the door. The male PC put all his weight against the door, however we were matched in strength and the only result would have been the door getting broken. I decided to relent. He asked me to hand over my key, which stupidly I did. I let them all in. The six of us went into my kitchen and I was asked a number of questions for around 5 minutes by the lead idiot crises team member called Kerry when I get another knock at the door. I answered, I was then greeted by two doctors, one Asian and one white. I let them in. I was surrounded by seven total strangers, whom I had never met or spoke to before. I can tell you it was very unnerving and uncomfortable being judged and assessed by all these strange people. I realised they had already decided I would be committed. I knew what was coming. With the doctors here, the assessment lasted another 5 minutes before they all asked if they could go in my front room to have a discussion, I agreed. I was left with the thick as fuck Police Gangster "Mongo" (I'm going to ask Mongo if he fancies a boxing match for charity when I get out, he's a heavyweight and I a light weight, I'm more than game) I chatted to him. After 10 to 15 minutes the 6 others, who I don't know and have never met, came back in and informed me that I was being taken to hospital under section two of the mental health act. I argued, how can you have the right to do that after only talking to me for 10 minutes? Under, what grounds? I asked. Because your family are worried for your mental health, was the reply. I shnortled. What, the family I do not speak to any longer and will never again? Laurencia I have not spoken to for 5 months and my sister Carla since October 12th. How can you do this? I will not go, as there is nobody to look after my dogs. Why do this on a Friday night anyway?" I said. What is the point? I am more than willing to submit myself for assessment on a daily basis, 10 hours a day if need be, I wanted a evaluation anyway to dispel these rumours that my family have spread about me. The doctor replied that he cannot assess me properly with only 10 hours a day. Errr you what? (I have only been in the presence of my consultant for a total of 30 minutes in 8 days) Kerry, the

student of life from the crises team butted in and said my "family" would be looking after my dogs. The fuck they are I said. I asked Kerry if it was the crises team that had rung me a dozen times from a withheld number. She replied no. I have since listened to my messages and have 4 from the withheld number and are from the crises team, so it's safe to assume the other calls were the crises team too. Why lie? One of the messages a man said "Hello Michael, I'm from the crises team, we are just wondering if you would like to come to Roseberry Park? Lmfao! Umm...what a dick...
At this point I realised reason and common sense have left the room and what's coming is coming. I instantly realised that if I just went with them or put up a fight without doing anything to let people know then not one person who cares about me, except my "family" would be aware I had gone anywhere. I then decided to do the Facebook lives. I wish I had the presence of mind to do that from the beginning.

After being forcefully handcuffed, dragged from my home and put in the back of the paddy wagon, Kerry, the leader and instigator jumped in. Well she got both fucking barrels all the way to Boro.

Looking guilty as fuck too. I asked the bitch if she had read the files about what had been happening to me? She said yes. I went mad. I said "How the fuck can you take from that, that I need to be put in a mental health institution? You stupid woman! It should have been the subject of a police investigation not with me in Hospital!"
She nodded at the PC's "They are just PC's and don't know their arses from their elbows, it needs to be proper detectives!"

Mongo messed up too, when I mentioned Gary and Carl McCarten he said as a matter of fact "I have never heard of them" Bullshit.

We arrived at Roseberry Park. I was un-cuffed and left with nothing but the clothes I was wearing. Within 20 minutes I had a medical, everything was sound and my resting heart rate was 72bpm, pretty fucking good under the circumstances I'd say. Since then it is usually in the High 80 low 90s. I woke up this morning at 05.30 and my heart felt like it was kicking out of my chest. I went to the medical room and was 103bpm resting. Now I would have accepted

anxiety as the cause except my dick shrinks, I am very glittery like I'm on whizz and I get a pharmaceutical taste in my mouth. I believe I am being medicated without my knowledge and against my will. It is always after food. If I starve for the day and only drink water my heart rate is normal and my actions and mannerisms are me again. It's all very curious.

On the Saturday, I was forced to hand over my key to my estranged niece Laurencia Wood. I was told, not asked, that she would be going around to the bungalow a couple of times a day to feed them and let them out. I said "THE FUCK SHE IS!" but because they had been alone so long I had no choice but to hand it over. Did she go that night? Probably not. We are talking pure evil here. My lovely, loyal and beautiful dogs were left alone and scared for over 36hrs +. I was at my wits-end with worry about the poor buggers, they are my family after all. Evil they are not. I said to the frankly incompetent people who work here, that "You don't just have a duty of care to me but my fucking dogs too. Get them sorted and in kennels stat and I expect you to pay!" They realised I was right. On Monday they were picked up and moved to a kennels near foxes farm. Now I could start to get a grip of my situation.

My niece Laurencia packed me a bag and my friend brought it in on Sunday. This consisted of 1 pair of boxers, 1 pair of trainer socks, 3 polo shirts, 1 pair of jeans. My coffee filter and coffee beans. Yeah proper caring she is the despicable human being. Big shout out to the professional dickhead Paul Dawson. Thank you so much for donating £100 to my go fund me. I know your reasons were not honourable but I appreciate it nonetheless. To her credit I did get my phone and wallet and USB's (though I fear that would not have happened without the Facebook lives.) I did try with a go fund me but was to no avail without that business page on Facebook that I have lost access to. I am fine. Handling it brilliantly. I catch the staff lying to me on a regular basis. They are trying really hard to convince me that my tribunal is my appeal when the appeal is in front of the Hospital mangers at my section and comes before the tribunal.

It's hilarious sometimes. I departed to my friend on the phone earlier today that when the staff change from worried to fuck and panicking in the office, getting red faces, then to them suddenly starting to smile at me, I think something has changed in their favour. Now you cannot have a private conversation on the phone in here as it's got two places capable of a signal and many people listening and the smiling only works with the heartless and incompetent staff in the office. Since then, every fucker I see, including the patients has been smiling at me. I can't help but laugh. It's so funny to see. Is it wrong that a part of me is actually enjoying this? I dunno, I am definitely not normal but mentally ill, I am not.

To the people who have got me here, Carla, Laurencia, Katy and her brother Darren, Gary and Carl McCarten, Cleveland Police, Rasheed and his Asian army, plus the NHS mental health teams involved...Karma is coming for all of you and she is a very patient bitch. If I do not survive this and anybody who is involved finds they are dying before their time and are wondering why? Oh God why? This isn't fair?!?! Why me? When you are in utter despair at this tragic and grossly unfair situation you find yourselves in and cursing god and life, just remember the name Michael

Elwood, the innocent and mentally strong as an ox man that you helped persecute and destroy...and you shall have your answer...

Much love

Mikey Elwood xx"

Chapter 9

Roseberry Park - The Bilsdale Ward

The Medicating

I was uncuffed by the Police buffoon "Mongo" He, being the nice guy he is had put one of my cuffs on way to tight. When I asked him to loosen them he put his finger through the gap in the slack one and professed it was ok. (I am serious about the boxing match!) My wrist had swelled so much by the time we got there that the pressure meant he had a right struggle unlocking it. I turned aggressively towards him, he moved and I put my hand out to shake his. What would hitting him have achieved? The Police and the student of life

Kerry left straight away. I sat down and looked around at my new surroundings. I was introduced to John and Peter, both care workers. I started a conversation up and introduced myself. Within 20 minutes I'd had a medical and my heart rate was 72bpm. I was shocked at this. I'd just had my home invaded and been unceremoniously pounced on and arrested then dragged here, I was quite proud at my calm. I started to introduce myself to the patients and was shown my new digs. More than a few said things like "Mate, you don't look, too mental"
"You don't look like you should be here mate" Even John said, "You don't look like you are suffering a mental illness, I bet you cannot wait to see your consultant on Monday" I realised there is nobody here except the care workers. I got angry at the obvious realisation and couldn't believe the reasons why and the way I was brought here. What does it serve to do that to people on a Friday night? What were my plans that night? Make lamb burgers, do some writing and watch a film on Netflix. Yep needs to be banged up right there. Proper danger to society I am. I thought back on the Facebook lives. Though I have deleted these video's I know they exist on WhatsApp and will

find a copy of both videos. They are quite harrowing to watch and I am glad that I had the presence of mind to take them. Not one person who cares about me would have known I am here.
I hit it off with John straight away and taking pity that I had no possessions he found me some toiletries and some backy. I was buzzing. He was very sympathetic and seemed like he cared, Peter on the other hand never said a word, nor portrayed any emotions. I went to bed in my plastic quilt and pillows in a room with nothing in it and no TV. I despaired at my situation and could not sleep, I asked Joanne, the other care worker for a sleeping tablet and got 5 hours sleep. When I awoke the next day I went for breakfast and started to get to know everybody. I, being the social and outgoing individual that I am, it did not take long. I made friends quickly and set about the task of being me. Later in the day I enquired about my dogs to Lauren and Bab's the nurses on duty that day. "Oh your niece is going to go around and let the dogs out a couple of times a day. She needs the key" Lauren told me. "You what? They are still alone? Not good enough" I said "You don't just have a duty of care to me but my fucking dogs too! You cannot just leave them all day and just let them out

twice a day, get them in kennels and I expect you to pay!" To the girls credit they did that and I was grateful. When it came to giving Laurencia the key to my home, I was fuming at having to do this. Somebody came to my cell and said "Your sister will be here in 30mins" Okay I said. I put my hand in my back pocket and realised I still had the key from when Lauren the nurse had gave me it. I walked to the office and low and behold there was Laurencia, stood at the other side of the office at the window. I looked at her. She looked like she had been crying. After a few moments, she smiled, not a normal smile more between a smirk and a surprised look. The guilt flowed from her pores. I said "You're evil Laurencia, pure evil"

"Karma's a coming, my girl" I said. I looked at her through the glass she looked uncomfortable to say the least. I walked away, disgusted at my family member. Later I and the nurse, Lauren filled out my forms for my appeal in front of the hospital managers and the tribunal in front of a doctor, judge and social worker who are completely independent of the hospital. I was excited at this. Oh yes I wanted my day in court, so to speak.

Sunday

Still I had no possessions at all. Just the clothes I was brought in with. I'd had a number of showers but was starting to feel uncomfortable in the clothes. I was informed that my friend Chris would be coming later with the items on the list I'd gave the nurses and they had given to Laurencia, who was supposed to have returned last night with my belongings and predictably she was a no show. Chris arrived around 6ish, what a sight for sore eyes was my good friend, now excited and high at the sight of my brother, I looked at what my niece had sent me. I was gobsmacked and angry. That's it? That's what I mean to my family? I did not dwell on it too much because of Chris being there and I wanted to make the most of it. I still had not been told why I was here other than your family are worried. Chris left but had lifted my spirits somewhat the Big Galoot. After he left I took the picture you see and went for a fresh coffee. I had not got used to the piss that passes for coffee in this institution. The coffee tub you see in the pic, had sellotape all around it. I asked Chris about the sellotape and he just said Laurencia had done it. Ok I thought, it's just to keep the coffee in. I pulled all the sellotape off and looked in the tub. I noticed that there was a lot less coffee than had been there on the Friday. About three cups worth left. I shrugged this feeling off and when Chris went I made my coffee. My first bit of caffeine in three days. Now I drink strong coffee and this was like amber nectar, satisfied I went and sat down and watched TV with the lads. My god I felt fucking unreal within 30mins. I knew the feeling. MDMA. I realised where it must have come from. That feeling is unmistakable. The chattering of the teeth. The warm feeling of well being, I felt worried but awesome at the same time. I went in to the little surgery and asked the nurses John and Joanne to check my heart rate and now please. They obliged. 88bpm resting. All my other stats were quite high too. I was told it was my withdrawal from cannabis. "I've not smoked any for 4 days prior to coming in" I said. "No, I know this feeling, fucking MDMA my love" I should have demanded a doctor there and then. I know Chris has nothing to do with this and remember Laurencia now has access to all my stuff including my files. It was an unmistakable feeling and I would have been even more off my face had I used what was left in the tub of coffee but because it was so little. I wanted to conserve it until Chris brought me some more and I only used one cups worth. I saved the rest of the coffee for future preservation. I have a sample of the coffee still too. I went to my room and was in a good place for most of the night. The next day Chris came back with all my other stuff and brought me my two full and unopened Co-op own brand No 5. It's full bodied and has great flavour, lovely. Except that I felt like I was on wizz after each cup. Chris came on the Tuesday too and I told him about it. He laughed and said make me one then. I did. He commented later that his heart was beating like fuck all the way home and felt off his tits. Chris being Chris, he put it down to the caffeine and strength. I countered that "You drink this brand around mine all the time and you or I have never felt like that before!" He agreed then suggested he get a drug test from work. I agreed and said that was a bloody good idea but as with anything Chris suggests if you don't remind him he will forget, guaranteed. I didn't remind him. I was very active making coffee for the patients. I gave one to Big Al on the night and I heard him shout minutes after I went into my room. I went back out and investigated as I liked Big Al and there were 3 unidentified men in the little surgery. I asked Al where his cup was and then noticed it on top of the TV stand. I went over and it was empty. Red hot it was too. Suspicious, I hung around outside the surgery and someone went in. They quick as a flash slammed the door but I could see the three men huddled around the counter and were very busy testing something. I smiled and I never did see those men again. I also decided to throw away the coffee beans. Did the feelings of being on whizz stop at that point? Nope. By Tuesday I had noticed after most meals and sometimes after a coffee I would get the same symptoms within 30 minutes or so. Now I really do have to stress the fact that I know my body better than most. I know the feelings were of a pharmaceutical nature and with similarities to an amphetamine based one at that. The increased heart rate, jittery-ness, dry mouth, taste and the big tell, my penis shrinking, there was a full length mirror in my room and I don't have one at home, I loved it because I had lost 2 stone over the period of being poisoned and well my Johnson had never looked more in proportion in my life, I could not stop looking at myself! It was so obvious when all of a sudden I had to virtually squint to see it, I was gutted, stood there bollock naked and thinking "something is not right here" I started to miss meals to test if I had the same symptoms and feelings afterwards. I did not. I then decided to fast for a full 24hrs. I went back to normal in every way. This fact confirmed it to me. I was not quiet about my suspicions. I noticed when a particular cleaner/food server was working that was when I suffered the symptoms after my meals. John and/or Peter would be on too. I told her my suspicions in front of everybody. The staff all went red. On one of the nights after my main meal my cousin Katie rang the ward. I had suspicions about the staff listening to my calls. Now this was the first time I have spoken to Katie for some time. I was particularly jittery and agitated, speaking a thousand words to the dozen, feeling the effects of the substance used. I then spent 25 minutes in the dining room, near the office but the other side of a 5ft high TV stand that divided the lounge and dining room, talking to Katie, I told her everything that had happened since I was committed and particularly concerning the medicating. I let it be known that Katie worked for the NHS, not that she did fuck all to help me like, in fact she was very nervous sounding. I watched the reactions in the office. Very animated, nervous looking and worried with bright red faces. A doctor started waving his arms up in the air when I mentioned my symptoms. Lauren the pretty nurse, her face was bright red. I moved closer to the office as I ended the call just as somebody was leaving and a nurse in the office that I could not see before had a phone to her ear and everybody looked very sheepish still with bright red faces. I smiled. I was amused and satisfied they did indeed listen to your calls. I mentioned this to Lauren a few days later and told her I had watched you all sneakily in the office, that I had taken the call on the office land line on purpose; I told her I'd seen you all panic in the office! I was laughing. She went bright red. I usually ring back on my mobile whoever it is. There are no places of privacy in this ward. No phone signal except outside in the gulag yard or next to a particular fire door. Never once did I have a conversation that was not listened too or overheard. You are denied access to the Wi-Fi if you own an iphone. It strangely worked on android. No access to a computer with internet. I even have suspicions my room was bugged, no I was certain. If I'd had guests and had departed sensitive information in my room, then in the office on seeing the guests out the staff would look very worried. They went from worried and anxious to triumphant or quietly amused quite a lot. I will explain the staff's roles in detail later on. I had been secretly medicated every day since 8th December through to Monday 16th except the 24hrs that I had fasted and I had only knowingly taken a Zoplaclone for sleep on the Friday night and Saturday night after I arrived. On this night I was starving and had a double helping at tea time. The date would be around the 14th I'd hazard a guess. (I have done some time lining and it was indeed) I really should have done a daily diary whilst I was in there but you know it was hard enough to deal with my situation and I just couldn't summon the will to do it. With the double helping of the same dish I felt really bad within 20 minutes and started to get really worried at this point. By the first Tuesday of being there the realisation kicked in at the dire situation that I find myself in because if the staff are medicating me in my food then that means I am exactly where my enemies want me to be and I am going to be lucky to survive this.

14th December 2019 - I had my food and within 20/30 minutes my heart was thumping in my chest but it had never been this bad before. I got pissed off now, why the fuck were they doing this to me? I don't think it was to kill me but more to make me look unhinged and jittery all the time. This night I'd gotten that worried that I rang my friend Annona. She is a nurse for the NHS and she is the most lovely person one could meet. I explained everything that had gone on and how I could go about getting my bloods checked independently? Annona told me that I could ask my GP surgery and they could send the district nurse out or I could pay BUPA, I explained everything else that had gone on and we were on the phone for quite some time. However, because I was in the gulag yard there were people around and hovering plus John the Smiling Assassin was stood next to the open kitchen window ear wigging, a private conversation it was not. That night was the last time I was secretly medicated. I had been very vocal about it. Two days later and under extreme duress I was forced to take other prescribed medication. I'll go into that in a moment. Why would the staff be medicating me against my will,

I hear you ask? Michael you sound like you should be in there! The screams echo all around me. Well you will just have to trust me and keep reading and hopefully it makes sense by the end, I am hoping so anyway. I will say that the overheard phone call kicked off a very stressful and long two nights as you will read…

…This all came to ahead on the 16th of December 2019 by way of forcing me to take medication. 10 minutes after a meeting with a Dr Martin, more on him later, I get a knock at my cell door. I answer to be greeted with Dr Edera, he looks panicked and hurriedly, he tried to tell me he was prescribing me some shit or another (Haloperidol). I told him to fuck off, I don't recognise you as my Psychiatrist. I am not mentally ill and don't come back. I will not take drugs. Ten minutes later I hear a lot of footsteps coming to my door. I had a gut feeling something was afoot and thought I had not heard the last of this. I unlocked and opened my door to find at least 9 people steaming towards me. Everybody except the weasel Dr Edera. Some of the men were big lads too. Bethan one of the nurses was holding a Tray with a couple of syringes and cups on. I knew what was happening and instantly started screaming *"I Michael Elwood am of sound body and mind I do not need drugs*" over and over again. I kept looking around at all the people present and pleaded with them not to do this. "You're all helping to persecute an innocent man, you're all going to hell" They all looked shamed except Bethan, no she was enjoying it. I went into a fight stance and thought better. That is just what they want is for me to fight. I'd be on a section three and banged up for 6 months potentially but what really worried me was getting a sedative injection and waking up to my phone being gone. Suddenly there was commotion from behind and I'd seen Big Al, a patient, fighting one of them, they all descended on top of Big Al. He is shouting "I can see what you are doing to the lad, I'll grass you all up you bastards" he got a jab in the arse. They came back to me. Bethan piped up "That's enough Michael, this has gone on too long, it's up to you, the tablets or we force the injection" I kept shouting but realised the futility of it. Dejected and under extreme protest I took the pills. I then proceeded to shamefully drench Bethan with the rest of the water in my mouth straight into her face. I dislike this girl. It was satisfying and I was gutted about the medication. Every staff member present that day got both barrels for the next 48hrs. Deservedly so, too. From that day on I had to take Haloperidol. This marked the day the secret and sly medicating stopped and the legal medicating began. I do not recommend it. I was not mentally ill. I was more than willing to submit myself to a psychologist and work through my mind and I even requested such. Should that not be a better avenue to travel down first rather than mind altering drugs designed for people suffering schizophrenia, mania, agitation and psychosis and by a psychiatrist who has spent just 30 minutes in my company (65 minutes in 24 days if you take away the tribunal time) and I had been in there ten days too. In my mind knowing how illegal my detention was and the ulterior motives behind it, it was a massive breach of my human rights.

The side effects, nothing at all to begin with but after 5 days I became very flat and stiff. Like my shoulders had locked and would not move. Every action was very measured and slow. It was hard to piss. Dry mouth, I was shaky. I got ulcers and just did not feel like me. I am sure if you were suffering any of the prescribed symptoms it treats it would be beneficial but for me, who did not, it was a horrible experience. The day before being forced to take these drugs I had decided to change tactics and while still maintain my belief I wasn't mentally ill, I was not, suffering PTSD yes but not one of the symptoms above but I decided I would be very civil and calm and keep to myself for the rest of my stay. I knew I had my rescheduled tribunal coming up. I had been really fighting my corner up until then and I would continue to do so but quietly. This was made easier by the fact the skulduggery with all the staff and patients had stopped by and large since the day of my forced medication. It really makes it look like it was the medication that made me calm down and stop fighting the system but if you research that drug it takes time to build up and can take up to a couple of weeks to take effect. I could see what they were doing and it didn't stand up to scrutiny. Dr Edera however, did try his best to help the drug build up as quickly as possible, the scoundrel. Within days he had upped my dose from 1.5mg twice a day, two days later 5mg twice a day and then finally 5mg three times a day. 15mg a day! I went nuts every time he upped it. Angry but controlled still. He didn't even tell me the second time. I found out from a nurse. Against the rules is that Dr

Edera. 15mg is a massive dose when it comes to Haloperidol and seems far too high a dose. Why did I need so much and so quickly. Why so sudden after my meeting with Dr Martin from the original tribunal? Why was Edera so nervous and flustered that day when he visited me mere minutes after my meeting? Why such high doses of such a personality changing drug? Why did he not seek me out daily instead of his once a week? You barley ever saw this "Doctor" on his ward. Why? What did he do all day? Skive in his office?

Chapter 10
The Poisoning Claims

After a certain amount of days, I don't remember exactly when but I had what is called a formulation meeting. 13th December 2019. Present were 4 people. My consultant Dr Edera, (I will not go into him in much depth yet, no, he gets his own chapter, does the delightful and lazy psychologist, The Psychiatrist Dr Edera) I looked like a lawyer and smart. That put me in lawyer mode, too. I introduced myself and asked everybody to introduce themselves and explain who they were.

Present were Dr Edera, Sue Williams community nurse, Kate Ball Clinical Psychologist and Lucy Appleton Staff Nurse, except Doctor Edera the others weren't involved. I cannot remember in great detail what was said though I do remember me telling everybody in the room quite pointedly "Make no mistake; I will be assessing you all at the same time too!" I then turned, looking each dead in the eye and for a couple of seconds. I did a lot of the talking. I was angry by this point. I did mention to them all that rather than Dr Edera could I please have a female psychologist as I know I would get no benefit from Dr Edera. He asked why? I said, "I am an Alfa male and you are not Dr Edera, also I did not want an Asian Doctor. Forgive me I'm not racist, no offence. I just don't like you doctor, I need a female because I would respond better with one, also I won't take drugs and as you are a Psychiatrist, you deal with the medication side and looking at your patients you rely far too much on drugs" Dr Edera smiled at this. I also asked to be moved wards. This was denied. I asked Dr Edera if he was willing to read my files. He would not. I said I will not give your qualifications the respect that they deserve in that case. We got on to the reasons why I was committed. I shut up and listened. "It was your poisoning claims Michael" said Dr Edera. Oh dear, I proceeded to go on a spectacular rant at all in the room, I cannot remember what was said but it was passionate. The gist of it was about it how it should have been the result of a police investigation and not with me in here! That type of thing. I ended the meeting with "Meeting over and good day to you all" then I walked out. I then had a conversation with an old friend who had seen my plight on Facebook and reached out to me. This person has worked in the NHS mental health sector for years. We had a good chat and I told her everything. She told me I am in a really bad situation. She said that "The more time you spend with genuinely mentally ill patients the more like them you will become. You will pick up their mannerisms and all the while the staff will try to convince you that you are mentally ill. By the sounds of the reasons and the way they brought you in, it was definitely illegal, you have to be strong and just keep telling everyone you are not mentally ill and keep away from the patients because once on a section there is nothing anybody can do to help you" I pretty much stayed in my room from then on in. I still left to do

whatever but I decided to keep myself to myself from then on. I bumped into the staff nurse, Lucy from the formulation meeting and informed her that my detention is definitely illegal! She replied "Now I know that's how you feel Michael..."
"No that's the legality of it"
"I understand that is how you're feeling but..." Patronising cow "No you silly woman, it's got nothing to do with feelings, it's bloody illegal and I'm going to sue the NHS and Cleveland Police" I stomped off. Its a lot bloody harder than it sounds unless you have £100k or your complaint is classed as medical negligence.

I knew my friend was right on the being around mentally ill people because of my nephew Martin who lived with me, you see he does suffer genuine mental illness and it did start to rub off on me after a month. I was glad when he left. I then realised that was the very reason that the staff stayed in the office most of the time. I mentally thanked her for that reminder later on because up to that point I was being social and organising domino games and helping people, in fact patients came to me more than they went to the office. I, on more than a few occasion averted world war three. Yeah, I nipped that in the bud. I put my now, abundant alone time to good use and wrote on Facebook about my poisoning claims because I honestly still cannot believe they used that against me to lock me up. I posted this on the day I was forced to take medication. The 16th December 2019.

The Poisoning Claims.

"I Michael Elwood am of sound body and mind. I swear on my ancestors souls and Stevie-Jayne and Benni my Great Niece and Nephew souls that everything is right and true and happened.

The symptoms

I would suddenly feel extremely lethargic and have an intense pressure and uncomfortable-ness in my bladder. Now that feeling was a much more uncomfortable feeling than I'd suffered when passing a kidney stone back at Xmas and New Year. It was intense. I would then go to the toilet and then urinate. Out would come what can only be described as very black and thick urine. Around about 200 to 300ml worth. I would drink lots of water and then I would be fine within a couple of hours. This happened to me very intermittently. Once a week, twice a week at the most. I, having suffered with kidney stones both immovable and passing. I was aware the blackness and shortness of the urine that came out was in fact a new and very strange symptom. Leading up to the 10th October 2019, it was so intermittent I never got tested or looked at by a doctor. I really should have...my estimation that it only happened 6 to 8 times for 4 to 6 weeks prior. I mentioned this to my sister Carla, usually full of concern with anything like that she didn't say a word, no she smiled...curious. It didn't happen for more than a week on occasion...

To tell the full story I have to go back to the Tuesday the 8th, though the symptoms went back around 3 to 4 weeks prior to that date. The 8th was the date I started working at XPO in Middleton St George. I was doing a class two pallet round in mainly the Newcastle and Durham areas. I borrowed a bicycle from a friend and I rode 14 mile round trip to work every day and then completed a non stop busy pallet round. On Thursday 10th October 2019, I suddenly had the symptoms described above and suffered the black piss. I just powered through and did my job. On the Friday the 11th, I suffered the same symptoms again. I just put it down to riding the bike so much and always being on the go. I was still concerned about the black piss. Saturday and Sunday I was positively fine. Not one symptom at all. Monday, back at work I was also fine, felt tip fucking top on those three days. The key point here is that Monday was the first time I was away from the bungalow...Curious.

Tuesday 15th October 2019.

I went to work and on my way to my first delivery I felt the familiar uncomfortable-ness in my bladder and Penis. I was travelling up the A1 and nearly passed out and crashed. I pulled in to Durham services and parked in the lorry park. I went straight into the garage with my water bottle. I pissed out the black bloody sludge, as I call it, filled it up and drank all of the litre water bottle and then refilled it. I went back into my truck and slept for 45 minutes on the bunk. I, now late for my first job, forced myself to get up and go. I cannot explain the exhaustion that I felt and could have slept in that truck all day. Though, I did feel a little better. I got to the metro centre and found where I needed to be and eventually I found the shops rear entrance. I found the staff and started to help with the delivery. The boss and staff commented to me how ill I looked and asked if I was ok? I told them I think I'm passing a kidney stone. As the delivery progressed, I got comments like, mate are you sure you are alright? You look like you are dying mate! I rang the office and spoke to the women who worked there and I told her why I was late and the symptoms I was suffering. I finished all my other jobs and went home. I slept well that night...

Wednesday 16th October 2019
I got up at 05.30 and did my tasks, shower, take dogs for a walk, make bate etc...I got to work sorted the load and set off for my first job. I had eaten my bate early again, I do it every time but when you think about it, I have been up for nearly 4 hours and not one for breakfast it's understandable really. I got somewhere near my first job and felt the familiar symptoms, did the whole piss and water routine, got my head down again and got up and powered on again. I wasn't quite as bad as on Tuesday, however I managed to

fuck my phone screen and as your phone nowadays is an essential item and I was using it as my sat nav. I had a little meltdown in my cab, which consisted of me punching the dash a few times and swearing a lot. I managed my last three deliveries with directions from the office. I got back and rode home. Still feeling exhausted I sorted Brie and Bear, then I forced myself to eat something. I didn't have much food and not a lot of choice. By 8pm I was desperately ill. I could not lift my head up. The exhaustion I felt was worse than Tuesday and that was extreme. I went to bed. I awoke at 04.30 without an alarm and still felt as bad as the night before. I got dressed but it was no good. I could not ride the bike never mind safely control a lorry. I collapsed back into bed and did not awake again until 1800. I got up sorted the dogs and went back to bed about 8pm. I felt a little better but not much. I woke the next day at 07.30 still desperately ill. What happened after I went to the bank that day is covered in "My Witness Statement" and no need to rewrite it. I had recovered fully by the Saturday and my bungalow became my prison right up until I was put in this hell called a mental health institution.

I was still only 80% sure that I had been getting poisoned until my birthday.

24th October 2019

I had suspicions that people were gaining access to my home. You know the feeling somebody has been in? Now with all the shit I had been going through with Cleveland Police, Rasheed, the McCartens, my Family etc, I decided that day to leave the latch on my front door and leave through the patio. Problem was the key is snapped on the inside of the conservatory door and I would be unable to lock it. I decided to put my garden furniture, pub style bench, old table and chimenea against the door and use a ratchet strap to secure it. This was a lot harder than it sounds. After 10 to 15 minutes of fucking around and a lot of swearing I got a perfect hold and it was as neat and tidy as can be. Why did I do this? I had a hunch that whoever it was would try to gain access and seeing the latch on from the kitchen window along with the duct tape they might assume I could not lock the patio and try to get in that way. I knew if they had no experience with ratchet straps then they would never be able to put it back the same. I was right. It goes into this in much more detail in the witness statement. The ratchet was under the seat on the pub bench, instead of over it and the strap was slack and twisted in the ratchet, the furniture had moved too. Busted. But who? When I left for town that day I heard two beeps from a car near my friend Katies mothers. Like a coast is clear beep, beep. They really should have waited until I got further up the road. I could not see anything strange so I continued. (Darren from over the road, his car was present) When I got back in the bungalow that day there was a birthday card posted from his sister Katie.

The Perpetrators

After realising I was right about somebody had been accessing my home and the fact Katie had been round in the 1.5 hrs I was in the town, I started to really analyse and wonder about my symptoms. I decided to send her a message of thanks for the card. This is a key point here so listen up at the back, I departed to Katie my symptoms, the black and short urine, exhaustion and the feelings in my bladder and penis. Her reply was "Sounds like you have a kidney infection, you need to go to hospital because it can lead to sepsis" I was flabbergasted, with suffering kidney stones, I have had a canny few kidney infections and the symptoms are definitely not those. Katie would know this because she is an ex-paramedic and works for 111 and the NHS. I never replied to her message. That was the last time I'd seen or heard from her until 01/12/2019. Now this is strange because she was always worried about me and in regular contact. The other very telling thing was the fact that she had been MIA from her mother's all that time too. Now she's a creature of habit, doesn't have many friends and I would see her car there on many occasions every week, even on her 4 night shift rota. It was very curious and extremely out of character for Katie. I began to get suspicious of her because I had given a key to Katie and her mother previously, I've been known to lose my keys and was sick of booting my poor door in, it's easier than it sounds, the middle section comes out quite easily with two good boots. Brie and Bear, the poor buggers are bit funny with me for a day after, understandable really. I did a little research into my symptoms and found out the feelings and short black urine was consistent with a foreign substance entering my body and being as quickly as possible attacked and removed by my immune system. Once I added all this up I was convinced it was indeed Katie, her brother Darren and possibly my niece that had been poisoning me.

Sunday 1st December 2019
I had a routine from the ratchet strap incident, I would always leave the latch on and leave by the patio door and climb over my fence and gate and confident that Katie and my niece did not have a key for the patio. I never really left my home for any length of time unless I had to go to town. I was safe at home, where I took my dogs for a walk and my local shop. A couple of days previously I mentioned to Aimee, that I believe Katie, her brother and Laurencia really need access to my home and I believe it's because whatever substance was used, there will be evidence under my sink, finger prints etc... On the 30th of November I took Brie and Bear for their daily walk, as I left, Katie's brother returned home. He nodded at me as he went past, then did a U-turn and sped back past me with screeching wheels and high revs. Forgot your key to my home? I mused. I

did not notice anything strange when I returned, except the latch wasn't on fully. Still doing its job but consistent with the door being opened with it on. The next day 1st December 2019 I went to take my dogs and booted them out of the front door, put the latch on and did my patio door routine. When I returned I put my key in the door and I opened it. It opened wide. FUCK!!!! I went in checked the patio door, it was ok. I went to the French doors in the front room and instantly noticed the key. Now my dad some years ago had watched a program about burglary and in the program it had said that if you leave your key in fully, a device exists that can turn your key from the outside. From then on in, we always left out keys half way in and got into a habit with it. I knew it was only half way because it's part of my checks before I leave the bungalow. This was a mistake, I should have had it all the way in and twisted to the side. What I found when I looked was the key was held in to the lock by 2mm like it had been pushed out.

(My nephew Martin Jon Jones has a key for the French doors, I know this because it was how he was able to burgle me on the half a dozen occasions that he did. The little bastard, I am

starting to realise my "family" maybe are really bad people. You think? Unfortunately all the good ones have passed, oh well, I'll just have to make my own won't I. I then noticed in the kitchen that a plastic bag from under the sink was outside the freezer door and it definitely wasn't there before. FUCK! I went outside got angry and kicked my recycle bin, sending dog food cans everywhere. I went back and started to process this new development. About an hour later I get a knock at the door. Still absolutely fuming, I open without my usual checks and fuck me I see Laurencia, my niece. Laurencia had a half smile on her face. I looked at her for a few seconds and just slammed the door and shouted "Don't ever come back" first time I'd seen her in 5 months. I think I handled it rather well considering. I then processed that too. She felt emboldened by the fact they had cleaned up whatever they have been trying to do since they realised I had figured it out? She looked guilty as fuck. She always will to me. I fear for my great
niece and nephew with a mother like that. (One thing that bugged me was, had my friend Aimee departed to Laurencia or Carla about my belief of there being evidence under the sink?)

Then an hour after Laurencia appeared I got a text from Katie for the first time since the 24th October! I could not believe it

"Hiya lovely, you've been quiet, hows you?"

To obvious my dear. I blocked her. She messaged me on WhatsApp

"What the fuck is going on? After everything I deserve an explanation"...Deserve prison cell my dear not an explanation. She then emailed me the same message just worded differently. I ignored it.

On the 11th November 2019 I had contacted and sent my files to Cleveland Polices finest department of incompetence the "Standards and Ethics Department" meant to investigate the wrong doings of Cleveland Police. I think that department would be bigger than all the others put together if they actually did. I realised this was a futile exercise. A week before I contacted them I sent the files to the IOPC (Independent Office of Police Conduct) I did this so it was on record with another government body and I thought they might help me. No. The IOPC legally cannot unless Cleveland Police refer themselves. You fucking what? Erm ok then. They had 15 working days and then I could appeal to the IOPC. I was predictably given the run-around by the Standards and Ethics Department. (Had they done what it was set up to do, we would have had evidence under my sink and lots of other evidence before they cleaned it all up) On the 2nd December 2019 I went to the library and wrote the letter you see below. At the same time I put in a pointless appeal to the IOPC. When I contacted them they had no record that I had even emailed to confirm they had received it...curious.

By the 6th I was committed here on the grounds of my claims above...Those claims should have been investigated by Cleveland Police. It's a bullshit reason and remember it is illegal that they brought me in, never mind my continued detention and now they have forced me to take drugs. This, mere minutes after talking to an independent doctor for 10 minutes about my upcoming tribunal. He was a twat and lost my trust straight away. I will not attend my tribunal. I am hoping this was to hide the fact they have been medicating me through my food. I guess I will see tomorrow...

The fight continues..."

***

I did not attend my tribunal. One, because I did not have a solicitor and two because I did not trust the reports of the staff and Dr Edera, I knew at that point I would lose. I also refused because I wanted my appeal in front of the hospital managers first too. Due process and all that...

Chapter 11
The Intimidation and Patients and
The Staff

The Intimidation attempts

I am going to go through each person individually and tell the story. I cannot think of a better way to do it and try to explain what happened. It is an unconventional way of doing it but let's see if it works.

Baraket - Patient

Baraket hails from Ethiopia, a persecuted and born again Christian preacher although there was nothing holy about Baraket. He sports a rather nasty scar down his forehead and cheek gained with an axe from said persecution. He was in on a section two when I turned up. Said he'd been living and then lifted in Sheffield and brought to Teesside. Never prescribed medication and only started to lose it towards the end. Always conflicted and under pressure. We made friends to begin with. He was always after borrowing every ones phone. Loud and nice at first but was under a lot of outside pressure. His claim to fame is he made me laugh at dinner time one time, he said to Bethan dead serious "I wish I was as fat as you!" he meant it and not in a horrible way. "You can't say that to a lady Baraket." I said. I looked at Bethan and said "Well erm" and chuckled.

John "The Smiling Assassin" Healey - Health Care Assistant

I met John the very first night I was there. He befriended me and found me some backy. I liked John to begin with and initially I thought he was a good person. By the Monday night, John's demeanour had changed from very friendly and natural to stiff and guarded. He had definitely turned but was a lot more devious and clever than the rest of the staff, John and Care assistant Peter were definitely on Cleveland Police and Rasheeds payroll. I hold John and Peter responsible for the secret medicating as both were always working when it happened.

Simon – Patient

He came in around 6 days after I did and a voluntary patient. He had a very disturbed aura about him. He had gaunt and spooky eyes. He was very skinny and bald. I was my friendly self with Simon when I first met him. It was not reciprocated. He was very animated and agitated. He made a rather obvious beeline for me. After our first couple of encounters I did not utter more than two sentences to him for the rest of his stay. He left the day before I did. Totally defeated.

Mohammed – Patient

An old school Asian around 60 in traditional dress, a false eye, religious, a vegetarian and with child like mannerisms. He, for the first few days always greeted me with "Michael" said in a child like high pitched voice. He would not leave me alone and trust me the at first charming and high pitched "Michael" soon got on your fucking nerves…

Ali – Patient

Quiet, Asian lad, early 20s. Just wanted a quiet life did good old Ali. Apart from a few bollockings from me for lack of manners, please and thank you mainly, he kept himself to himself. He was beginning to get pressure from Baraket but just locked himself in his room and ignored him mostly. He really did not want to get involved despite Baraket and John the Smiling Assassins best efforts.

Baraket had started to change somewhat. Some days after I arrived, I had stopped lending him my phone and he had begun to get visitors. Three burly black men would visit. They always spoke in their native tongue. The tone was quick and heated, like they were putting pressure on Baraket. It was strange; he became sullen and stressed looking after that visit. He didn't seem to sleep any longer. One day he disappeared for 10 hrs. He was loud and it was so peaceful without him there. I found this strange because he was brought in around the same time as me and I had not even talked about leave. We had a few arguments over my phone after I refused to continue to lend him it. I did not trust him, especially after a patient, Big Al, whispered to me "Mick, don't trust that c@?t Baraket, especially with your phone" I decided nobody gets access to that phone apart from me from then on. He would always try to borrow my phone but it was futile. He got a basic mobile phone from somewhere after one of his disappearing acts and would speak really aggressively into it. You could hear him all around the building. He started doing this at ten at night. I confronted him but in a respectful way and he got aggressive. I realised he was doing this on purpose right near my room. I surmised it maybe was to draw me out and get me to attack him. So for the next few nights when he did this near my room, I ignored it and he give up. He would always be asking me if I wanted to go for walks. I would tell him that the people who got me here would get to me too easily on the outside. I really started to get suspicious of old Baraket. He was not prescribed medication and forced to take drugs like I was, yet as time wore on he did indeed seem quite ill, no ill is the wrong word, more under extreme pressure, before he disappeared. Once he got a mobile phone from nowhere it was hourly and very aggressive conversations he was having. After receiving the phone, I realised he was given it so John could text him my location around the building as he would pop up out of nowhere and he suddenly started to follow me menacingly with a very devious look on his face. I have to say that Baraket, though extremely physically fit as he is, is around 9st ringing wet and I just did not fear him. He told me he was a triathlon athlete and to be fair, he used to do 200 laps of the gulag yard daily and he would not have a bead of sweet on him. I started thinking that someone from outside maybe pressuring poor old Baraket and the mad thing? You could tell he liked me. He started to bug Ali a lot too, knocking on his door day and night. Ali's door was two doors down from mine. I think Baraket knew he would need help.

When Simon arrived I clocked him in the gulag yard having a fag and decided to introduce myself. We started talking and his demeanour was cocky. He suddenly told me he had killed someone in the past and had been in and out of institutions all his life. Not impressed I asked who he had killed? He said, "I cannot tell you that!" I looked at him for a few moments and said my fair wells. His cocky and patronising demeanour, coupled with his strange looks and psychotic smile, I took an instant dislike of Simon and felt he was targeting me purposely. When I was next in the dining room he walked towards me and I quickly went around another table to get away from him. I was amused but he didn't realise and it emboldened him. Simon had a smile on his face, a really sinister one whenever he looked at me. Later on that night he

stepped towards me with intent, slamming his foot in my pointed direction. I laughed. I was not finding him unnerving or intimidating but I could not react either. The next day at breakfast one of the patients, Ricky told me "Watch it Mick that Simon is hard as fuck and be careful" Now Ricky on the other hand was definitely a hard man before his stroke and sadly he was half numb down one side of his body, he really suffered the poor bugger. I laughed "Fuck off Ricky, there is nobody hard in this whole place. Baraket has unbelievable stamina but I have strength and aggression and as for Simon, my big toe is harder than him" Later on that night I went to do some laundry and Simon was about to follow me into the laundry room, I span around, he stopped dead at this unexpected move and I looked him in the eye and with quiet aggression and through gritted teeth said "You know Simon there is not one fucking molecule in me that is scared of you, you know that mate, you will not get me to attack you, you have to attack me first, I will only attack you, if you are a threat"
"Am I a threat?"
"That depends on you Simon" I moved towards him and he flinched and stepped back. Simon, you

fucked up mate, now I've got you mentally beat and you know it. I did not get much bother out of Simon after that. He used to stand outside in the gulag yard outside the window closest to my door with his dressing gown on and hood up and striped pyjama bottoms with slippers on and trying to look all Psychotic, waiting for me to leave my room. Other than first clocking him and shnortling, I didn't pay him any heed and he gave up eventually. He did do something else that was strange, John in the cell next door, told me about a ghost that roams the halls at night. I laughed and didn't really take any notice. That night I heard shuffling past my door and down the hallway. I heard it again. Then it happened a third time. Fuck this I thought, I have to have a look. I opened my door and 5 metres up the hall or so was clearly Simon stopped dead like a statue in his dressing gown and slippers on and with his hood up. Not facing me. I shnortled and called him a weirdo and went back to bed. It never happened again funnily enough. My ignorance to Simon's existence really started to get to Simon by the end of his stay. His many attempts to get in my head were always met with Good Sir humour or indifference; he should have admitted defeat to me when I stood up to him outside the laundry room that night.

Mohamed changed significantly too. He was harmless enough and after trying a little to intimidate me he was more on the funny side than what he was intending. He would step into me like Simon did, with his hands in his pocket and suddenly remove them. I just laughed at him. I did notice that Mo did not need his hearing aid that he wore at the beginning any longer and seemed to be able to hear me from 20 yards now. Though thankfully he dropped the high pitched "Michael" I did hear him speak normally to his daughter in Arabic. She was a frequent visitor to Mo and a couple of times left an assortment of Greggs. "It's Ok Mick she has done it before, help yourself" said John the smiling assassin. I always left the Greggs. Even though he changed and was clearly more compos mentis than he portrays. I still liked Mo and in reality what could he do, he wasn't a threat. On three occasions he did knock on my door in the early hours. I would never open my door unless you identified yourself and never did, I didn't actually see him but I knew because his cell is next door. I just told him to behave and fuck off. He did. Eventually he admitted defeat and went back to being five year old Mo, so I went back to being nice to him.

14th December 2019 - 7pm.

I ended the call to Annona, where I departed everything that happened openly and discussed getting my bloods checked, I walked into a worried looking John outside the office, who had overheard my conversation with her, he was stood with Baraket who in turn was shouting and being aggressive, he was stood next to Ali. John nervously shouted at me "Michael, come here, your friend wants a word with you"
"He's no friend of mine" I said
I hurried to my room. It felt really wrong that did. I wondered what would have happened if I'd have stayed and confronted John, Baraket and Ali. An hour later I was in my room and heard Baraket say something and I heard keys jangle. I then heard Baraket knock on Ali's door with some urgency almost whispering "Ali, Ali" Knock knock. "Ali, Ali" Fuck this if he's got a skeleton key from John. I opened my door and went out into the hallway. I looked at Baraket who was maybe 15 yards down at Ali's door. "Baraket, did John just

give you a key for my door did he? I wouldn't mate, I know you have been told to hurt me or get me to attack you but I promise you Baraket, I will see it coming and you will be in a fight for your life! It doesn't matter if it's with Ali and Simon at the same time. I beg you don't do it" I looked at him and he looked at me the whole time and didn't say a word, still stood facing Ali's door with his head turned towards me. He looked conflicted. I went back in my room, locked my door convinced that Baraket, Ali and possibly Simon might be planning to storm my room. I stayed awake all night. Around about 7am, John opened my door with Baraket sat on the hallway window sill opposite my room and looking angry and staring at me menacingly. John had a smirk on his face and asked if I was alright, I was distressed at the situation and at this point really started to see the bad situation I found myself in. I despaired at my luck. I was upset because I had done nothing wrong and did not deserve to be here and with the secret medicating and intimidation, plus knowing Baraket is being pressured from outside, I realised my situation was a really fucking bad one to be in and Cleveland Police, Rasheed, The McCartens and my family have me right where they all want me, facing what I was facing. It's me against them again but again I have not done anything wrong to make them, erm, them. I am always reacting and I am never a step ahead, why? I am not devious or built for that, I just don't have it in me to be that underhand and frankly evil to people. I am here because of Cleveland Police the NHS and my Family and friends. I told John to "Fuck off" and shut the door. He did.

The next night I stayed awake again. I was already tired but I felt I had to be ready. I felt safe during the day and that day I'd slept around 6 hrs. At around 7am I was about to go to sleep when I get a knock at my door. I shout fuck off. They keep knocking. I get up angry and open the door. I am greeted by my neighbour John who is stood with a black female nurse. "Wtf John! I'm trying to sleep what's up?" "They're shutting the ward down Mick, it's over, come on"
"What do you mean they are shutting the ward down John?" "They are shutting it down come on!" I looked at the mute nurse "What's going on? Are they emptying the ward? She nodded. I shut my door. I did not like this. There was a lot of noise and movement coming from the hall way.

After half an hour I looked out and the ward was all but empty except the bad staff members involved and were all sat at the dining room table and I could see Simon, a patient called David and another patient Joe also involved. I admit I got a bit scared, lack of sleep, whatever but then I got hopeful, I actually thought people might be here to save me. I quickly realised this not to be so but then I thought they were emptying the ward so they could kill me. Just as I was facing my morality again I got a text message from Tracy my nephew Jamie's mum asking how I was. I was surprised because I didn't get a usable signal in my room usually. I told her I thought they were going to kill me. She calmed me down and told me she'd phoned the ward and told them she knows I'm here. This made me calm down and I ventured out to make a coffee. Apart from the few patients and the staff the place was deserted. I got a grip of myself and I went straight to bed and slept for 7 hrs. After the 16th when I was forced the medication the intimidation stopped just like everything else. It was ten days of hell in that place, between the secret medicating and intimidation. Thing is it was worse after because now I was left alone, I had nothing to fight for or keep me occupied. It became a boring count down to my tribunal. It really started to get on top for all the staff involved at this point.

I was sat down using my phone next to the fire door when Baraket approached me all menacingly and I quickly stood up, he was at his most problematic concerning me at this point, I jumped up quickly, stood aggressively into a fight stance and pointed at the line in the floor where it joins and said "Come past that line Baraket and I swear to god it will be the last thing you ever do, I fucking dare you!" My face must have brokered no arguments because he stopped dead in his tracks and after awhile he turned and left. I sat back down and watched him walk away. I was out in the gulag yard one night after the incidents and Baraket was there, after greeting him I said to him "Baraket, you have been persecuted before have you not?"
"Yes"
"Well what do you think I am suffering right now? That makes us brothers more than enemies, doesn't it Baraket?" He looked down at the floor nodded and said "Yes" He had his hand in the left pocket of his coat and he went to remove it

"Leave that hand in that pocket Baraket, don't fucking do it!" Moving away from him, I smiled. He smiled back and pulled out a metal key ring on a fabric chain, "It's just this Michael" We both laughed. We were good with each other after that and I continued to engage with him even though I knew he was under pressure to harm me and it was highly likely he was admitted for one reason only. I made a point of shaking his hand everyday and asking after his well being in front of the staff. I did, however keep a respectful distance. I knew from his mannerisms and reactions that he really did not want to harm me and he knew I would likely be victorious if he did attack me on his own, the people putting pressure on him did not care and just wanted him to put his life on the line and have a crack at it nonetheless. He did vanish in the end. A couple of days before my tribunal, he had not slept for two days and had a meltdown and was really aggressive to the staff but it was more in desperation and panic. I noticed this change and my sleeping patterns were all over the place, I would get up at 4am and he would still be up. I chatted to him but I really couldn't be arsed with him for too long. He was a great speaker but a deaf listener. He looked exhausted and extremely stressed. That morning he was shouting with two translators and was agitated and worried sounding, almost in tears. I heard in English that some Muslims had been ringing his phone and threatening his family. He disappeared that day. I just got a "Dunno" from the staff when I asked where he had gone. This was the day before my rescheduled tribunal. A good few patients vanished without a trace or were released in my time there. There was always a little anxiety when somebody left as I wondered who would be replacing them and would they be genuine. It was a big concern for me.

Bethan "Pure Evil" Story - Staff Nurse

Bethan was on the day shift for my first 5 days in here. My gut screamed to me something was off with this girl. She was always looking over with a strange look on her face, a sinister and slightly amused look. I felt like I had seen her before and she had familiar features. She never tried to strike up a conversation. I found her odd but there was something else that was bothering me, I just could not put my finger on why but my good old gut was screaming at me again. On her last shift it suddenly hit me. Holly shit! I am gobsmacked as it dawned on me where I had seen this girl from. I could not believe it when it suddenly hit me. I remembered an ex friend that I always had suspicions about being a grass but as I wasn't involved in that industry I was not bothered and surmised that its part of the job description and kept my thoughts to myself. This friend had a wife, who I was friends with on my blocked Facebook and I remembered seeing Bethan on my news feed in pictures with my old friend's wife on more than one occasion. They have similar features, sisters or cousins maybe? Coincidence, you would say? Me too except of her actions since I'd been here and the big one, who was this ex friend? Well, well it is only another big drug dealer in Stockton who has connections to myself, my family, my friends and Gary and Carl McCarten! Welcome to this sorry tale of woe Mr Stephen Frost. I've known Stephen Frost for around 4/5 years and we used to be quite good friends until I realised he was not trust worthy. He is great friends with my now ex friend Lee Russell and is connected with all my other friends too. Funnily enough I got a visit a few days before from a close associate of Frostie, he was all full of fake concern but it was a strange visit, he also works for the NHS. The connection with Bethan and Frostie means Frostie is in on this too, an unseen player until now. Suddenly it all made complete sense to me and he must be working with the corrupt elements at Cleveland Police also and is definitely a C.I. This connection with Bethan proves it was a set up because I do not for one second believe it to be a coincidence. It ties everybody together in this. Proof! Finally! It was obviously Bethan who recruited the other staff members involved, Joanne, John the Smiling Assassin and Peter the Cyborg mainly. It's the smoking gun I need for people to believe me. I have to say, I do not go out of my way to befriend drug dealers but it is the top industry for employment in Teesside and I only know these people because of the pubs I drank in. It's just a coincidence really. I have never sold drugs. I could not believe the connection. I couldn't help myself and I let it slip. I am not purposely trying to take down these boys and the corrupt elements at Cleveland Police but you all have left me with no choice but to go down this route. With the secret medicating, the intimidation attempts and realising the new players involved, this knowledge just proved how precarious my situation was and still is. The secret medication they were giving me made me a right gobby fucker and I blurted out information like confetti. I didn't see Bethan again until the day of my forced medication. One thing I have to say is maybe her last shift before, I was walking past the door to the ward and lent out of the main door was Bethan, talking to a man. This man was in a smart suit, around 6.2, bald and looked high up. CID I would say. He definitely had some Norman in him. They were having a heated discussion. Those gut feelings again and it is screaming he is the top man, the corrupt element at Cleveland Police. I would be able to recognise him straight away so if he works for Cleveland Police I can very easily identify him. I hope this explains why I spat water into Bethan's face that day. While on the subject of Cleveland Police, on around the tenth day of my incarceration Cleveland's finest gave good old John, the care assistant a visit in the office. Brendon another assistant told me not to worry they are not here for you. Fuck off Brandon. 2hrs they were there, looking at a computer and talking to John for 1.5hrs then another staff member for the rest. Listening to the recordings from my room

I expect. They were very red faced and worried looking when they left. It was around the time after my overheard conversation with Annona where I had departed quite a lot of information in the open. They were all very worried at that point. If only I could get people to believe me. It's a lot harder than it sounds. At least now I have proof and can connect mostly everybody in this sorry tale of woe.

Joanne " The Liar" Taylor - Nurse

I did not like Joanne one bit I have to say. She was patronising and thinks she is really clever when really it's the opposite. Clearly recruited and involved with Bethan up to her neck. Now my natural dislike and gut feeling about somebody does not mean I will be horrible to them and it was so with Joanne in the beginning. However, she lied a lot. She had a stupid grin every time she lied, quite an obvious tell. She was the first one to try and convince me my tribunal and my appeal is the same thing and tried on multiple occasions. Yes a tribunal is an appeal but not the appeal in front of the managers, that comes first. She was infuriating. I eventually proved to her and everybody else who had tried to convince me and

I was permitted to submit an application. It was a well earned win, even if I did not get it in the end. Other times she tried to convince me that things didn't happen. She was stood next to me when I recognised Sue the acting ward manager on the staff board, "That's the one who made me sign the paperwork" "Now that didn't happen, Michael"
"Oh but it fucking did my dear Joanne" The second time she tried that I shut her down; I looked her in the eye and said *"Just Don't Joanne!, Just Fucking Don't"* She shut up. Joanne also lied to me saying I am not permitted to look at my medical records and drug charts. "Something to hide I said?" I asked the next shift if I could look at them and they let me no problem. Why lie? Because the one she had at the time had obviously been doctored and updated with the secret medication that was used.

I got my most pissed off with Joanne on the 18th. I was handed a letter around the time of the start of my tribunal that I didn't attend, in the envelope contained three reports. One from Dr Edera, one from Lauren Jackson and one from Joanne. Joanne's was appalling. I have a copy now, it went missing when I attended my tribunal but I got the

solicitors to send me a copy, I should have taken my paperwork with me with hindsight. In a nutshell she claimed I was having a psychotic episode and definitely suffering psychosis and needed to be in hospital. You what? I stormed to the office. There were two hospital workers from other departments in there at the time, completely not giving a fuck, I knocked on the door and Joanne was sat at the desk next to the door. I said "What, Joanne, fucking qualifies you to make a diagnosis that I am suffering psychosis?" she went bright red. "Erm, I think you are" she said sheepishly
"You know you are helping to persecute an innocent man?"..."This isn't the time or the place to discuss this Michael, let's go to the…" I butted in "Why? I have nothing to hide, no it's not me that has something to hide is it Joanne?" I looked at her for a few seconds for effect and she looked ashamed and red faced, fuming I walked away. She changed somewhat after that and I had no real issue with her from then on. You see the staffs days off would kick in and a new staff cycle would begin. You would go through periods of not seeing people for days or ever again in some cases. The exceptions were Peter and John. It is

my estimation that I had spent no more than 1 to 2hrs in Joanne's company in the whole 24 days I was held against my will. She is a nurse. She is not qualified to make that assessment. Her report alone confirmed I was right not to attend my tribunal on the 18th.

Lauren – Care Assistant

Lauren was my friend, she was only 22 but was mature and not yet corrupted by time and the system, a fresh egg and cared, or so I thought. She is an intelligent girl and capable of so much more than the despicable mental health sector. She filled out my application for the appeal and the tribunal. She would come to my cell and talk to me. I would tell her about myself. It was Lauren who suggested a particular female psychologist. I said yes. I kept asking for her. I never did meet her. I would have been willing to see her everyday and a much better course of action and treatment than Haloperidol if that is what the staff and doctors genuinely believed, I know they didn't believe I was mentally ill for one second, you could see it in their eyes. New people like work experience students, new young employees they stopped appearing after a week of me being there and I believe that was because they could see straight away I was okay and started being vocal about it. Lauren was a good egg I believed. We did fall out twice. The first week I got a visit from the Psychosis team from the NHS and met another Lauren, I did not know where they were from and when I found out I was fuming. Lauren Jackson from the psychosis team, she comes and visits me now in a professional capacity and with my consent, glad of the company, though I know the NHS is worried I am going to sue them so she might be a spy, probably is to be honest. They should be worried. I went and found Lauren after Miss Jackson was dismissed. I asked who had diagnosed me with psychosis and why were those people sent to me? She said...wait for it..."It's because of your bizarre beliefs, Michael" I'd of laughed if I wasn't so angry. "Bizarre Beliefs? What the fuck does that even mean Lauren? That is the most peculiar term I have ever heard. Did you make it up or is it an official term? Oh Lauren I had high hopes for you" I stormed off. After I calmed down, I had a good laugh about it. I christened Lauren BB from that day forth. I was pissed off because I had asked her on many occasions to read my witness statement and told her you will understand and it is that big I cannot possibly tell you about it all and it not make me sound like a nutter. Everybody just wanted me to tell them the story. I cannot do it justice without written words. I believe it might be one reason I am still here. I did tell her about the poisoning. No one except Kerry ever admitted reading the files when it came to the NHS. They had copies because they printed it all out for me and I did not ask them to nor send them the files. Did they read them? I can only speculate. The night after the forced medication Lauren came to my room and tried to talk me into taking some medication that was prescribed but optional. It was an antihistamine with sedative properties and helps with agitation, I wasn't agitated. This was Laurens second attempt after the last night. Around 9pm my door opens and Lauren comes in with a nurse and a cup, I was half asleep. "I just want you to try this drug and I will tell you about it…" I snapped "Lauren you are 22 years old and cannot tell me anything about fuck all, you are a student of life compared to me now get out and fuck off" I remember shouting at the suspected bug in my room "Fucking sucker for a pretty face you Mikey my boy!" That was the last time I'd see Lauren. She disappeared and I never got to thank her. She was the only one who cared. I would love to know what happened. From the 18th she was nowhere to be seen. Did she change wards? Quit? Take some holidays? Maybe one day I will find out though she knew what was going on, on that ward concerning me and with hindsight not as trust worthy as first thought.

Peter "Cyborg" Armstrong – HSA

This man always seemed to be at work. Stiff as a board and emotionless he was like a robot. I never once caught him engaging with a patient. Now on the ward they have to check your cell every hour. You have some blinds that they open with a radiator bleed type key and the staff use a light switch on the outside to light your room up. It is really annoying. It meant broken sleep every single night. The key is a square key and has round balls as tumblers and makes a thucking machine gun type noise as it travels through the lock. Peter, on a night would always come round and check but it wasn't every hour, more like every half. Another thing I noticed was that his and a lot of other staffs footsteps to my door were mostly continuous. Strange as you would think he would be stopping every few metres to check on the others. He would always put his key in the door at the same time as doing the blinds. I disliked this man and his demeanour immensely but kept quiet. One night I was up late and decided to ask him about it. "Peter! Why do you put the key in the door when you open the blinds? Now I was expecting a reply like "So I can gain quick access if you are in need" Something like that but what I got was, "I'm not I am just doing the blinds" Umm, oh dear Peter, both sounds are very different to each other and unmistakable, why lie? I did get him talking a few times and even made him laugh a couple of times too. He seems like he was a very different man than the one he was portraying to me in the main. On two occasions he was present when a new non ward staff member unlocked my door on a night twice and left it unlocked. It woke me both times but is another example of the tactics used to annoy me. He was always messing with my door and always mute and emotionless, I disliked this man greatly. He was always present when my food was medicated.

Babs – Care Assistant

She was lovely for my whole stay really. She was just a naturally bubbly and caring creature. I started to get to know Bab's and befriend her. I told her the story of Peter and the key door incident and the attempts at intimidation. She asked me if I felt safe here?

"Would you?" I replied. She seemed really concerned. I was awake that night and noticed she was sat at a computer in the office, and concentrating for some hours, looking at the camera footage maybe, I thought? I do know she was more stiff and guarded with me from her next shift and stopped her attempts at getting to know me but was still lovely. Was she recruited by Bethan or warned off or both?

Carl – Care Assistant

Not too much to say on burly Carl, a late comer he tried to gain my trust but lied to me in the first 3 minutes of meeting him and lost my trust straight away, another who tried to convince me that my appeal is my tribunal. When I complained about the Wi-Fi he lied that we have never given out Wi-Fi. "Carl, there are fucking patients with android phones using the fucking Wi-Fi, it's just not working for iPhone. You have just told a lie you did not need to tell. Full of shit, you Carl" The only other thing of note was when I was complaining about the forced medication he flippantly said "It's ok we can do it under the Mental Health Act" my reply was "Just because you could doesn't mean you should Carl" He didn't really engage much after that I think he knew it was futile.

Brendon – Care Assistant

He was the nice guy of the team. He was always playing good cop. He was involved in my opinion but did not directly affect me and he only told a couple of fibs so I am going to go easy on dippy Brandon. One of the nights I thought my cell would be stormed, at around 7am the shift swaps over and Brendon came to open my blinds to find me stood 6ft away and directly under the light above and stood in a fighting stance ready for fucking anything and all psyched up and looking evil under the light. He looked at me for a second and quick as a flash he shut the blinds. I being revved up, unlocked my door and went in the hall way to find Brandon doing a running walk up the hallway looking back every few steps with a scared look and bright red face. I burst out laughing. He stopped at the end of the hallway and said "Hi Michael, are you okay? I was just checking on you"

"Top of the world Brandon, do me a favour and drop the fucking good cop act I know you are involved!" I went back in my cell, chuckling to myself and I went to bed.

Simon – Care Assistant

Told me a few porkies did Simon. His face was the easiest to read out of all of the staff and especially lies. He was mostly ok and did not really harm me, plus he let me keep my pillows and quilt that I'd had smuggled in so he gets a pass too. One instance I have to tell is Simon had let slip to me that a female had phoned the office to say she would be sending them my files. I said "Who?" He couldn't remember.

"Well it will be in your notes if you took the call. After an hour of looking flustered and lost in the office, he eventually came out and said "Lauren Jackson" I didn't believe him and told him that the reason I want to know is because my niece has had access to the original files now so if anything that I wrote that didn't come direct from me needs to be checked and cannot be taken as genuine, if anybody does send any files from outside, you give me copies so I can check them as I have the originals and they come from me"

Sophie – Care Assistant

Always in the thick of it was Sophie but still in the background all the same. I believe her to be involved. She wasn't good at lying and she is quite portly and her emotions betrayed her easily. She was present at the forced medicating and I let her know a good few times that "Karma's a coming for you my dear, I have forgave you but unfortunately there is nothing I can do about Karma, she has you locked in her sights and is a patient bitch Sophie" I said that in front of her colleague from another ward. She looked shamed and a little worried to her credit. Though a good person underneath, I could not stay angry at her for long.

Erica and Sue - Care Assistant and Ward Manager

My tribunal was booked before my appeal in front of the hospital managers. It was done on the sneak. On the Monday or Tuesday after being sectioned I had a knock at the door. I answered and it was a blond short woman that I did not recognise. I invited her in. she was holding some paperwork. She asked me to sign the already folded over to the sign page form and told me it was just to confirm my appeal in front of the managers. Why would I need to confirm my appeal I asked? She said she didn't know and would I sign please. I snatched the forms and unfurled them because I wanted to check, as I did I noticed my sister Carla was down as my next of kin. Furious at this realisation, I borrowed this woman's pen scribbled Carla's name out and put my step mother Jan. I then very stupidly just signed the document and due to my anger and my secret drugging, I handed it back. I realised my mistake when all of a sudden people were talking about my tribunal. I did a bit of investigation and found out that you do indeed have your appeal in front of the hospital managers first. I also found out through a good friend that the form I needed for the tribunal was a T110 form. I asked for one. I got one and within a minute of looking I recognised it as the form the blond woman had asked me to sign. I believed the fact I had signed the tribunal form meant it cancelled my appeal in front of the managers. I never did get my appeal. I later recognised the culprit who made me sign as Sue the acting ward manager, the dishonest but really nice cow. It's funny, even before I realised this fact about Sue, I was very vocal about the signing of the forms and appeal and in the office and listening to my rant were Lauren and Erica a staff nurse, there were two others present but I cannot remember who. I was telling Lauren about it and demanding the application for the appeal when Erica butted in "That wasn't Sue, that was me"

"No it wasn't"

"It was, I remember you scribbling your sister out and putting your step mother, how would I know that?" I am extremely sceptical but initially accepted the explanation, for around 30 seconds. By the time I had reached my room I had replayed in my head the encounter and did an about turn and stormed back. I knocked on the office door. Lauren answered and Erica was bent over doing something. "Erica, the thing is it definitely wasn't you, no this lady was younger and I towered over her and I'm only 5.7 and you're what, Erica? 5.9? I have told many staff members about myself removing my sister's name from the form. Nice try though my Dear" The only thing Sue and Erica shared in common was blond hair. The looks on the faces of Erica and the others present were priceless. You fucked up Erica and everyone knew it.

Big Al – Patient

I liked Big Al. he looked the spitting dab of Mrs Bucket's brother from Keeping Up Appearances. He was obviously a boyo back in the day. He was the only one who was definitely genuine. The day I was forced my medication and he stuck up for me was not the first time he earned a jab in the arse for my benefit. He used to sit in the lounge for hours and either people watch or sleep. Fiery but with an old school soundness about him. He had begun to see what the staff were doing to me and had been vocal about it. He had been privy to my conversation with my cousin Katie and pieced it all together. I think they might have paid him off for his silence or made a deal of some sort at least. Some of the times I would hear him shout and go check on him but nothing was a matter when I got there and he was acting. After the 16th he just clammed up whenever I asked. On the 17th I came into the lounge to see Al all dressed up in his best and with his belongings in a bin bag "Going home Al?" I asked "Yeah Mick, they are getting me a taxi now!" "Made a deal Al?" I asked in front of another assistant Julia. Cue a rather comical interaction between the two and an argument gathered pace and before Big Al knew it he had to stay. Sorry mate I definitely ventured out of my room at just the wrong time. I would love to interview the old bugger. The day of the forced medication and Big Al's actions meant that the way the staff had been treating me was now being noticed by the patients not involved already. This was bad for them and another reason I believe all the skulduggery stopped that day, for if the patients can put it together then how long before others do? I was ever so grateful to Big Al for his support and if he did use the knowledge to make a deal then good luck to him. I would love to interview him. He told me after the forced medicating he enjoyed the tussle and it was exciting. "I haven't got a clue what was in that jab, Mick" He did not like Baraket one bit and even threw a full coffee over him once. I couldn't believe it, I was stood next to Baraket and he didn't get a drop on me. It was a pleasure to meet him and you never know maybe one day I can interview him. He told me not to trust Baraket especially with my phone.

Joe and Al – Patients?

Now Joe was an elderly man. He mumbled and shuffled around a lot. He disappeared regularly and would return with some odd things, a women's fur coat, hand bag, a kid's hat, things like that and lots of sweets usually. Now I thought this guy was cool as fuck and harmless and I had that view until 3 things happened. First I opened my door one morning and just watched everybody on the other side of the building, it was busy but I spotted Joe and gone was the stoop he had and he was stood up tall. Gone was the shuffling walk, gone was the daft hats. If it wasn't for his clothes you would think it was a different man. I shut my door and was now suspicious and started watching Joe much more closely. Second, in came a new patient called Al. he was a very short man and funny looking and made a be-line for me. Always talking and following me around. I had to tell him to stop. He departed to me at tea time in the dining room that he did not feel safe in here. "So why are you here?" I asked. "Because my house was broken into and I don't feel safe at home"

"But you are voluntary Al and if I didn't feel safe, which I don't as it happens, I would be straight out of here!" Al had a limp, only it seems the limp was fake. I caught him walking normally on more than one occasion, once he never knew I was watching as he was walking in the gulag yard and a patient called David told him I was looking and just like that his limp returned mid stride. I creased up laughing. I was present in the lounge and noticed out the corner of my eye that Joe was whispering to Al. Now this was at least two weeks into my stay and I have never understood Joe's mumbling, or seen anyone try to engage with him. I got fuck all when I tried. Later Al approached me and told me that Joe had given him 40 fags and that he was scared because Joe got aggressive when he tried to give them back. I said "Don't worry, just keep hold of them until the morning and at breakfast give them to me and I will give him them back" He tried to hand me the cigarettes. I refused to take them. Al was nearly in tears. I told him to man up and if he is that worried to go give them to a staff member. The next morning I asked Al about it and he flippantly told me, it's ok he sorted it. I found this funny as he nearly had a nervous breakdown about it last night. The secret whispering really made me start to wonder about Joe and Al. I remember talking about Garry and John McCarten being Cleveland Polices C.I's and Joe then doing a sign of the cross. He would disappear a lot too. Most nights he vanished after a certain time. I'd say he was present around half the 24 days of my stay at most. The third, was when the ward was emptied and he was still present and there was an occasion where I had departed the information about everyone smiling at me in the office and it getting to me as I think something has changed in the staffs favour, the day I said that Joe started pointedly smiling at me, something he had never done before. He showed up after an absence of over a week for a couple of days towards the end and I used to just study him. Joe used to smoke in the canteen and nobody minded, I once watched him from the gulag yard writing Xmas cards and could see the neatness and care he was using. It just did not tally up with the man presented. If he was a fake patient, which I believe to be so, he was a fucking good one and needs a pay rise, that's for sure and I respect his craft. Strange one that.

Jonathan – Patient

I met Jonathan on my first night, very friendly and warm guy. He had a lot to say and it all made perfect sense to him but was total bollocks to everyone else. All about astronomy and energy, being grounded, how symbols affect your soul, shit like that. I always tried to make sense of it and a little bit of it actually did. Other than talking bollocks he was alright was John. On the first Sunday morning and still feeling the effects of the suspected MDMA I mentioned this to Johno. I said I felt like I have had a rap of MDMA, he didn't say anything and just smiled and his eyebrows rose. We always talked and the only other thing of note was when I mentioned being secretly medicated to him, in front of all the other patients, John the care assistant and the cleaner/server Marie that I suspected of doing the medicating. Johno said this "Well Mick, they must have a good reason" and smiled. I looked at Jonathan. "There is never a good reason to be secretly medicated Jonathan" I said. I could not believe he just said that. I looked at the other John and he looked like he had stopped breathing. The cleaner/server didn't know where to look. I mulled it over all that night. The next day I walk into the lounge to see Jonathan's possessions and him and his Dad. I asked "Are you leaving John lad? Out of the blue? Never said yesterday? Nice one mate!" He just said "Yeah" and we said our goodbyes. I think he was shipped out before I could get the chance to tease what he knew out of him, I'd say. He had recently told me that he was not on medication as he didn't need it. I used that as a reason why I don't need drugs either, it worked for a few days. I was sad to see good old kind hearted Johno leave; he had given me a jig saw shaped coaster with "Dream Big" stamped on it. I still have it and thought it was very apt.

Peter – Patient

Peter was a big lad, super friendly and super anxious which could turn to violence quickly. I got on with him. He was good to talk to and was always sound with me. His attempts to befriend me did seem a little forced. On one occasion he was having a fag and seemed extremely agitated. He was really jumpy and a little aggressive. I spoke to him and smoked my fag but didn't linger just in case. By the next weekend he left for a four day trip home. He came back on the Tuesday and we got talking and he said out of the blue "I don't think you are right Mick I can tell" I looked at him in the eyes and I thought, you don't even know me, what an odd thing to say. I stood up and shook his hand, said "Take care Peter, see you in a bit" and walked off. That was the last time I'd see Peter. He'd just got back, where did he go? I did ask him to go to the shop for me for some backy but my friend Chris said he would bring me some in, when I told Peter he looked anxious about it and tried to talk me into letting him get it for me, almost in desperation, I'm betting I would have received spiked backy had I agreed. Another strange one, that was.

Ali No 2 or "UJ" – Patient

He was a late arrival but came with a bang. Firstly he looked all psychotic and aggressive, like he was about to pop then when I mentioned this to the staff he changed to patronisingly friendly and made a beeline to try and intimidate me. Following me around, getting in my face. I fronted it out. I awoke one morning and went for a fag outside in the gulag yard and he got right nose to nose in my face. Stared me down did Ali. I told him, the same as I told everyone in there "You have to attack me first" I laughed at him. Later on I opened my door and he was stood across the other side of the building looking all menacing and staring at me. I stared at him right back. After a minute I raised my hand to my cheek and smiled creepily and waved my hand in a clasp and spooky wave, all the while still staring. He looked away to the side "Got you dickhead" I thought. He looked back. He looked away again "He's fucked it" My eyes never left his. He looked down. "Boom he knocks it out of the park" I had won again. Turns out he was alright in the end was old Ali, although he was a natural bellend but not a bother after that the boyo.

John my Neighbour

He was a good egg was John. Not that much to say other than we were quite friendly and I looked out for John when I could. I was his protection against Baraket and him wanting John's phone. He was in his 60's and his first time in an institution. Mine too mate. His wife and her sister who visited were lovely and seemed like they cared. John did try to be a silly bugger, I think someone talked him into it but I just told him to behave and stop and he did. We got on with our lives. He disappeared a few days before I left and I was sad because we didn't say goodbye.

Dillon

This kid was around 6.4 gangly with big, size 14 flat footed feet. He played rugby and was athletic. He made forced attempts to befriend me but they were too obvious and I sensed not quite genuine. He was a university student he told me. He would walk past my room on a night stomping with his flat feet, it sounded and felt like a baby elephant. I bollocked him a couple of times because late at night was the only time he did it and he only went 10 metres either side of my room. On the third occasion I, in my boxers went right out in the corridor looked up at the harmless giant, looked him in the eyes and said quietly "Dillon, behave mate it is 10.30 at night, people are trying to sleep and you're stomping up and down the hall way like a baby elephant"
"I've got flat feet Mick"
"I bloody know you have I can feel the vibrations you twat" I smiled. He smiled.

"It's what I do Mick"

"Not at bloody night and not past my bloody room Dillon you don't. It's about respect mate. Look Dillon you are a good kid but don't let these fuckers use you to piss me off" He looked a bit ashamed mixed with embarrassment. He did not reply. He stopped that night. I commented one night to Dillon that "I believe I will only leave this place in a box" He replied "At least you will be out, Mick!" I chuckled "Touché" I replied.

One time, late at night I opened my door when Baraket suddenly started screaming into his phone at 10pm, to see what was happening and Dillon was there with a pack of chocolate digestives. He offered me one, I took two. I felt off my tits for a few hours. I am thinking it can't be the sugar? Next morning I awake to an extremely ill looking Dillon wrapped in his quilt in the lounge being looked at. I had to wonder. Has he unwittingly eaten a full pack of spiked biscuits? I laughed at the thought. Baraket brought them in from the outside, he was absent most of that day, gave the digestives to Dillon, started screaming into his phone to draw me out and positioned Dillon with the biscuits outside my door, all the while not telling Dillon they were spiked! He munched on them all night! I could not stop laughing at the thought!

That's it on the main people involved except the despicable Dr Edera...

Chapter 12 - Dr Edera

Well, well, well, what a boyo this dude is. I met Dr Edera on Monday 9th December 2019. I took a dislike to him instantly. I did not want an Asian doctor. Not to be racist but I was hoping for a white female. I just connect better with a woman when it comes to feelings and such and my past experiences with the male Asian community didn't help. I just knew the Doctor would be Asian. I was right. I told him I am not willing to talk to him until he reads my files. He said this was not possible but I can tell him about them. I said that will not be possible. I said, I didn't want a male doctor and could I have a female please. I did not see him again until the formulation meeting. In all I'd seen the doctor on maybe 8 to 10 occasions totalling 65 minutes in 24 days. That is fucking ridiculous. Alright, I didn't make it easy for him and he usually got both barrels and was told to fuck off most times. What does the NHS pay him for? Should he have not tried to see me every day Monday to Friday, much deserved abuse or not?? You didn't bump into him on the ward much either. If I was a doctor and had my own ward and a patient under my care as difficult as I was and all the patient wanted was another doctor I would sign him over straight away, it would be the right thing to do.

The day of the 17th when he made all those people force medication on me after prescribing the drugs he never got a chance to explain because I wouldn't talk to him. He cannot force the drugs on me without talking to me first. When it comes to medication under the Mental Health Act, I think you should be able to appeal the decision before it's forced. I really hated his visits. He tended to annoy me just by being there. Until the 17th I was an uncooperative patient. It was only after the forced medicating and my decision to change tactics and be less obtuse that I became slightly more accommodating towards Dr Edera. It never lasted long because he would infuriate me every time. I just knew he was a bad person and was part of the set up and responsible for my situation, in my opinion the set up was pre planned days in advance. If I am right, which believe I am and have proof, then Dr Edera was definitely involved and I could feel it from the first time I met him. Ultimately this set up could not have happened without the Doctors full knowledge and consent. He knows Rasheed, undoubtedly.

I attended a meeting with Edera and Brandon the nice guy. It was some days after the medicating but before the final dose was upped. He told me he "Wanted to see an improvement in me accepting the treatment." He said "I want you to be calm and accept you are ill" I asked what he had diagnosed me with exactly? "Mania" I went mad. "How the fuck can you come to that conclusion when you have only spent 50 minutes in my presence the whole time I have been here doctor?" It's better than psychosis I guess. "I want you to spend more time out of your room so we can assess you and Michael I'd like to hear less swearing" "Fuck off Doctor, that's who I am and I don't like you so I swear more. Let me get this straight, you want me to change myself from me to how you want me to be, you don't even know me, don't forget and when I have achieved your perception of how I should be, you will release me? Is that the gist of it Doctor?"

"Erm"

"I will give you an hour a day socialising but you will have to convince your lazy staff to leave the office" He didn't know what to say. I did not give them the hour. I added "Some of your staff need to be in here I think" Brandon piped up. "I have a problem called (I cannot remember the name) and needed help mentally myself"

"Case in point, thanks Brandon"

That was the most civil conversation I and Dr Edera ever achieved.

Dr Martin

I have been saving good old Dr Martin's story. Three days before the tribunal that I did not attend, I had a scheduled meeting with a Doctor from the tribunal, a Doctor Martin. I get a knock at the door and I am greeted by a ward staff member and a fat middle aged and portly good old boy. We went to the quiet room, the staff member asked if he could stay. I said no. Pointless as they just hung around the door and listened, dopey bastards, I could see his shadow under the door. I didn't say anything and was used to the constant spying by now. He introduced himself. We shook hands. I started to tell him the story of how I was brought in. After 5 minutes he butted in and said "You are quite an intelligent and articulate man aren't you?" I didn't really say anything and just shrugged. He changed the subject to my past drug use, I told him and then asked why that was pertinent? He said "Because it explains why people go around the bend" What an odd thing to say I thought. I told him "I would like to continue with the story please" He replied "I was hoping for a break from it actually" I looked at him for some seconds. "Oh dear Doctor, you have just lost my trust" I stood up "Meeting over, I will not be attending my tribunal. Good day to you" and I walked out.

Ten minutes later I get a very flustered and nervous looking Dr Edera at my door banging on about prescribing me Haloperidol, I told him to do one and shut my door and then ten minutes after that I was forced to take them under extreme duress. I think they were that worried about me being me at my tribunal and the secret medicating that it became imperative to get me on Haloperidol and/or Olanzapine. Both drugs treat the same thing and when I pointed this out it just became Haloperidol. The third drug, the anti histamine I think, maybe that had something to do with the secret medicating but those symptoms were amphetamine like and this had sedative properties. Maybe they shared some of the ingredients. I never once knowingly took it, despite the staffs best efforts. I believe the drugs were prescribed, not to help me or because I needed them but to suppress the fight in me and change me as a person in the hope I would not have my usual ability in something like a tribunal and let's be honest, I love shit like that.

When I got the three reports on my mental state a few days later I noticed on Dr Edera's file that the attending physician, or proper Doctor unlike Edera, was, you will never guess, Dr Martin! Holy shit that whole meeting was a set up! I later realised the tribunal doctor has to, by legislation be totally independent of the Hospital. No connections at all and he would not visit me three days prior, no, no but on the morning of the tribunal. I was flabbergasted. I could not believe it. I still cannot.

The Dose Increases

After a couple of days Edera knocked at my door. I, still fuming told him to fuck off. I think I shouted that he was a despicable human being. He is. Later I get another knock at the door and was informed by a care assistant Julia, that my dose has increased from 1.5mg twice a day to 5mg twice a day and can I come to the surgery to take them. I went mad. I stormed to the surgery and went ballistic. How can he be able to do this with no recourse of action at all? This is wrong. I was shouting and I realised how angry I was, I went outside the surgery and took a deep breath and counted to ten and went back. I was calm. The two nurses who got it in the neck had looked at the floor mostly but did not look scared and they knew I was just angry and venting and of course, very luckily for him, Edera was safely at home by then, he really is a pathetic little pussy. Some days later, Edera himself came to tell me he was upping the dose to 15mg a day. Predictably I went ballistic. He was a lucky man that I can get so angry and still control myself. Perhaps had I not been aware of the consequences of my actions it would have been different. After suffering a tirade of abuse he walked off. After a minute I followed, he was in the surgery.

"So Doctor, so what is the justification for upping my dose 50%?"

"It's not 50% Michael"

"It fucking is you thick c**t, if it was 10mg a day before and 15mg after that's 50%, Arsehole" Please forgive my French.

"Oh yes, yes you are right yes, I apologise"

"You're a piece of shit doctor, I think you have ulterior motives, Dr Edera" He walked the 10 yards to the office, not saying anything he looked scared. Good. There were 4 staff members in the office and a workman changing a lock on the door. As he got there I continued *"I am going to make it my life's work to get you struck off Doctor, I will be suing you, the NHS and Cleveland Police".* I think we were up to 55minutes in my company at that point, I can't remember. *"55 minutes in your company now doctor and I have been here weeks! A fucking lazy psychologist that's what you are doctor"* Edera now safely in the office and looking relieved, I looked at the startled and kneeling down workman, took a deep breath and walked away.

The Room visit about the tribunal

Friday 27th December 2019 I had a visit from Edera and a junior doctor about my tribunal. I can't remember much about that meeting other than he pissed me off as usual and I descended into my usual arsehole mode. I did remember him mentioning that my family are worried about my Facebook posts. This delighted me! "They are worried are they? They fucking should be" I also remember telling him that the posts stay for public record and it is my right" I cannot remember much else. Sometime later I was queuing for my dinner when I was approached by Edera and the junior doctor.

"Michael, Michael, I have just finished reading your posts and I really think you should consider deleting them."

"I told you Doctor they stay though I will delete the post with Big Al in"

"Michael, you should reconsider, I worry for your home as you said your address in the video"

"There is nothing in it worth nicking Doctor so don't worry about my bungalow"

"Michael, I worry about people putting their hands on you when you leave" I'd be more worried about me putting my hands on you, Doctor.
"For fuck sake Doctor Edera it is not I that you are worried about and let me worry about other people's hands"

"Michael…" Jesus wept…

"Just fuck off Doctor, they stay"

He finally walked away.

The next visit from Edera was before my tribunal and we had a discussion about how it would work. I asked him some questions about his report and then asked him "Are you going to say I need to be in hospital Doctor?"
"Yes"
"I thought so and what is your diagnosis again?"
"That you are suffering mania and bipolar"
"The fuck I am Doctor, I not suffering anything but being me, you have spent no time with me Doctor Edera and forced drugs on me without due cause. What exactly are you basing your diagnosis on?" "Because you are quite forward, confident

and grandiose, you never let me speak or answer questions (for your own safety that is Pal but of course I am guilty of all of the above but well, that is just me) and you said you were an alpha male"

"I am an alpha male Doctor, the times I have been a leader, people followed, I am a leader Dr Edera not a follower and one reason why I requested a female psychologist. Those reasons are just not good enough to base your diagnosis on. I believe you have ulterior motives for wanting to keep me in here" "It's okay to be ill Michael, it's not your fault" Like a red rag to a bull that was.

"Fuck off Doctor Edera you piece of shit, I bet you are angling for a section three, aren't you?"

"I cannot discount it"

"Just fuck off doctor"

As he walked away I had to fight the urge to run and go to town on him. I hated this man with a passion. I shouted after him, he turned. "I really do not like you Dr Edera and say hello to Rasheed for me" as he turned back I noticed a smirk.

"I seen that you piece of shit"

"What"

"The Smirk, you know you are not a good person Dr Edera, Karma is coming for you pal"

Chapter 13 - The Tribunal
Monday 30th December 2019

I had a visit by a legal representative from a firm called Punch Robin. A nice lady had informed me that it had been declared that I did not possess the mental capacity to arrange my own counsel (sort of true) and they had been appointed on my behalf. I was ok with this. She left saying not to worry I can see you are alright. I would be getting a visit from Rachel my solicitor on Monday morning and have to be ready by 9am.

Monday – I was up by 6am and did my daily exercise routine. I then went and got a coffee and the ironing board and iron, sorted my shirt and two piece and hung them up. I watched my TV but not really watching it my mind elsewhere. I kept thinking what it would be like to be stuck here for up to 6 months, how soul destroying the thought was. I fully expected to lose after Joanne's and Dr Edera's reports. I knew I had done enough since my change of tactics on the 17th that there would need to be different reports but knowing Joanne and Edera, I knew they would be angled to paint me as unstable and mentally ill. I went for a bath, dressed and then at 9am I went to the lounge. I was expectedly told there was a Doctor waiting to speak to me. After 15 minutes he showed up. I forget his name but was greeted by the polar opposite of Dr Martin. I will get all the names. He was smart and well spoken, private school educated, definitely. He looked after himself and I liked him instantly. He was witty and funny but you could tell a good person. Real doctors who save people generally are good people. He was interested with what I had to say and was the first person to really take what I was saying seriously. He was asking probing questions and getting to the main points while we discussed things like how I was arrested and brought in, my Parmo's, the business, my family and the reason used for my incarceration. He was never patronising. Predictably the subject turned to drug use and I admitted my use of marijuana. He said was that wise? "I am not mentally ill doctor, if by smoking cannabis you develop psychological problems then I would say that you have something under the surface to begin with and it is brought to the fore by smoking it" "Erm no that's not right" He thought about it for a couple of seconds then said

"Erm actually it is" he paused looked at me and nodded in my direction and then said "Doctor" We both started laughing and then he shook his head and said "Nooo…" He brought the meeting to an end and left. I felt better. It was almost like two equals in the meeting but that cannot be with a Doctor for what have I achieved in comparison? Nothing. He is a healer. I am working on it though. I walked away respecting that Doctor, the first one in 24 days.

Next up was Rachael my solicitor. She was a petite woman, mid 20s, brunet and with, this is going to sound like a contradiction, piercingly pale eyes. Blue that ringed her pupils. Frankly they were fascinating and beautiful. We went through the three reports and marked down what we needed to mention. She worked quickly, we only had 15 minutes. She left and at 10.30am I was escorted to the main building. Doctor Edera was 30 yards walking ahead. If looks could injure and maim! We entered and went into the tribunal room. This consisted of a table with chairs either side. Nothing like a court room. It was more of a conference room. We went in and present were the three judges, the doctor from the meeting, a judge and an experienced care worker. On the opposite side was Edera, Joanne Taylor, myself, Rachael and Lauren Jackson from the Psychosis team. There was another woman present but I have no idea who or even why she was there. She was probably there as a witness. The Judges introduced themselves and explained who they would speak to first and that was Dr Edera. It would be the Doctor from the meeting that would be grilling Edera. I noticed a familiar look on the doctors face and I got the feeling he felt the same as me on meeting Edera.

"Hello Dr Edera, can you explain Michael's diagnosis please" "Yes certainly, Michael is suffering mania and bipolar but we have seen some improvement from Michael of late"

"What were Michael's symptoms?"

"He was showing signs of mania. always interrupting conversation, not letting people answer questions, he could be angry and always walks out of meetings, he claims the staff on the ward were poisoning him" I turned to Rachael, "Medicating, I never once said poisoning" I whispered. "Is Michael violent?" "No, Michael has not attacked anybody, he says he will only attack if provoked, though I do worry about people putting their hands on Michael when he

leaves hospital" That was the third time he said that and I often wondered if they were really thinly veiled threats "Would you say Michael needs to be in hospital?" "Yes that is my opinion" "Has Michael had a history of mental illness?"
"No this is his first time"
"You prescribed Haloperidol?"
"Yes he is on a 15mg dose"
The Doctor recoiled and said with some surprise "15mg!?" he looked at Edera for a few moments and the weasel did not say anything but I guess it wasn't really a question, more a statement.
"It is mentioned in your report that one of the reasons Michael was brought in was because he answered the door with a knife and attended court for this in June?"
"Yes"
"Michael denies this and tells me he has never answered the door with a knife in his hand and in fact attended court for a speeding charge in July. Another reason he was brought in was due to his poisoning claims. Do you accept that Michael did not answer his door with a knife and attend court for it, where did the information come from and did you ever consider the fact Michael may have

actually been getting poisoned?" Go on Doctor, I was smiling and looked at Edera.

"The information that I receive is from the family and social workers involved in the section, I accept that it might be wrong" Only every part.

"Does Michael need to be in hospital Doctor Edera?"

"Yes that is my opinion"

The doctor finished his questions. I have to state that this is from memory and there will have been more dialogue than written here. Dr Edera made his excuses and left the proceedings. He was very hard to hear and nervous sounding the whole time was old Edera. The two Doctors did not seem equal. Not his finest performance or maybe he could tell the doctor did not like him? If I could tell then I am sure he could too. The three judges moved on to Joanne. We had an okay relationship by now, she had dropped the act after realising I had worked out her involvement and was being herself with me and was actually quite pleasant but I just knew she was going to side with Edera.

I cannot remember the conversation as such but I'll write the questions and answers that I do.

"What does Michael do on the ward?"

"Michael is friendly, he engages well with others, he keeps himself to himself, he sleeps a lot" I butted in "Nothing else to do"
"Does Michael get many visitors?"
"Yes quite a lot actually"
"In your opinion is Michael mentally ill?"
"Yes"
"Do you think Michael needs to be in Hospital?"
"No, I think he is ok now and can leave"
Wow I could not believe it. Erm, thank you Joanne, I was not expecting that I can tell you. I think everyone heard my intake of breath. They turned to Lauren Jackson. I had no idea what she was going to say. "Do you think Michael has mental health problems?"
"Yes"
"Do you think Michael should remain in hospital?"
"No I don't think so, he needs the chance to prove he is ok and I think Michael is capable and deserves the chance to try. He has indicated that he would be willing to work with us and we are satisfied for him to be released"

Gob smacked. Thank you, Lauren.

Now it was my turn.

"Hello again Michael, do you feel that you are mentally ill?"
"Not one bit Doctor no"
"If you were released would you pose a threat to your family and neighbours who may have poisoned you?"
"No doctor, I have a natural ppp…sorry I really struggle with this word, I'll start again. I have a natural propensity for forgiveness and have decided to forgive them, I am only ever a threat to anybody who wants to do me harm, in self defence. As for people who want to lay their hands on me, well there is nothing I can do about that. As for my Doctors diagnoses, he has spent a total of 65 minutes in my presence in 24 days so I don't know what he is basing his diagnoses on. I have to say that I have never said the staff, were poisoning me but medicating, I always felt like I was on amphetamines and was very jittery, my heart would thump in my chest. I had a pharmaceutical taste in my mouth and my penis was almost inverted. This only ever happens when drugs have been consumed. I fasted for 24 hours and these symptoms dissipated. The symptoms

seemed to happen after a meal usually" I could tell they were fascinated. I guess they could see my conviction. "What would you do when released?" asked the Judge.

"I would get my dogs back, redecorate my home so I can sell it, get a job and move away from Teesside"…and it's poison.

"Is there anything else you would like to say?"

"Yes, concerning the reasons I was brought in, in the report it states that I was abusive to my family, I have to state they were estranged and I had not seen my sister since October and my niece, apart from very briefly, for over five months. In the report my family stated I train excessively and have lost a lot of weight. There is no such thing as training excessively and we can see I am a good weight. I have never answered the door with a knife, ever. The poisoning happened and should have resulted in a police investigation and not me being in hospital. I tried to get it investigated but I had to go to Cleveland Police and as it actually concerns Cleveland Police, I was predictably given the runaround. The only people who can investigate Cleveland Police are Cleveland Police, you see. I then appeal to the IOPC and then three days later Cleveland police force their way into my home and I end up here after five minutes with two strange doctors."

The Judge asked "What makes you think Cleveland Police are involved?"
I told him the basic outline of the speeding case and that the performance was so brilliantly shite it was awesome, all three judges smiled. I told them about Cleveland police using their CI's against me and a brief outline of what's been happening. The Judge asked "But why are these people doing this Michael?" I looked him in the eye and said "Believe it or not Judge it's because I reinvented the Teesside Parmo good enough to take nationwide and when people with means and business sense tried them they realised I was right and then I pissed off Cleveland Police" They all smiled. The judges asked us to leave them so they could discuss the decision. We went next door and sat at the table, Lauren started to quiz me about the Pc Tim court case but I got three minutes in and Joanne piped up and said "But he could have had a gun Michael" Jesus, does she never learn?
"Shut up Joanne you weren't there and the whole bloody point is that he didn't"

There was a knock at the door, we were called back in.

We sat down.

"Okay Michael we have decided to lift the section"

I cannot describe the sheer relief I felt.
The judge asked about how I know Cleveland Police are so corrupt? "I couldn't tell you anybody who works for them but I have my horror stories with them judge and I know plenty of people with their own too. It's rotten from the top, plenty of good people work for Cleveland Police but they don't have the power, it does not matter how many good ones there are if it's bad at the top"
"Will you get your Parmo business up and running again?" "I'll get there Judge, of that I have no doubt. I have many business ideas and just need one to work"
"What are the other business ideas?"
"I learned the hard way to keep them close to my chest nowadays Judge" They all smiled.
"Will you keep taking the medication Michael?"

"Honestly? Not if I don't have to, no" I didn't. When a section is lifted it is the equivalent of it never happening and your rights going back to as they were before. They are not saying you are not mentally ill but they are saying we don't think you need to be in hospital.

Finally the Doctor asked me this "Michael you know three people, all have said that they think you are mentally ill?"
"Yes Doctor and not one of them know me or know anything about me, please forgive me if I don't hold much stock in their opinions"

All three judges smiled.

We wished each other well and shook hands and left.

When I got outside at the entrance, I gave Rachael a hug told Rachael her eyes really were unique and beautiful and take care, I thanked her, I said goodbye to Lauren Jackson and thanked her too, "See you soon" I said.

As I walked back to the ward, more like floated I turned to Joanne and said "Well lass I wasn't expecting that, thank you"
She said "Ah well there you go and you are welcome" If she had not been a bitch for the first ten days and clearly on the take, we might have been friends Joanne and I. I went back to my room and had a triumphant cry. I was so sure I was going to lose and be stuck here but my ancestors keep looking down on me, I think. I packed up and got my friend Trev to come and pick me up, as I am packing I get a visit from Edera.
"They lifted the section I hear Michael"
"Yes Doctor, good isn't it?"
"Well Michael I do worry about you on the outside"
"Don't you worry about me mate"
"I really think you should continue the medication Michael"
"Not a fucking chance"
"I just don't want to see you back here Michael. How about you come back for a medication meeting?"
"Nope" I never stopped packing and didn't look at him once. If I had reacted I might have ended up staying.

"You have had enough of listening, haven't you Michael?"

"Yes, goodbye Dr Edera"

He left. I went home completely elated but stiff as a board and my anxiety, depression and despair for the last 24 days was over and replaced with anxiety for real world problems, food, my family, money, gangsters, dogs, the police, mortgages, evil Asian business men etc. I much prefer that type of worry. I do worry about it happening again. I wonder what new hell my enemies are cooking up for me as we speak. I am always chasing my tail.

I got the dogs back from the kennels the next day, that was emotional and I figured out what I was going to do. I could not write, I did not feel like writing, not for 10 days after, until the Haloperidol wore off. Did I start to write this straight away once I got the urge? No I wrote a new business plan for Cheeky Devils which included a pitch to Aldi. I then started to think about my time in that horrible place and was suddenly compelled to start writing about it. I am getting quicker but I think you can tell from Fuck You PC Tim to this that it is not inspired writing like the first part of the book. Though my writing skills are getting honed and I am so much quicker than I used to be. Unfortunately there was a heartbreaking side effect to my anxiety. My dogs Brie and Bear started to lose their fur. I could not bare to watch this and seeing them suffer, I had no choice but to get them rescued and they were taken by the lovely people at The British Briard Club. Brie was particularly bad because she is a naturally sensitive dog. £300 vet bill later (Thank you Jenny from the Briard Club) and the vets confirmed it was not pest related and Brie had picked up an infection, basically confirming it was my anxiety. It breaks my heart to think I was making them suffer with my own despair, although I was never outwardly anxious. The more I watched them both suffer the more anxious I became, which in turn made them suffer even more. It was a vicious circle. There is more to dogs than we realise, especially when I see bear staring at the corner of a room. He can definitely see something but not me, it's freaky when a dog does that. They are much happier now and I am happy because of that fact and it helped me with my anxiety. However, people now know they are gone and an attempt was disturbed by myself between 1/3am the other morning. I was up and when I switched the hallway light on, I heard somebody jump over the fence and then the resulting flickers as the culprit ran off with a flash light in their hand. Though I only heard this and saw it through frosted glass but suspicious still. It may have woken and spooked my neighbours because a few days later they got two bright security lights installed.

Chapter 14 - The Family

On Christmas day I decided to send my sister Carla a message. By then I had read the report for the reasons I was brought in or the lies shall we say. By this point I'd had a lot of time to think about everything and had already decided to forgive my sister and eventually Laurencia. There was something else driving me to do this other than them being family. I wanted to see how they reacted to things, the mannerisms, would they try to be my friend or would the lies and manipulations continue? I wanted to go through it all and ask them questions. I wanted to be mistaken about them.

"Hello Carla, I wish you a merry Xmas and wish you all the best.

I have forgiven you for the things you have done to me. I love you and believe you were driven and controlled by Laurencia. I can never forgive her.

You are welcome to come and see me.

I love you and even your daughter though I am devastated at her actions.

Have a good one and speak soon.

Love Mikey xxx"

Her Reply

"Hi Mikey!
You won't believe how happy I am to hear from you.
I'm so pleased you've got in touch.
I'll give you a ring later if that's ok?
Merry Christmas bro. Love you xxx"
I phoned her that night and instantly realised Laurencia was in the background with Paul listening. I said I will ring her when she is alone. I

rang the next day and we'd had a good 30min chat. It was natural and nice. We got on to the reasons I was here but only touched on them and the only thing she said to piss me off was "I hope you are getting the help you need" and "Grandma hopes you are getting the help you need" What she said made me angry for at least a week. Cheeky cow, your lies got me in here and you are clearly telling Big G that I am mentally ill. I have not seen Carla since October.

Two days later Carla visited me.

I get a knock on my cell door, it's Carla, I am not going to lie it was genuinely good to see her. We hugged and exchanged pleasantries and we had a nice conversation for the first 5 minutes. Carla then steered the conversation on to Laurencia.

She told me Laurencia had come around that day because I was so worried about you. "You know what she is like, 'I'll go and see him, he will talk to me'... She was not poisoning you" I said "Well it could not have been a worse time for her to come around sis, an hour after somebody had been in my home!"

"She wouldn't do that Michael and nobody was poisoning you Michael" I went mad and slammed my arms on the bed. *"Do not try and convince me it did not happen, Carla. It did, you weren't there and your brother nearly died I was that ill, never mind that I nearly crashed my lorry! It should have resulted in a police investigation Carla. Don't ever try to convince me it didn't happen, ever again"*

"Okay I am sorry"

"Now where did this knife claim come from and the weight loss and excessive training, the reasons used to put me here and when was I abusive to you or Laurencia? These reasons and the poisoning are why I am in here Carla" She wasn't expecting that question. "We were worried about you, Michael, I got messages from your friend Aimee and Katie. Aimee said you have been carrying knives on you. She was in tears! (I had not and why didn't it say that in the report?) Chris also messaged me. (I know it was the other way round) Katie messaged me really worried about you too, saying you won't talk to her and that her mum had witnessed you put your car in the garage

and she thought you were going to top yourself. (Three weeks prior and when I made a run for it to Ambers) We were just really worried Michael"
"If she was that worried why didn't she come over?
"What about the excessive weight training and weight loss?" "Well you have lost weight" I took my top off and showed her my well toned and healthy looking body. "Well your stomach is as flat as I have seen it in a long time" I shnortled.
"Carla, do you think I am ill and need to be in here? "Erm I think you need help Michael and it could be good for you"
"So you think I am where I need to be?"
"If they can help you yes"
"Carla, there is nothing wrong with me, I am the same person I always was and I do not deserve to be here"
"Where I have been working there was a GP and I asked his advice, he said you might be a danger to yourself and others and to contact your GP but we didn't know who your GP was, so I contacted the Crises team instead" It would have been sorted straight away if I had spoke to DR Barlow.
"So I was admitted under false facts and given a diagnoses from a GP I have never fucking met

Carla?" I left it after that because I was getting angry and by now I had leave and we went for a drink in the local pub and had a nice hour. I pondered this conversation a lot after and how everything was deflected to other people. They knew they had no right to do what they did. Their lies are in black and white and on official papers now. Instrumental in setting in setting me up to be murdered in a mental hospital. Carla, Laurencia and Aimee set me up! People who are supposed to love me! We have met up on three occasions and not one thing has ever been mentioned about the last 6 months. If I talk about it, I don't get any questions or answers. I have never lost that gut feeling that I am still right about Carla and her involvement. Though, she continued to encourage me to sort it out with Laurencia. Funnily enough I bumped into Laurencia in my local park the day after my release on my way to the job centre. She had seen me first and looked scared. I had approached her and apologised for my behaviour, I have to state that I am still convinced she was involved and still is, I would say. I wanted to see her and study her. We hugged and got emotional. I had an appointment and had to leave. A few days later I was going around my sisters and Carla said

Laurencia is coming round and she would pick me up. Nice one I said. I rang her and she picked me up an hour later. She was her old self the entire time. We went to McDonald's and mentioned how much better I was looking. I looked at her and said "I was not mentally ill Laurencia, I did not deserve to be in there" She did not say anything. We then went to Carla's. She stayed an hour and nothing was mentioned about anything. Now if she was innocent and with what I had publicly stated about Laurencia on Facebook, I would have expected fireworks, shouting, tears, a fucking discussion. Then interest in what has been happening. 2018 Laurencia would have been setting up an investigation and planning our victory against these enemies who wanted to hurt her beloved uncle. Not even a question of what it was like being locked up. Nada, it was if you had gone back in time to around June and nothing had ever happened. It was nice actually. My gut tells me I am right still. Carla continues her probes into my life from afar. Getting people to message me secretly on her behalf and is fake as fuck on the phone. I am very careful about the information I illicit to her but when I mention anything about this subject I am just met with silence or trying to convince me things didn't happen. My family are incapable of being honest with me and it just confirms their guilt in my eyes. With the constant lies and manipulations and now I've connected it all with Bethan and Stephen Frost, I know I was right about Carla and Laurencia and are definitely right in the middle of all this. I got a visit from an old friend Daniel. He showed up unannounced and it was good to see the rogue. We traded pleasantries then the subject got around to recent mad shit happening in Teesside and then my incarceration. I told him a bit about it and the forced medication when he piped up with this belter "Maybe you needed those pills Mikey" Oh dear. *"Don't even try it Dan! Don't try and convince me I needed to be on drugs, just don't fucking do it Dan, how would you even know? It's been what, more than six months since I have seen you? Be careful Daniel!"*

"I wasn't mate sorry" He went on to say "You're wrong about Carla and Lauren you know Mikey, they would never do anything against you"

"Thing is Dan there are just too many unanswered questions, I have decided to give them the benefit of the doubt and want to believe it but my gut tells me different. You know what I have done Dan?

I've forgave them but it will never be the same again" I then told him about the "evidence" used to section me and then we said our goodbyes and he left. A week later Carla let it be known that Daniel had told her that I'd told him I still thought Laurencia had poisoned me. I think she was involved but I never mentioned anything about poisoning to Daniel when he visited me that night. I'm of the opinion that he came to see me at Carla's request.

I messaged Jan while I was in there and before she went to Australia to see if I could ring her. I had to wait three hours and she gives me a time. I messaged back that I just want a normal conversation and let's do just that. I rang her.

It was really nice to speak to her, for the first five minutes but Jan kept steering the conversation to the poisoning "Come on Jan, I just wanted a normal conversation remember, can we just leave it please?" Jan persisted and of course I eventually started to explain the poisoning in full. Towards the end she got very, erm, Jan and started to shout at me, well I say shout but when Jan gets emotional she has, what can only be described as a "High pitched screech" A quite a bit higher than Carla and to the point she is almost unintelligible.

I did catch "But you have not explained any of my questions" "Sorry Jan but I have answered every single question to the full" I had, too. Jan called what I had written "Mumbled Garbage" at that point I hung up. I was so disappointed in Jan. Jan never reacted like this in November when she read it and was so out of character. She never mentioned if Martin did or didn't pay for her holiday. She would have told me straight away if I was wrong, it's a confirmation for me. I can't help but feel that tragically my family have got a good egg like Jan right in the middle of all this skulduggery. The question I would love to know is, have my family read the first half of this document and all the others too? I hope so but they are keeping it close to their chest if so. I cannot see how they have not. I hope it makes them ashamed. My sister keeps encouraging me to get in touch with Katie. I eventually noticed her at her Mums and I decided to message her. She rang me back and we had a good chat, I explained why I had suspected her, the messages and the absence and popping up with the card just at the time people had unmistakably tried to gain access to my home. She did not give me any reason other than to state it definitely was not her who was poisoning me. At least she is not trying to convince me it didn't happen. I explained what happened while I was in hospital and the fact people were trying to get to me in there. The thing is, it's the same with Carla and Laurencia, there are just too many unanswered questions. I will say if it genuinely was not Katie or Laurencia then it has to be her brother Darren. His car has always been at his mothers and fathers the time I know people have been in. I have to fight the urge to confront him, I know better than to do something stupid like that, but still. There is someone else who has always been at home when people have been in my bungalow, I was really trying to give this person the benefit of the doubt but I can no longer discount him unfortunately, though that will be explained in the yet to be written, part 4. Oh yes this book only covers up to the end of February 2020 and the war I don't want to be in and do not deserve, sadly continues with vigour...

My Friends

Craigy, my old friend rang me the Saturday previous from me getting sectioned, the first time in a couple of months and we ended up arguing because I would not go to the pub across the road, Craigy was unusual in his tone and manner and I ended up telling him to fuck off and put the phone down. I messaged him to apologise.

"I hope nobody was listening in, on that call. Sorry for telling you to fuck off but I don't really care if you believe me or not. It's the truth."

"M8 it was me and u listening nobody else, u are being crazy not being funny, who would want to kill you. I would like to be there for you but I fear the road you are going down will only lead to one thing x"

Was that a warning? I felt it was Lee Russell talking.

I replied "Have you read it? It's not a road I have chosen to go down Craigy. Honestly you need to stay out of it. You haven't lived this the last 5 weeks, how would you know? Ffs, you've been in Southampton for months, how would you know really? I'm the only one being honest mate and that's the truth of it. Read it!"

My friend Aimee it turns out was instrumental in getting me sectioned. Carla told me it was Aimee that rang her in tears and told her all the bullshit reasons they used, though that does not explain when exactly I was being abusive to Carla or Laurencia. The thing is Aimee and two of my other friends Trev and Louise came to see me a week before I was sectioned, unannounced and out of character. Looking back it was a fishing expedition. I had not seen them for months and it was very out of character. I told them what had been happening. I reminded Aimee that I had sent her my witness statement and asked if she had read it. She hadn't, although she can read, Aimee doesn't have the concentration levels it requires. It was nice to see them and I was in regular contact with Aimee from that night. I said Louise can read it too and Aimee had asked Louise to read her the witness statement. I phoned her when people had been in my home and the day previously I had departed to Aimee that I believe there is evidence under my sink and they need access. I also spoke to her the day Laurencia came round and she was fine, she never mentioned any worries about my mental health. I didn't know this until Carla told me. She said Aimee had been in tears on the phone to her and told her all the bullshit but then ceased all contact with Carla after I was sectioned. Why would my friend go to someone who she knows has been working against me for months and I am estranged from, then instigate myself being sectioned? Just doesn't add up until you realise it was all a set up and every player has good reason to want me there. The Bethan and Stephen Frost connect ties it altogether and was a major mistake. It implicates my family, my friends, Frost and the McCartens, plus the guy I don't know and his companion (Tony Carter), all with Cleveland Police, the Crises Team, the Staff at the Bilsdale Ward, Doctor Edera and Rasheed. Clearly they could not foresee I had seen Bethan before on Facebook. It is the break I've needed. It is the link that proves my innocence and my story. I got many visits from Aimee, while in hospital she even spent around £50 in sports direct on me, guilty conscience maybe? Louise, Trev and Chris came regularly with Trev saving my life with a TV. I went from barley seeing them for months before my sectioning, then became the most popular friend and saw them more in hospital than I did for the last year. (Trev fixed my boiler when

I got home and the only thing in reality that Trev, Louise and Chris have done is gather Intel for Clevelands finest, the McCartens, Frostie, my sister and Laurencia. I know that those three friends know more than they tell me, which means they are hiding information from me so how can I trust them?) Since, I have been released I have not seen hide nor hare of any of them for the first two weeks of being out. Then out of nowhere they all contact me over a couple of days and I realised from then on, I always get contacted by them in waves, like somebody is directing them. All fake on the phone and all asking probing questions. Nothing for a week or two then they all message around the same time. I know Lee is best friends with Frostie and saw recognition in Bethan especially and a little in Louise when they bumped into each other when Louise and Aimee were leaving after a visit one day. My gut says Chris, Trev, Louise, Craigy and obviously Aimee know a hell of lot more than they let on, even Annona. Maybe they thought they were helping to shut me up without people having to kill me, to save me maybe but not realising they had just set me up to be persecuted, drugged and potentially murdered by the staff and patients in the Bilsdale Ward. My god if I had lost that tribunal I would have really been in the shit. You just did not know who would be getting admitted next and still being under the care of Evil Dr Edera. I think I would have eventually ended up doing time for Doctor Edera if I had to remain. I was not in a good position and I am devastated at the realisation that my family and friends where complicit in me being set up and believe this has been what my family and some of my friends have been setting the stall out for and working towards for some time.

Chapter 15
My Thoughts, Fears, Dreams and the Mental Health Act

The manner in how I was arrested and the evidence used against me for the section does indeed mean my arrest and detention were illegal, the fact I had genuine accusations against my estranged family who got me sectioned means the person in charge of the Crises team had a duty of care to step back and think "Hang on a minute there might be more to this than meets the eye" Especially after reading my Witness Statement. A detailed discussion with me about it at the least would then be expected and the accusations would have been explained and proved to be false thus avoiding my section. In the end all I had was a 5 minute phone call and 5 minutes with the two doctors who sectioned me. I hate to say this but the staff at the NHS, from the Crises team right through to the Bilsdale ward staff, allowed the Mental Health act to be abused and used against an innocent man. This also makes the forced medicating illegal too. Imagine the Police forcing their way into your home without a warrant and then seven strange people surrounding you, what a horrible experience it was being judged by all these strange people in your home. Five minutes with the doctors who sectioned me, Five! I protested about the poisoning claims repeatedly and told them over and over it's a genuine complaint. I told them about my family, all to deaf ears. Complete strangers can come into your life and rip you out of it on the whim of family, who I might ad I had serious allegations against? All the while, using false evidence to section me? If they had departed to me the other actual reasons used at the time instead of just "Your family are worried" and then asking me about the poisoning, I would have been able to debunk the claims and avoided this section but they knew that didn't they. I believe in reality that it was decided some days prior that I was going to be sectioned no matter what I did. I feel Carla, Laurencia and Lee Russell have been laying the ground work for this play since August. My sectioning was a tactic by everyone involved to shut me up and make everyone think I am crazy, while at the same time attempting to actually make me crazy and potentially murdered. For if Carla said I am mentally ill to my face then a betting man says they will be telling everyone else the same too still. Well they all have been since August. I wonder if they tell people that I won my Tribunal?

I know Dr Edera knows Rash. My family and friends used what they could against me to help get me locked up in a desperate attempt to end this in their favour. It has backfired. I told the staff repeatedly that the mistake everyone has made is fucking with a writer. If I did not have the ability to write it all down I could never in a billion years be able to explain all of this and do it justice. Whenever I have tried with spoken words I sound like a nutter, even to myself and because of the subject, I do get jittery and seem manic when I talk about it but change the conversation to anything else, then I am fine, I guess its all been that traumatic that whenever I mention the subject I get very anxious.

I have truly learned that the power of written words is astonishing.

The staff in the Bilsdale ward should be ashamed of themselves for everything they helped perpetrate against me those first 10 days. It was simply persecution and psychological torture. The secret medicating, the constant lies, you would be constantly fobbed off, the staff messing around with my door and my blinds. Can you imagine your light being switched on every single hour of every single night for 24 nights? That the foot steps were continuous to my door, when the staff should have been checking everyone and stopping every 3 metres? If they notice a particular action was getting to me, the staff stepped it up ten fold. They patronised you constantly. I would estimate that out of a 12 hour shift they sat in the office up to ten hours. Just picking pay checks up most of them while others, like John the Smiling Assassin and Peter the Cyborg really enjoyed their work but not in a good way. Truly the nutters are running the asylum on that ward. The staff looked at you like you were a piece of shit if you knocked on the office door. It is my opinion that, in general, I found the staff to be suffering mental health problems themselves. A very different breed are the people who work in the mental health sector of the NHS compared to the Hero's that work in the main hospitals who possess, compassion, humanity and are driven by a will to help and save people, all these noble and valiant traits are simply missing in the mental health sector, they really are the poor relations of the proper health professionals in the big hospitals. The big hospitals are pure cocaine and the mental health hospitals are stepped on whizz. There were a few good eggs. I think the staff, were definitely not expecting the man they got and with the fighting spirit I displayed. They more than met their match and they simply, even collectively, were not clever enough to get much past me. They had plenty of victories mind. My mistake was leaving my notes unattended when I went to the tribunal. I didn't even look when I got back. I get home and all gone out of my folder. Schoolboy error, Michael. I think they definitely bit off more than they could chew and were glad when I left. They can get into a long line of people who have underestimated me. My problem was because you are in a mental health institution no one takes you seriously, as soon as they hear section two and mental health they become deaf. You have absolutely no rights. If I had my rights and been able to get my bloods checked independently then I would have been out much sooner and the staff members involved arrested and would be unable to do this against another innocent person. It was funny watching people who didn't work on the wards come in, workmen, other patient's families; they treated you like you had the plague. They didn't even want to look at you. Some looked scared to be there, I am guilty of playing on that a bit to pass the time. It was funny. I did get confused as a staff member a few times. It did not take long for outsiders to start to wonder because he doesn't seem very ill? When you join a ward on a section your doctor is simply your God. It seems you are beholden to that Doctor. He can make you take the medication and fuck with your head. He failed with me...Really Michael, its taken you two months to get over it, he did a blinding job, you fool...Dr Edera is a weak man that has been given a sinew of power. Weakness and power don't mix and is always a bad combination. I am sure he can be good with people but only if you bend to his will. He relies on drugs too much. His problem was I had him sussed out and mentally beaten the first time I met him. However, given enough time and drugs and that might just have changed. I asked on many occasions to change psychiatrist and to see the psychologist but they could not let me do that, could they? The new Doctor and Psychiatrist would not have been involved and it wouldn't do for her to see I am not mentally ill now would it? Actually break all this down and god forbid they actually believe me. I requested a mental health advocate on the 17th but never heard anything. On many occasions I would be having good conversations with patients and then it was medication time, within 20 minutes they were either jabbering gibberish or asleep. Some patients looked forward to the drugs, fair enough and good luck to them but I did not want to be one. That was the biggest and scariest thought was becoming an institutionalised Zombie. I believe Edera, already set the stall out for that with his forced medicating. If it was not for winning the tribunal I would undoubtedly still have been in hospital under the care of that dastardly man.

There is absolutely nothing to do on the wards. No mental stimulation at all. A couple of board games, some books and DVD's but no DVD player. I mentioned a few times that either somebody is skimming off of the top or the Conservatives had definitely been raping the NHS the last 10 years. There was one TV in the lounge that you cannot hear, No TV in your room unless you sort one yourself. Your room was pleasant with its own shower room but no door. The bedding was plastic and made you sweat all night, apparently the bedding has to be fire retardant, whom ever wrote that regulation never slept in plastic bedding before the fucking Norman. No activities at all. I called the gulag yard, the gulag yard because it's just bare and life devoid concrete. You spend most of the day with your thoughts. You could get escorted to the recreational centre. Brilliant place, a pool table that should have been re-clothed around 15 years ago, a music room that consisted of a non working electric keyboard, non working electric drum kit and three bongo's. There was a clay modelling room. There were two PC's with word but no access to the internet and you are not allowed USB's! The only good thing was the table-tennis table. Frankly it was depressing and consequently I only went once. Boredom and over thinking were your enemies and were a constant battle. You could easily start to crack up just by being there. My tactic was focus on the little things, my daily exercise routine, coffees; laundry was a good one, meals, baths and blessed sleep. I ended up doing a lot of that after it calmed down on the 17th after the forced medicating. Everything, apart from Barraket, being fobbed off, patronised, lied to and fucking around with my lights and door truly stopped that day. I do not care if anybody says "It was the drugs" No, just like antidepressants and vitamins you don't get any "benefits" for some time as the substance needs to build up. It was a conscious decision to start being introvert and polite, I had an eye on my upcoming tribunal. It was also helped by the skulduggery with the staff and patients stopping. I did not feel any change until he upped the dose to 15mg a day. That's when I became stiff and overly measured in my actions. The best analogy I can come up with is... "Imagine your mind being detached from your body, you are still you but in a slow and painfully measured and suffocating cage"

If you are genuinely ill then I am sure there are massive benefits to people who do suffer psychosis, schizophrenia, mania, bi-polar etc...but to somebody who does not suffer any of these illnesses then you just get the side effects and it can end up changing you to the point that now you are mentally ill because you are not you any more due to the drugs. Ironic isn't it? Go in ok come out mentally ill and is what happens to many sane people who for whatever reason find themselves wrongly locked up in a mental health institution on a section unless you have strong mental strength. Case in point is good old Baraket. To see him deteriorate and be so conflicted about what they were pressuring him to do, I felt really bad for him in the end. Ironic isn't it?

From as early as Monday 2nd December it was planned that I would be getting sectioned, concerning my family, much further back than that even. This was a set up plain and simple, involving quite an array of actors. The best thing I did was not go to my original tribunal because it is likely I would still be in hospital or dead. The food was absolute tosh, The best meal was breakfast and Weetabix on a morning. The other meals were the most un-nutritional food. The food was oven ready meals that the servers cook in a convection oven. Not one meal you would purchase for yourself. My stool was like Mr whippy. I had not eaten 3 meals a day since I last trained properly. I lost weight while I was in there. Nothing really had any protein in. Utter shite. When I left and had my first decent meal my muscles instantly grew. What a feeling it was, I looked massive and all because I'd had a couple of great quality, home made burgers, it was like all the results from daily exercises over 24 days were released with some proper food in me. I got asked by Lauren Jackson on her last visit if "I plan to sue the NHS" I believe I have a water tight case if I did. They really fucked up with Bethan and when you think the manner, grounds, secret medicating and the forced medicating, the fact it was a set up, that I can now PROVE and link everybody together, means it was illegal and breached human rights laws so yes I want my day in court, after all Cleveland Police's resources and the Mental Health Act were abused and used against me. I need to be out of this situation first. I hope to get a book deal, I need a proper job but that will not happen in Teesside. I need to relocate and breathe easy for the first time in months. My life has been on hold for over a year, just remaining static not going forward. It needs to change but I cannot do this alone. I am hoping the writing is good enough that I hopefully get an advance and pay off my debts and relocate from Teesside. The only thing keeping me safe I believe, is the fact I sent copies of all my files to The Sun and the Evening Gazette, Teesside's local rag and I asked them to keep a check on me. If I disappear, get killed by a patient, stabbed on the street then it becomes a big story to them with national interest and at that point I believed that was where it was heading and still is. Both publications know of Michael Elwood, because of my posts on their respective sites and a really good Brexit article I sent to The Sun back in August. I then told Dr Edera and mentioned it in my room a number of times to my friends. The staff knew. There are a lot of nervous people out there and yes I am concerned for my safety and definitely need to relocate from Teesside ASAP but still I am determined to tell this story, even if it means my life is the cost of people finally believing me. I accept the risks and deem the endeavour to be worth it. They have left me with no choice. Fuck em.

A few days before I was sectioned a post popped up on Teesside live, the Facebook website of the Evening Gazette on my news feed proclaiming Ross Kemp, AKA Grant Mitchell was coming to Teesside in support of the Labour Party and its candidates, instantly I knew this to be the post to settle a promise I made to my Stockton South Labour MP, Dr Paul Williams. In that public Facebook promise, I wrote that I would make sure he did not get re-elected. Dr Williams, you see, he is a Remainer and voted with remain tendencies in Parliament and Stockton South voted overwhelmingly to leave. My comment explained this and told Mr Kemp not to bother. I don't think he did in the end. The comment got nearly 200 likes and was by far the top comment. Not the first time this has happened, what was a first was being set upon by labour supporters. Over 100 comments including my replies, everyone was in support of Dr Williams and Labour, some were abusive. I replied to everyone in a respectful manner and with sound reason and argument using facts and figures and owned every single opponent. I explained how socialism does not work in a capitalist world, how Corbyn would be a disaster for the UK economy and the NHS and asked repeatedly to give me examples of Dr Paul Williams good work as an MP, I did not receive any. I even shamed a couple of the abusive ones into apologising to me, I was persuasive. The thing is when I thought about it I might just have achieved probably more votes for conservative candidate Matt Vickers in Stockton south than all his door knockers put together. The post got 600+ likes. My comment got 200 likes, The post was shared 100's of times. Some of my replies to comments got over 20 likes. It is safe to say a good few thousand will have read my comment and to a lesser extent, the replies. You can times likes many multiple times over with actual views and I wonder how many undecided voters I may have persuaded with my sound reason and argument in such a marginal seat as Stockton South? Not to mention reminding voters of his voting tendencies concerning Brexit. I told a doctor about this the first night I was in hospital. She was a young Asian woman, you have to be examined when you first get there and she was nice and I explained about it. She and the nurses went in to the office and looked it up. I remember the looks of amazement at me when they were reading it all. It made me smile. I'd love Facebook to look into the analytics of it. I knew the post would get many views in Teesside as everybody on Facebook has it here and with Ross Kemps name it was the perfect post to enact my evil plan. With my gentlemanly and Good Sir style of debate I have developed, it worked a treat. People who usually get the top comment, never actually reply to anybody and just tend to sit back and marvel at everybody else arguing whilst basking in gleeful relevance as your clever comment starts world war three underneath in the comments. That is not I. No, I answer every single one with respect and sound reason and argument. Stockton South was taken by the conservatives by just over 5000 votes and I like to think I did my bit for the Brexit cause because if you voted Brexit then there was only one vote, though I was unable to vote myself due to being in hospital. From the moment of the doctors and nurses reading the post that night, word spread and every staff member at Roseberry Park knew who Michael Elwood was. A couple of staff members I had never met before started to tear into the Tories on meeting me straight away! I was amused and all I said was Boris will sort it out don't worry and shnortled. I had become the NHS's hated Tory poster boy! I wondered if they knew Dr Paul Williams? I am betting so. I wonder if he had anything to do with this? A lot of connections has Dr Williams. Teesside live have deleted the post sadly and I will be asking them officially why, when I send them and the Sun this draft. Right now I am hemmed in but hoping this book will give me the means to escape this hell. Every second, of every minute, of every hour, of every day I am in Teesside I am in danger.

I was messaging my friend Annona the other day

Me healthy happy and eating, training and 2 months before the poisoning started.

and she was asking me to go to a local pub for her birthday, I would have loved to go but told her I could not because I wouldn't feel safe because I know some of my enemies drink in there. I then thought about the enemies that I have accumulated and I remembered a thought I had whilst in hospital. I had not done a single thing to make any one of them my enemies, no they made me theirs. Now I can prove the Bethan and Frostie connect and potentially identify the corrupt element within Cleveland Police and if they have used 4 C.I's against me, which a judge would be able to find out straight away if they are, all whist setting up an illegal detention to a mental health hospital, at which I was secretly medicated, forced mind bending medication, intimidated, psychologically tortured and set up from the beginning, it does not make good reading, does it? Bethan, Joanne, John the Smiling Assassin, Peter the Cyborg and the Evil Dr Edera have a lot to answer for here. Not to mention the unanswered questions surrounding the poisoning and the fact I had gifted the detectives a guide on where to start.

Pics below in the middle of being poisoned

Hi Facebook it's
Mikey Elwood
Please let me in
the withdrawal symptoms
are painful help n Beat
out please.
Mikeyelwood@xmail.com

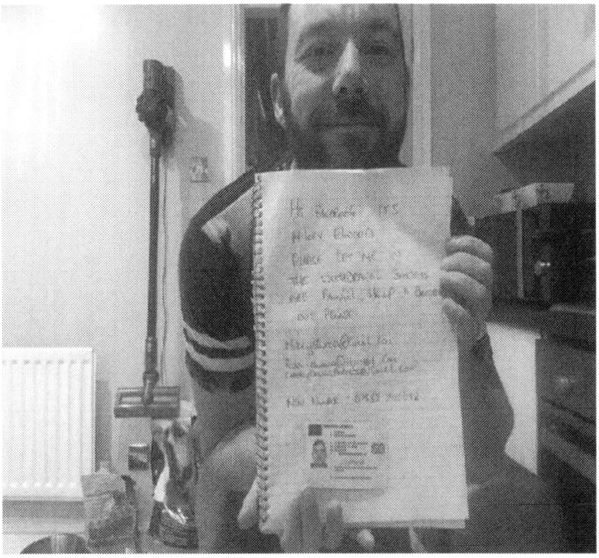

...the investigation and all the evidence that would have been found at that time of me putting the complaint in to the Standards and ethics department.

The final Irony? I have been waiting for bailiffs to force their way into my home to repossess my possessions, not that there is anything worth taking but why? Well I forgot to set up a repayment plan for my court fine for the PC Tim fine! Shit! Two weeks I've been expecting him, two weeks! It's my own fault really but what next? I never lodged that appeal because all this shit started. I wish I had done.

What I really want to happen is I get to interview the patients and staff, everybody involved even in court and on the stand. There are so many people that know more than they let on. A proper Police investigation would back up everything that has happened, indeed if the standards and ethics department had done their job then, I might be living a different life now and free from PTSD, severe anxiety, messed up sleeping patterns and constantly looking over my shoulder every time I leave my home. I have to state I have always suffered depression and have been suicidal on more than one occasion so yes I have been mentally ill but not in the respect Dr Edera and Joanne Taylor were trying to portray me as. Am I mentally ill now? I have mulled that question over significantly lately and all I can say is, I am suffering PTSD, severe anxiety, messed up sleeping patterns and constantly looking over my shoulder and all are classed as suffering mental illness then, well, yes I guess I am? You cannot go through what I have this past year or so and it not touch you mentally in some way. All I know is a change of scenery as many nautical miles away from Teesside as possible and finding love will be my cure. As soon as I know that I am sorted, I can reach out to my girl and finally ask her out. She is still single, she's waiting for me to sort my shit out, maybe. Though she will have heard a lot about me by now and honestly I am not in the least bit hopeful. If not that's okay too. She has saved my life on more occasions than I care to remember now. She got me through some dark times in that place, I can tell you. It's still a story of love and my road to her. Too find out. Now though I am sick of her being a memory, a thought, a picture in my mind, a photo, a fantasy, none of it is good enough any more, I am getting impatient and just want to get on with my life and love her, hopefully. Reach that potential. Be allowed to be fucking me. Be a success. All I know is the constant throughout this sorry tale of woe is my integrity and truthfulness and ultimately I am the only one in this whole fucked up episode who is being honest. For the world is not kind to people who tell the truth and do the right thing..

~~The End~~
This story isn't finished by a long shot, part 4 coming soon.

PRIXTURIOUS

Part 4

Chapter one

Well, well, well, what can I say the chapters above are not the end of this story, not by any means and I can assure you the story does not get any better, I am afraid not no. No happy ending for this boy yet, though fighting spirit and a will to live is still undoubted. What I am about to walk you through is the time period of 1st March 2020 through to the present day, currently at the time of writing is the 8th July 2020 and is as shocking to me as it should be to you once you have read it. Let down is not the term I would use to sufficiently describe what has gone down over that time period. It was a rather calm period between my release on the 30th December 2019 and March.

The 3rd of March I was on a course for my SIA security badge and was also marks the day I fell out with my sister, Carla and we spoke for the last time. After being released from the hospital and writing part three, I was just hoping for some calm and a chance to do something positive after all the trauma I went through before and during the hospital stay, I was understandably quite wary though and I was very apprehensive about this course. An argument with my sister over messenger that morning probably didn't help, she told me I was ill and should seek help. By this point she was getting very pushy with trying to convince me I was ill and nothing of what went on before happened, she was silent if I ever mentioned anything to do with hospital or poisoning, not one question or any concern, I laughed because I had been studying her closely for a coupe of months now. There was an incident were I went to hug her and she flinched and went all stiff, she was still acting the whole time, I had begun to get sick of her continued manipulations and falseness and I was ok actually so decided that this was it for us, I called her poison, wished her the best and bid her farewell, though my distrust of Carla showed because I had lied to Carla about my course date because I did not trust her and did not want my location for the next 5 weeks to be known. It hadn't escaped my notice that a man with a routine is an easy man to set up. Catching the same bus every day and taking the same route to home and after my recent struggles I was nervous about this. I remember walking into the class room at the learning centre in Billingham and noticing the people who I was doing the course with and could see that they were jack the lads mostly and I recognised the course instructor, he looked so familiar and it turns out I knew his bodybuilding brother and he told me that he knew everybody who there is to know in Teesside as he had been on the doors since he was 15. Shit. My guts turned a little after gaining that knowledge. Thing is his demeanour towards me changed by dinner time, he kept disappearing for long lengths of time and his looks and body language, there was a clear difference from his friendly self at the start and I realised he knew exactly who I was because the jack the lads demeanour changed with his also. Shit, shit, how does he know? His wasn't the only demeanour change that had happened to me recently, I'd given my work coach at the job centre my book, hoping that he would maybe help me in some way as he seemed nice to begin with but his demeanour changed also after he read it. I have to admit that I am getting very skilled at reading people and their subtle changes by now and had an unease feeling especially with the instructor. My heart sank on the way home as the boys I was friendly with never said a word to me on the bus and I realised that normal activities would be like this all the time in Teesside, I am never going to be able to trust in this town again and will always be looking over my shoulder. I decided not to go back to the course but no matter as Co-vid 19 reared its ugly head and the course was cancelled anyway. When I went to my next meeting with the work coach his attitude and demeanour change means I cannot count him out of being the person who informed the instructor or maybe the instructor found out another way, I don't know. It was gutting to realise my life had become this way. This also remains the last time I talked to my sister.

At around this time I had an email from the Care and Quality Commission that I had started a complaint with when I was in hospital and I had a good think, well if Cleveland Police wont help me then I will follow through with this complaint and see if I can't stop this happening to another innocent citizen at Roseberry Park Hospital. So I did and had to give consent to the CQC to hand over all the paperwork to the complaints department of the NHS trust that covers Roseberry

Park, The Tees, Esk and Wear Valleys NHS Foundation Trust. This is when everything started to kick off again, this and falling out with Carla is the pin point after the calm of when the switch was flicked and it re-starts the campaign against me, that and the fact Carla had lost control of me.

This is when we meet my neighbours, who we will call Fred (Dominic Turnbull) and Rose for the purpose of this document and just because I can, though not really as bad as the real Fred and Rose they are a very different kind of evil or should I say the male of the two is at the very least. I have withheld her name because of Roses dad who is an old friend and I would love to know what he makes of all this? Now Fred my neighbour has been under suspicion with me for sometime now, you see I gave him a very first draft of my book or part two, when I was writing and living that part of the book back in October as I needed to get the document among many others, from my USB to my emails and at the time I had no other way of doing it but using somebody else's computer and internet. The problem was I realised by now that every time somebody had been in the bungalow as well as Darren Wilkinson across the road, Fred was also always in and his car was present and at this recent realisation everything sort of fell into place and I realised Fred was involved. Now I had decided to keep that knowledge and give him the benefit of the doubt because Rose at that time, I was sure she was a good egg and was my friend up to that point and I think highly of her dad who was at least, my friend, I don't know now. It had niggled at me about how people were getting in and not use the drive, that people would surely notice comings and goings from my home, People in the flats Fred and Rose, neighbours across the road etc, but the only way in was through the bushes at the back of the shed and Fred's, you could squeeze through but it would be in full view of Fred and the four flats that face the bush so I didn't think it likely that was how they did it but it was how they did it as it turns out. I've extended the fence and blocked it up now, made it so you have to jump over the shed roof which makes it too risky. The Flatts all looked empty I'd noticed, no coming and goings, blinds always shut on all 4, never any lights on, just empty but for how long? Why? Who owns them now? The last time I remember people there was back in summer. Seems strange to have four conveniently empty flats and people just so happen to be using those same bushes that face all 4 flats to enter my back garden. Startling coincidence wouldn't you say? Wouldn't surprise me if my uncle Martin has purchased them waiting for the bungalow to come on the market after repossession because who has 4 x £145k+, £600/650pcm flats sat there empty? I think maybe he sees a massive opportunity to purchase the various houses and build either his dream home or a few luxury homes and make a fortune. It is a brilliant location for it and I am literally the only thing stopping it from happening. Ill give 2 to 1 that as soon as my home is repossessed that planning permission goes in to demolish the bungalow, next doors and the flats...just a little theory and I may well be wrong on that, another thing a proper investigation would uncover...

Out of nowhere and quite startlingly there was suddenly a big loud banging sound down the side of the bungalow and on Fred's side of the property something bounced off of the bathroom window it sounded like, quick as a flash I was up and opened the front door and had a look, nothing except the security light was on from next door that good ol'Fred had installed after someone had recently tried to break into my home and I spooked them after I disturbed them one night. They are ridiculously bright and light up the bungalow quite intrusively. I was fuming when I realised it was him. I have never quite gelled with ol'Fred, he is not a good person is Fred, the type that feeds from others misery and not caring if he is causing the misery while maintaining an on the surface, respectable, nice guy persona but really is a petty, selfish and arrogant sad man because on the surface he's got it all and should be content and very happy in life but my experience is this is not a man capable of enjoying the good things and he once told me he has had previous with past neighbours and I just felt it the second I met him that I sensed he actually suffered an inferiority complex regarding me, I am not to bad at doing things like brakes and discs on cars or bikes, building fences things like that and he's not to clever with his hands really and I realise now that he has always disliked me because of it. I really only bothered because of Rose and thought "Well if she is good and she loves him he can't be all bad so I always at least tried with him but I would catch him being a dick sometimes like setting the dogs off on purpose making cat noises things like that. I caught him bang to rights one night, Brie and Bear were fast asleep in my bedroom and I could hear him making cat noises and giggling only the dogs never reacted because they were asleep, so fuming about this as I had suspected it was him for sometime but the dogs always reacted quick as a flash and covered the noise but you don't get many cats in this part of Hartburn as there are so many dogs. The next time I'd seen Fred was when he came for a package sent to mine by mistake, I confronted him and told him what I thought of him, I got quite heated and I was calling him a child and how patheticly childish and petty he was, I actually shouted at him on purpose because I didn't want them involved at the time and I thought they were trying to help me. At the time I thought I could trust them mostly well Rose at least. Anyway after 2 weeks I went round to apologise, I got Rose first and she told me that Fred (Dominic Turnbull) had assumed I had mistaken him for somebody else and got the wrong man. I didn't say anything except to apologise and quietly amused I let it go. When I ran into Fred next I apologised to him he told me the same! Fred pal, I used your name multiple times and gave you a package with your wife's name on it, he didn't mind lying to my face in the hope it would stay plausible and I wouldn't point out the obvious and all because he was ashamed to admit to his wife he regularly sets my dogs off on purpose to annoy me and takes delight in the process. This big bang on the side of the bungalow marked the day I realised Fred and later on his wife Rose's involvement in this sorry tale of woe and a rather horrible period to live through at the bungalow. I sent Rose a message on Facebook...when I still thought she was a good person...

31st of March 07.51

"Hiya Rose, I am reaching out to you so that you might be able to talk some sense into your husband. I suspect it was him that threw something at my home last night, to see my reaction maybe? Take pictures of me investigating? Who knows. It was obviously him because the security light was on and I got out there within seconds. He seems like a very unhappy person that feeds off of my misery and really he should be the happiest man in the world. Lets look at this objectively. He has you, a beautiful and successful women who is a good person, he has a brilliant job, he has a beautiful home...why then is he so unhappy in life? Please tell him to leave me alone, just forget I live next

door to you both. I am no danger to him, I have to be better than that and it goes without saying that you are not in any danger either. I need to be attacked to justify violence. I suspect your husband is not a good person underneath and just hides it well . I have thought this the moment I met him and only really bothered with him because of you...for if a good egg like you loves him he can't be all bad...so I gave him the old beni. He needs to become a half full kind of guy and look at what he has and be fucking grateful.

I'm sorry I have had to do this but with these new powers the police have and the fact he is who he is, I am expecting trouble at my door at some point. I hope it doesn't happen but we will see.

I hope you are well and I am sorry it has come to this but we all have enough on our plates without any unneeded bullshit"...

I got around 4 days of peace then the slamming doors started and the set ups and security lights only I realised Rose was in! No I was gutted because Fred, bless him had just confirmed to me he was involved and might have been from the beginning and that Darren Wilkinson across the road was acting as the lookout while whoever gained access through the bushes at the back of Fred's and is how nobody had "seen" people enter my home from the drive and the fact the flats are all conveniently empty and now I realised his wife was involved too, I was so furious but I had come to realise by this point I could trust nobody and consequently I had by this time cut out everybody from my old life and there was no way into me by this point and thus started my realisation of next doors involvement. Then it clicked that in fact would explain how people are getting into the back of mine that and the four empty flats out the back. I'd really love to know who has bought them. The loud bangs happened again another couple of times and I realised it was to get me outside with weapons, I started to think maybe they are trying to get me set up so I end up back in a mental hospital? With the benefit of hindsight I would say that what it was all about for next door and by association Cleveland police. The lock down started and so did all the skulduggery with next door. It was almost like they both started to crack up with lock down and really start to lose it. Constantly slamming his back door which reverberated through the bungalow each time, I used to call him "the big hard door slammer" endless games of morse code played using the switches on the stupidly bright security lights, you can hear everything they do when they are out next door and would talk loudly and laugh and joke but it wasn't natural and was done with so much acting that I realised it was just to antagonise me. You could tell. Sending people around the bungalow with the aim of taking pics of me breaking lock down, I could see Rose up in the windows opposite the side of my home with a camera phone on one occasion and I was never stupid enough to open the front door and always came from the back. I'd say six attempts at a minimum and always marked with renewed slamming doors every time it failed. Basically everything and anything they could do to provoke me they tried and failed. That door slamming used to amuse me though. Fred is a pussy but listening to him slam doors on a daily basis you would think he is as hard as they come but it always amused me because usually it was in anger when I had got one over him or something hadn't worked out as planned and it was a little victory of sorts. The skulduggery was daily for weeks interrupted by periods of quite when something hadn't worked out or I was close to winning. During lock down it was annoying and the more I didn't react the more desperate next door became.

They made complaints to the police but I was not reacting to anything at all and that failed, they even had the mental health teams round. I got a letter addressed to Rose come through by "mistake" and it had Cleveland Polices stamp on the envelope, they really were putting the effort in and I cannot help but wonder what on earth they were offered to do this against me, me only having ever tried to be friends with them, ok I didn't like Fred but still I was nice to him generally. I am now convinced of their involvement in this conspiracy and that they are involved with the corrupt elements of Cleveland Police and there is a large possibility Fred has illegally been in my home and more than once or at least helped and enabled other people to do so. I remember telling Laurencia about Fred and Rose just before all this started and remember how she whispered it back to herself "The next door neighbours" she said softly. Umm.

It was around this time I thought enough was enough and I wrote a couple of Facebook posts threatening to release my book if they didn't leave me alone. Called a truce even, I spent some time preparing the book for a self published release on amazon. I followed through with the threat when they didn't leave me alone. No ones bought it but I have sent out a far few free copies up to now and people out there believe me which is good to see. Lots of people know I am telling the truth by now.

Next door especially. I would love the whole street to read it as they must of seen some things by this point. All cannot be oblivious to the strange and sinister going ons across the road and at the neighbours. Though the reality is they just think I am a nutter. The highlight of releasing the book was the silence for a few days from next door. They seemed to take it personally and really must have been worried at that point I would say, they would always go quiet and if something changed in their favour they became all loud and cocky again. I would love to grill them both and wonder aloud what they both said to the police...

Chapter 2

Now what I am about to depart to you will sound nuts and highly unlikely even to me, however the statements are true and actually happened. I am always telling it how it happened and as always I could not make it up, I tell it like it is and stand by every word I say, rather it is not fiction but a true statement of what happened and my experience of living it. No bending of the truth to fit a narrative, no lies, just the truth of what happened.

After the skulduggery of the neighbours I had by this time in April, around the 9th endured nearly 10 days of next doors campaign against me and I needed supplies and having sussed how people were getting in through the bushes at the back and behind my shed then using the French door key they could only have been sought from my nephew Martin who burgled me those times further linking my family in this story and how they knew about the bushes in the first place, I decided that all keys must be inserted on the inside and twisted out. I then thought about how am I going to achieve this and completely forgetting I have an electric remote garage door decided the best course of action was to jump out of the bedroom window which face the other neighbours side and they are always out in the back garden working since lock down and means nobody would be able to get in the house without being noticed because all the locks would have keys in them and would have to use that same window as it was the only way in. Of course the neighbours noticed me doing this and must of thought I was mad but actually I didn't mind as maybe it will make them keep an eye on the house. Now that I knew the neighbours were involved I could not trust somebody wouldn't be entering my home like in the recent past and I have just found a major suspect in Fred you see. Top of the list of suspects just like that numpty across the road the lookout Darren Wilkinson. Anyway I wondered how I could block the gap at the back of the shed and make them have to climb over the shed roof and massively expose those getting in and making it too risky when I remember I had some boards left over and other bits and pieces left over from some fencing and maybe have enough to build a fence and block it properly! Bonus but first supplies. I am skint and borrow £20 and walk to the shop, I get there and the shop is shut because of restocking shelves but the shop looks deserted and the shelf's decidedly empty, it was 4pm and they would reopen at 4.30pm. I walked home, when I get back to the shop 30 minutes later I walk to the meat fridge and all empty except a very tall pile of mince, the exact mince I buy stacked so high it went higher than the next shelf. Finding this unusual I picked up the mince and I went and got my coffee and milk, potatoes, carrots, leaks etc, I pay and I went home. I made a stew. It was bloody lovely until the next day, the next day I felt the symptoms of October but just not as brutal and without the black sludge in my urine. How could this be? I'd bought this from the shop myself and I have been nowhere since so nobody has had access to the food other than me. I know how this sounds but its true, I promise you. I ate the rest of the casserole just to be certain and because it was so nice. That was a mistake and I paid for that the next day. Though nowhere near as ill as back in October. After I recovered I decided to borrow some more money and go back to the shop and buy the same stuff and see what that was like. This time I had to wait outside the shop for a good solid 10 minutes in the queue to get in with social distancing. I went home and made the same stew and low and behold I was ill again. I could not believe it! They had figured out how to professionally reseal packets and must have bribed people that work in the co-op. Easy to pull off with the lock down. The symptoms are extreme dry mouth, lips sore, a thirst you cannot quench no matter how much water you drink, a metallic taste in your mouth like you have been sucking on batteries, extreme lethargic-ness and uncomfortable-ness in the Johnson. Unmistakable and bloody unbelievable, every symptom except the sludge. This means people in my local shop who I have suspects, have been recruited and the methods used mean a rather large upscale in equipment too if they are able to reseal packaging.

I was ill and dumbfounded but also needed to borrow money again for food that was not contaminated. The fact I cooked the food in a casserole probable saved me as it was so cooked through that the symptoms were mild but chronic and long lasting which was different to October because now I had properly ingested the substance but back then they were putting it on food I would eat directly out of the fridge an not cook you see. Over a week I ingested 4 contaminated meals and was ill for another week after. As far as I could tell, the mince, the potatoes, the carrots and my coffee were contaminated and all things I buy regularly, I borrowed yet more bloody money for food, £30 from someone I thought I could trust and don't know if she was involved in this but on the 15th of April 2020 20mins after the money was transferred I was set up at the co-op down the road from me at Hartburn Parade. They would of needed 30 minutes minimum to set up this play which means they knew I was going to the shop before I had decided I was even going to the shop. There was a 30 minutes gap between me asking for the money and getting the reply. I don't know what to think.

I was so happy my friend had helped me out with the money as I didn't get paid for another week, I opened the gate at the side when I notice Fred talking to a deep voiced man and sounding excited, whenever him and now Rose sound excited I always get worried as it means they are up to something, its a shame I would have smiled not so long ago at hearing the same noise, I looked through the gap and noticed the CSI guy who always seemed to be at Hartburn garage. Anyway I do all my checks and leave, I get to the shop and just as I get to the door and low and behold out walk Fred and Rose hand in hand to the point I had to stop mid stride to let them out, I had not noticed them walk to the shop, immediately I was suspicious and watched them as they walked across the car park they kept looking back and laughing and smiling, Clearly excited by something. If looks could injure and maim it would have done for them that day. I was in the queue, I was watching them walk away and in front of me was this big fat ginger security guard they were forced to hire after all the robberies and shop lifting happening in the shop, just as Fred and Rose went out of view I turned to the security guard and said my hello's and he pointedly said "I think there is some kids smoking ganja out the back of the shops" he said this so matter of factly and on queue it was comical and just like that I get a drift of cannabis but not from behind, like it would if they were at the back but from around the front of the shops, I, bemused then laughed and said "Good for them I have not had any in ages" I never smoked during lock down as I couldn't trust anybody to not give me spiked weed and backy from people I used to get it from but that's another story. I went about my shop buying things I would never usually buy and paid for my things I went home and it was strange, all the skulduggery with next door stopped for at least the next 5 days, in fact I didn't hear a peep out of them, no excited ramblings or frustrated door slamming, no security lights going off every two seconds and clearly with the switches as they are on a 10s timer usually the wally.

So here's my theory of what went down that day...

CSI guy was supposed to gain access to my home and retrieve anything he can, my laptop and the evidence I now have with all the food from the shop? While Fred and Rose went to the shop maybe to try and get a rise out of me and in glee at what they thought was certain victory and being witness to my reaction on finding my possessions or me gone if I'd of gone around the back of the shop. There were people around the back of the shop but I bet not kids smoking ganja. The silence from the neighbours was in total devastation at not succeeding on any of those points. I felt for you, I really did...this confirmed to me that employees at my local shop had indeed been recruited and my friend who leant me the money had a hand in the set up.

The lengths these people are going to is quite impressive, they must really hate me and have a really good incentive to try to kill me though I can only speculate on the why and who aspects of the campaign against me, the real shot callers. I'll state again, I am telling nothing but the truth no matter how unlikely it seems and I am not making this up and now I had all the evidence I would need to make a complaint to the police and try and put an end to this absurd situation. I had bought everything twice on my shops so had I good lot of unopened and packaged food, mince, potatoes, carrots etc, from the co-op with whatever the substance used contained within. The writing on the wall with next door meant I knew they were trying to get me sectioned again, I smelt Laurencia would be involved somehow and now was the time to start being public about this, try and get the main force to start an investigation and take me seriously. I decided the first thing I needed to do before that was make a complaint about the poisoning to Cleveland Police through the proper channels and I tied and failed to get a solicitor to help me but I was giving the police a chance to do the right thing. I even rung the Standards and Ethics department again though predictably I was given short thrift with that and was a waste of time. I rung the 111 number and tried my hardest not to sound like a nutter, unfortunately I got a new starter and was then put through to the most inept and patronising man who did not take me seriously and was rude mostly, it did make me wonder what they had written in the notes about me on file. I was pissed off because he was seemingly just showing off to the overhearing new girl and she got a very good lesson in how not to handle a call. I told him what I thought of him and I ended the call and waited for a response. That was Thursday night 23rd of April 2020. I even rung at midnight so they wouldn't be that busy. The response came on the Sunday 26th with a knock at my door from two uniformed officers. My heart sank as I was expecting CID level officers, you know befitting a conspiracy to commit murder claim that would normally encourage. Nope I was again given officers who wouldn't even give me their names, the same patronising manor as the call handler. The conversation predictably turned to my mental heath, immediately I was suspicious and asked them to leave as I could see what they were angling for. They just wanted me to talk to a colleague for a second. Yeah a mental health professional I said, they lied she wasn't. They would not leave so angrily, I snatch my phone and threatened them with Facebook live, they left at that thankfully. Angry to the point of seething that my local police force are this shit and wont help me and just want to put me in a mental hospital again. Remember this is a genuine complaint that I have evidence of, crystal clear fucking evidence, not to mention the oodles of evidence that would be found with a proper police investigation. If I could just get them to do the right thing?

The next morning still shocked at Cleveland Polices attempts to get me resectioned and knowing what I faced if I went back to that hospital I decided I needed to try and gain public awareness and force Cleveland Polices hand. I wrote out an open letter and then posted the letter on the most recent 5 posts from Cleveland Polices and Teesside Lives Facebook pages at around about 0730 in the morning...

"Dear any honest coppers at Cleveland Police, I have been suffering persecution at the hands of your corrupt elements since August last year. I have recently found substantial evidence that proves everything that has happened to me. I then decided, after previously trying with your standards and ethics department twice, to make a formal complaint of "Conspiracy to commit murder" I was unfortunately for myself put through to the most inept person you have working in your call centre, he would not give me his name and all I have is 8866, he was obtuse and patronising. I then get a visit from two uniformed officers on Sunday the 26th, they also would not give me their names, 2387 and 2638, they then patronised me and tried to trick me into being sectioned into a mental health

hospital. After a lot of arguing I eventually got them to leave by threatening to film them on Facebook live. I am not mentally ill. A proper police investigation would substantiate my claims, there is so much evidence out there, the evidence needs lab testing, phone records, bank statements and people to interview and put pressure on. The problem is your corrupt elements are getting nervous and need the evidence I have in my possession. I ask you to please read a book I have wrote on the subject called Prixturious, It is on amazon or contact me via email, mikeyelwood@gmail.com and I will send a pdf copy, do not look at it as a book more a gift and guide to an investigation, a lot of people stand to lose their liberty if I succeed and I am truly in danger. The man at the top running the show against me is I believe a chief inspector, I do not know his name, he is around 6.2 tall, bald, wears smart and expensive suits and around his early to mid 50's. I implore you to take this seriously and help me save my life. This man has spent a considerable amount of money taking me down and running your C.I's against me, all of whom I know personally. Please take me seriously, I will from today be making quite a lot of noise publicly about this and I implore you to take me seriously and help me.

Yours Truthfully Michael Elwood"

The only thing I missed out was that the book on Amazon the names had been changed but what happened next was totally unexpected and surprised even me. I was sat in the front bedroom waiting for the police and mental health teams I just knew to be coming around at some point in the future, a little scared at what I had just done, at around 0830 I heard next door. I heard Fred suddenly pleading with Rose "Don't go please, I beg you don't leave, please Rose don't go" I could not believe my ears, my instant gut feeling was on her seeing "Conspiracy to commit murder" it dawned on Rose what she had got herself involved with and being a fundamentally good person, I like to think she went straight to the police because at 0930 there was a few loud van door slams and a knock on Fred's door and it sounded official and heavy handed, there was no noise other than the dog barking for 4 days after that apart from people in and out but not Fred, the steady bored and stressed bark of a dog who doesn't like being alone, it was unusual. Fred would not arrive home until 10pm every night and no sign of Rose and dogs are never really left alone at ol'Freds. I thought I had cracked it, my phone was alive with notifications and Fred had been arrested, I just had to wait for the police to come around and interview me and test the evidence. Finally I could breath and it was all over now, I would be able to be the man I know I am meant to be, be allowed to be me again and use all the potential I have to succeed. I would obviously get compensated and who would mind with what I have been through. I started to cry, big loud guttural cries, the tears streamed down my cheeks, its done, the nightmare is over...

Yeah Na Fuck, because Monday came and went, then Tuesday, nothing, then Wed, Thurs, Friday, Sat and finally Sunday...Nothing. All the while there are CID cars at both neighbours and I even witnessed them across the street. The fact Fred was absent all day and all the van doors slamming and people in and out of his gaff, that Rose was MIA and a dog left alone all day it was obvious. I went to the shop and on my way across the road there was a man on the phone walking on the path he said pointedly and loudly "They have had him two days haven't they? Have they actually charged him?" while looking surprised to see me. I knew an investigation had indeed kicked off and for them to interview Fred for those long days I knew they now know I am telling the truth but by Sunday it suddenly hit me that the investigation had hit a snag or two so here is what I think happened.

Basically Cleveland Police realised I was telling the truth and they uncovered the wrong doings of the corrupt elements and in so doing proved my conspiracy but then they realised the consequences of that being true. A conspiracy involving serving officers using secret resources and clandestine assets and using profits gained from criminal activities in the pursuit of attempting to destroy and murder an innocent member of the public, using false and set up mental health ward and all the members of the public surrounding the innocent party who have been bribed, enlisted and involved, all could be charged within the conspiracy. Simply it was so much easier to paint me as mentally ill and not interview me. Very important that the police did not interview me. I would be classed the same as a lead detective and the expert, had they got me into a interview room I would of backed up everything and pointed the police in all the right directions and left them with no choice but to charge people and fucking rightly so. Parts two and three of the book was a gift of a guide to an investigation! Any detective worth their salt would find it hard to mess up. There is still so much evidence out there even to this day! To them it was one innocent man against the liberty of quite a lot of guilty people and saves the embarrassment of it all for Cleveland Police and resulting publicity, plus a lot of compensation to me. Basically they decided it best to continue to fuck me over and limit the damage. Shit its not over. Can a guy get a break...

Reading the cards right and at this realisation I knew what would be coming next and that was the mental health teams. Seven days after the Facebook posts I decided that I was now going to do was follow through on being public as I had held off during the investigation because I didn't want to influence it, it might have been a bad move with hindsight. Hate hindsight...I should have been public and pressured the Police more. I was so certain I'd cracked the case on the Monday I decided not to for now.

I decided to do Facebook lives twice a day, one in the morning and one in the evening just to let people know what is happening and did my first one on the Sunday after I realised it had back fired and by the next day I had my first visit from the Police and mental health teams. Scary that first one was but got it all on video. I did not need a mental health assessment I needed a bloody police investigation and the evidence I have testing and for me to be interviewed by detectives, I am telling the truth and I should at least of been interviewed. Three days in a row they came from Monday the 3rd of May until Wednesday the 6th but I was getting very ill over those days and was nearly dying by the 6th. A few days before I was messaged out of the blue by my old friend a female, who we will call Laura Calvert she was being overly nice and I was suspicious as she was pretty much the only person who I had not fallen out with from the old crowd, she offered to go to the shop for me as I had run low on supplies and was desperately trying to keep the evidence safe and could not leave after the mental health teams had been around I could be arrested at any place I went, I was refusing to answer the door to them and wouldn't speak to the doctors. I think you can see from the videos that I am fine mentally but needed people to believe me and be on my side. I was scared at times. This was all desperately unfair because again, I am telling the truth and being honest. That became my motto during my videos actually. Anyway not really trusting her but curious at the same time, I gave Laura my shopping list which consisted of 2 x 4 pints of milk, 30g amber leaf, 2 x filter tips, loaf of bread and some shorties and or malted milks. I got everything except the biscuits, which had changed to caramel digestive, I was immediately suspicious as I had not asked for them. I felt fine and tried the bread, that was ok and had two cups of coffee with the milk in and was ok. The backy had a funny taste to it but first night I was fine. Next day not so good. I realised after I poured a lot more of the milk on my Weetabix and continued to smoke the backy I got the unmistakable symptoms as before and the more backy I smoked the worse I got. You can watch me steadily get ill around 6 videos back, please watch them, my Facebook is public and all video's are available to view, I would say if you are reading this then it is essential viewing you don't have to watch the full lengths but watch for my deterioration. I was fine on the Sunday but desperately ill by the Wednesday and looked at deaths door. I immediately looked at the receipt and at the time in particular 12.22 and Laura delivered it all around 20mins later. However I had put the order in at 0930 and would have left plenty of time, 2.5 hours to nip to the shop and buy everything unpack, contaminate and repack all the goods using professional re-sealers, which I wonder are the tools available at the co-op, although this was from Sainsbury's but obviously the contaminate would be added off site, I also wonder if the cops had responded would there be video camera evidence of Laura going to the shop twice? Or one of the other suspects buying the same shopping list? That is just one example of how much evidence out there that there is, if only Cleveland Police had took me seriously and done their jobs, there are countless examples of the evidence that would have been uncovered with a proper police investigation. You have failed me Cleveland Police. Royally fucked me over. I still have the contaminated backy and challenge you to come and test it! It just needs investigating, but they know that don't they. There is still time for Cleveland Police to do the right thing and re-start the investigation.

I was so disappointed in Laura but not surprised and it was a little predictable but had added all the new evidence to the list plus my blood.

Chapter 3
Wednesday 6th May 2020

I awoke desperately ill and with an idea. With me now being so ill and now in the third period of poisoning and with all the evidence I now had in my possession I would phone my doctor and get my bloods checked and find out the substance. Then the Police cannot ignore me and start an investigation! I was ill but excited and felt this might be it! I rang the Alma Medical Centre and spoke to the on duty doctor, while on Facebook live and she told me the only body that can do the test needed on an unknown substance is a full Police work up and battery of tests, she told me the NHS only tests for 40 odd substances and would not have the facilities or expertises of that of the police. Bugger! (She lied!)

Again defeated in the jaws of victory. I had a think. I decided to try with the Police again and Live on Facebook. Waste of time of course. I pleaded with them to take me seriously. My god I felt ill. I broke down at this loss of victory and knew that the Police would be round again today with the Mental health teams. I was very week and upset at this point. Next door was always spying on me and listening to my phone conversations and sometimes I would talk at the door if I knew he was there, one time it was funny because I guessed right, I could feel someone there and said something rude and despicable about the man and I would hear a shifting and quite shutting of his door, the big bright security light conspicuously absent. This day after I pleaded with the Police to take me seriously I broke down. I had reached boiling point and was so ill. I cried and said things like "What did I ever do to you two apart from try to be your friends?" things like that. I hope they were listening good ol'Fred and Rose and I hope they felt it and it shamed them. I know for certain it would Rose because she is good really. I am of the opinion it would delight Fred though, he is just that type of man, he'd have a big smile on his face, listening in on his own and loved it. He wouldn't dare show it in front of Rose though. Keeps his dark side under raps does Fred. I got a hold of myself and made a stew, 30 minutes later there is a loud knock at my door and I can see the silo et of a couple of coppers. I said my usual and asked them to leave unless they were here about the case. The police officer informed me they had a warrant to enter the premises and if I didn't let them in then they would have to break the door down.

Fuck!

I was so ill and should have run to my garage but what I did was open the door, I was greeted by two cops, a psychiatrist (she never spoke once), a mental heath professional and a Paramedic. I let them in and they informed me there was an ambulance here and I was going to be checked out and then I had to accompany them for a mental health assessment. I knew what was coming and not sure if I actually had to go or not I grabbed my laptop and my phone and both chargers and I went with them. I guess I had no choice and in my weakened state, I could not fight much. The Paramedics never even checked my pulse or vitals and I kept telling them I needed to be in hospital. We went straight to Roseberry Park in the ambulance and I was grilled for 5 minutes by another doctor then had to wait while they made the decision. I kept protesting I am telling the truth and this should be a police investigation but of course mention poisoning to mental health professionals is condemning yourself in the "suffering mental health bracket" in their eyes, it is inconceivable for anybody to actually be getting poisoned or that in 95% of cases they are not actually getting poisoned and they see that a lot. I was angry at the absurdity of my situation and after an hour of talking to the two police officers I was told I was being committed under section two of the mental health act...again! I was dumbfounded about this after my last visit and this enraged me and frightened me but also I was still so ill I just wanted to sleep at that point. On my way to the room I heard the mental health professional depart to his colleagues that they should take my laptop and phone from me at the earliest opportunity. Over my dead body pal, I remember thinking, My laptop and phone never left my side from then on. I went in my cell and could not believe I am here again and I am telling the truth and being honest. I cannot describe to you the sheer frustration of telling the truth and nobody willing to believe you. Its is infuriating yet I am getting used to it by now.

I slept for 48 hours. I barely drunk any water or ate any food, I was badly ill and never even seen a doctor for those first 48 hours. I was also forced to take mind altering drugs again, this time Risperidone. I was not informed by a psychiatrist but a ward nurse and without even seeing or talking to anybody by this point. I did not and never have needed drugs. I am not mentally ill in this regard, I have only ever needed some therapy and someone to actually listen to me, after what I have been through. My new psychiatrist Doctor Kuma never even spoke to me for my first 2 weeks in there. I was understandably very nervous and worried after the last time and I admit I was very difficult for the first week but after a while I realised that this time it was different, non of the skulduggery of before happened and it was how it should have been, I was on a different ward this time. The staff were well intentioned and the patients all alright and friendly. I was comfortable after realising that it was ok this time. I needed to recover and it was two weeks before I was totally ok and back to myself. I can only say having two periods of being poisoned so close together had taken its toll on me and I was extremely ill. I really need to go for a few scans on my liver and kidneys and kept asking but was denied. In a way I was grateful to be in the mental hospital and given this opportunity to get out of the situation and myself better. My only real gripes were the medication and the fact that Dr Kuma only spent 35minutes in my company the whole 5 weeks I was there. Dr Edera 65 minutes in 24 days and then this new doctor blows that record right out of the park with his 35! 35 minutes is ridiculous. 65 minutes is ridiculous! If I ever do take the NHS to court then I wouldn't even let either speak on behalf of my mental health after such little time spent with me. Psychiatrists are lazy and rely on drugs far too much. No discussion of what I think is best for me, nada! Its shameful, you are effectively in prison without trial and then forced on the whim of a doctor to take mind altering drugs that in all honesty were not needed and all on the back of nurses reports (not sure there was much to report after 48 hours of sleeping that I did whilst prescribed the drugs) and previous notes by a dishonest psychiatrist like Dr Edera, like he can be trusted. The psychiatrists think they are gods and too good to be bothered with spending actual time with patients. Not once did anybody try to believe me or listen to what I was saying or bothered about the fact I am telling the truth. In the end when I realised I was safe I decided to just play the game and do what they wanted me to do. I kept myself to myself and kept my head down for the remaining time. I never mentioned anything really as it was all a waste of time. I effectively decided to play the game and do what was needed to get myself out. There was a time when I actually didn't really want to leave and it all just kick off again, I even enquired about re-homing. I realised that was not possible with me owning the bungalow. It's not long before it gets repossessed now and homelessness abounds.

I feel I have to mention an incident while I was in there, a ward assistant who does the cooking and cleaning, now I will try to be nice but she was a big lass and when I went to get my food there was already a plate made ready and what do you know it was exactly what I would have picked, macaroni and cheese, I asked why she has prepared a plate and she replied "just to serve quicker" I didn't think anything of it until an hour later and I got the symptoms. I could not believe it. I went to the medical room and got them to check my vitals and I was in hyperbolic state and my blood pressure was high. I went to bed quite ill, though I was ok by the morning. The worker was not in for the next two days but when she got back next on the third day she had put another plate off at dinner and it was just what I would have chosen. I looked at her and told her never to put a plate off for me and I will always want to see you serve it in front of me. I was always suspicious of her from then on and realised that Bethan Story was next door and could try to recruit someone she knows who works on the ward and this lass must be the weak link. I worried about that happening but other than that incident nothing else happened so I gave the big skulduggery laden and shifty worker the benefit of the doubt and put it down to delayed reaction ultimately knowing that worker spiked my food! She knows what they have been using and is somebody to put pressure on if I get my investigation. Lots of people to put pressure on!

After a couple of weeks I decided to put an appeal in against my section and around three weeks after being admitted I finally got my reports from the staff and doctors. I got as far as the crises team report and Doctor Kuma's. The doctors was ridiculous, in it he had wrote that I am very ill suffering paranoid delusions, delusions of grander, psychosis and lack any insight to my mental health, he reiterated the last one three times in his report. Strange as I would say the same to him. I was never given any insight to my mental health from reading that report as I only exchanged pleasantries with him until I was released after reading it, you never saw him. The psychiatrist see themselves as god like and full of their own self importance and just not very good. How much insight could he possibly posses after 30 minutes in my company up to that point? In his report I also got some information on why I was detained. This is where it gets very interesting. Laurencia popped up as expected. She had re-used the answering the door with a knife in my hand, which never happened but there were two new ones. One, apparently I had been suffering with my mental health for 3 years? Depression? Then yes I guess she is right I was struggling for a time. Then this beauty...I had been seen walking around my home with an axe! There is only one way she could have known that and I have only done it the once. Here's the story of what happened, it will make me sound like a nutter but you had to be there and see and feel what I felt, I will try my best to explain...oh, after reading the reports I decided not to go through with the appeal, I was happy to stay a bit longer and continue to recover and after reading the reports I didn't think I would win this time anyway and didn't see the point...I really was not excited about coming back to this hell that is the bungalow and my life.

I don't know the date of this story, it was around the time before I instigated the investigation and was releasing the book and there was a lot of worried people out there like next door, my family and the corrupt elements at Cleveland Police and

C.I's and I had noticed both neighbours had a lot of visitors and they were not friendly visits. I got up one day and heard the wife on the other side talking loudly with a man. I can hear pretty much most things from both neighbours when outside and they can hear with me too, not that much privacy really. I looked out the bedroom window to see a big ginger man talking to the wife. I look out the front bedroom and see a Vauxhall Nevaro van parked outside. I think nothing of it because it looks like he's a workman just pricing a job up. Around about 4pm that same day I am doing something in my kitchen and look out of the window to see through the gaps in my fence that same ginger man using a hose pipe and looking through the fence at me, on noticing that I had noticed him he seemed startled. I could tell nobody was home otherwise except this ginger man and the same for Fred and Rose, no dogs barking, doors slamming, security lights etc. At around 7pm, all the lights were off and the kitchen window was wide open at the other neighbours, both very unusual. On Fred and Roses side there is noway to see into the bungalow as it only has the bathroom and front door on that side but on the other it has all the bedroom and kitchen windows and you can see quite a lot and next door that side. the kitchen windows face my windows and is higher up. Now I was very suspicious of this ginger man and the wide open kitchen window and the fact Fred and Rose were out too. I smelled a rat and felt skulduggery afoot and something was not right. So I decided to patrol my home in the dark every 20 minutes and opened all the curtains in all the bedrooms and the only light was from my laptop that I was using to watch Netflix in between, my night vision was tip top. I could feel something was not right. At 8pm still no lights next door but the kitchen window from its widest setting was shut now. On fire and ready for anything, confident that both neighbours were not present and just the ginger man but maybe somebody in Fred and Roses, I shouted out in a "Here's Jonny" like way "Somebodies going to die tonight boys and it ain't gunna be me!" I have visions of the ginger man looking through my windows and just seeing me patrol the bungalow with my medium but very sharp axe and then hear my "Here's Jonny" speech. Makes me smile even now.

Ten minutes later I hear I van start up and with a fury of revs and screeching tires it sped off and I knew I was safe. I smiled. 20 minutes later next door came home and kitchen lights were on, then literally 5 minutes later Fred and Rose came home, suddenly the security lights came on and dogs barking, doors slamming...just like that, normality resumed...

My theory? Well 25% of me thought I was a paranoid lunatic but the other 75% knew I had saved myself that day. The corrupt elements got next door to leave under some pretext and ordered the same with Fred and Rose, well they are on the payroll after all and situated the ginger man in the neighbours house, they could even of had somebody in Fred's for all I know. The plan? To do me in and get the poisoned evidence I have, plus my laptop and phone. That is my feelings on it anyway and stands as the only time I have walked around my home carrying my axe unless I have been using it. It was the only time I did and a bit of a mistake by Laurencia to use it to get me sectioned because how the hell would she or anybody else know if she/they were not involved and the ginger man had not departed to them about the axe?? Yet more evidence of her involvement. There is more if any were needed.

On the 2nd May 2020 I mentioned Laurencia a good few times in the Facebook videos to do with shame and the next day I get a loud bang at my door. I go out the back and am confronted by Laurencia! I laugh and say...

"Not interested Laurencia, please leave and don't come back you are evil" I go back inside.

She proceeded to jump over the gate and start slamming on the French doors and screaming at me. I got her to leave when I picked my phone up and threatened her with Facebook live, though she did something very curious did Laurencia, you see when I looked out the front of the house her car was parked half over my side and half over Fred's side and I could see her car. I expected her to leave straight away but she didn't. Her car did not move for a minimum of 50 minutes...She was next fucking door! For 50 minutes! They know each other! Only the very people who blew themselves up and confirmed to me to be on the corrupt elements payroll and she went and had a cuppa for nearly an hour! Silly girl. Her visit was just to provoke me and she expected me to open the front door. She was at this point very nervous and nervous people make silly mistakes. She has made a fair few now and it is all mounting up. Broke my heart you have Laurencia, you have been key in getting me sectioned twice and helping the corrupt elements and you know Fred and Rose personally. Now how do I know Laurencia, it is not you who has been gaining access to my home because how do you know them? Not to mention spiking me with MDMA in my coffee the first time I was sectioned! You have been working together is the only explanation and your finger prints are all over this Laurencia. As far as I can see you have a pivotal role in this conspiracy, more so than your mother, even. That's the truth of the matter...I want to know what you and Fred and Rose know. I want you all in an interview room with detectives, somewhere Rose and Fred have already been as well as Fred in my home I believe.

Anyway back to hospital. Two weeks after I cancelled my appeal, I was released. A total of 5 weeks internment, one that did not resolve anything and was not needed at all. Both times I've been honest and both times I did not need to be in hospital. Though I was grateful of the chance to recover, I ditched the drugs straight away after being released and knew from last time it would be a 4 week recovery from being in hospital. You need time to adjust and to get yourself back and let the drugs wear off. Horrible are the drugs, I am sure if you do suffer paranoid delusions, psychosis etc, then yes they have a benefit but to me who didn't it is horrible. You go really stiff, get really agitated, cannot relax and this time I lost my libido to the point I stopped producing sperm. I had been prescribed drugs against my will again and would not continue to take them of my own free will. Ever.

5 weeks later and I am back to my normal self and can relax again. No skulduggery afoot as of yet and I have not heard a peep from next door. Their recent experiences must of made them realise the error of their ways. Rose you broke my heart when I realised you had gotten yourself involved because I was so sure you are a good person, which I still believe you are underneath. To Fred I say, I hope you learn some humanity and how to be sympathetic to a fellow human being. You need to realise what you have and be grateful for it before you lose it all and I hope your recent experiences you take that away from it and learn a valuable lesson. I will never forgive you but don't worry, if I was going to retaliate and boy how satisfying that would be, I would have done so by now. I hope you are ashamed of yourself Fred my boy. If the shoe was on the other foot I would have bent over backwards to help you out and do what I can for you. I would have read part two

back in October and been round yours asking what we are going to do about this. Not you though Fred, no you joined the other side or perhaps where already a member, only they and you know that...

So what became of all the evidence that I had acuminated? Did it disappear? Nope it was all still were I left it before I went into hospital though I threw away a lot from my freezer but still have key evidence. I was shocked and surprised when I got home and it was all still there. I am thinking that they might not have a front door key or just knew nobody is going to test it why bother trying to recover it. I still want this investigated and evidence tested, there is still time Cleveland police! Too many people involved and to put pressure on to not bear fruit if an investigation was enacted today. Lets look at the facts...

1. I have survived three periods of poisoning. Fact.

2. I have survived multiple non-poisoning attempts on my life - Fact

3. People have been entering my home illegally- Fact.

4. I have tried on multiple occasions to get the police to investigate and use my evidence, if they had my life would be very different by now - Fact

5. Police clandestine resources used against me by the corrupt elements of Cleveland Police – Fact?

6. Cleveland Police have had me sectioned under section 2 of the mental health act twice rather than investigate my genuine claims – Fact

7. I was not interviewed by Cleveland Police after making a formal complaint and spamming the Facebook Page. I should have been interviewed in either scenario

even if they thought I was mentally ill and making it up – Fact

8. I have been forced mind bending medication against my will twice due to Cleveland Polices incompetence – Fact

9. Cleveland Police abuse the mental health act to their benefit? - Fact

10. I have been fundamentally failed by both Cleveland Police and the mental health teams – Fact!

11. It was easier to paint me as mentally ill than admit the polices wrong doing – Fact!

12. The corrupt elements used Roseberry park namely the Bilsdale ward to set me up and used staff and patients to intimidate me and potentially harm me including secret medicating in my food – Fact

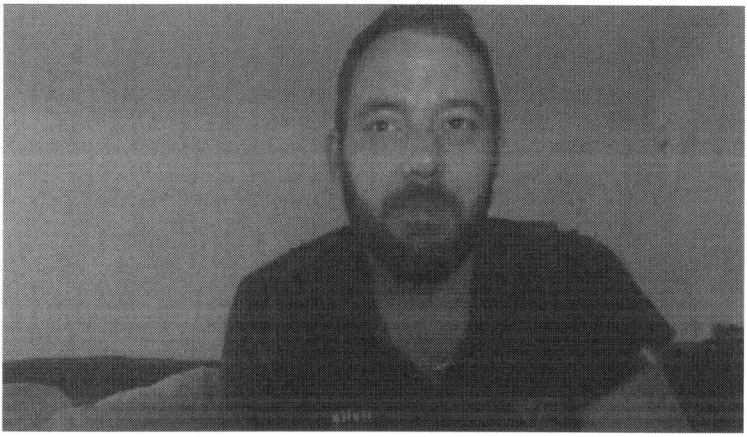

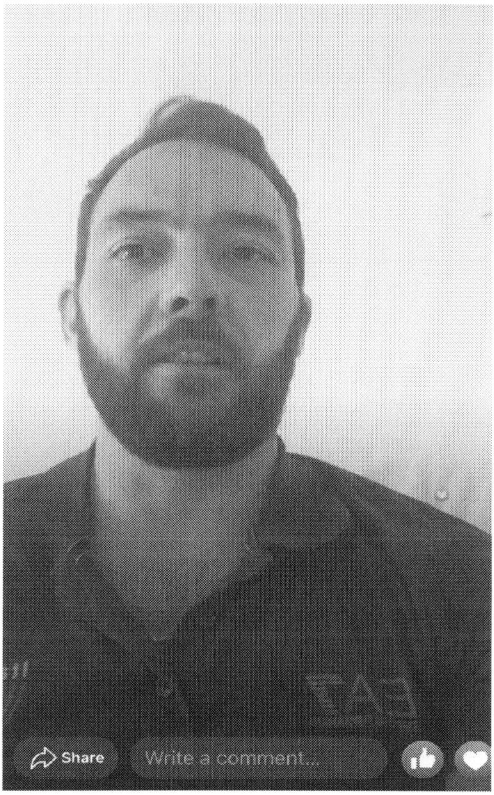
Share
Write a comment...

Totally fine after recovering from the second period of poisonings and the day Laura brought me my food.

Starting to look ill.

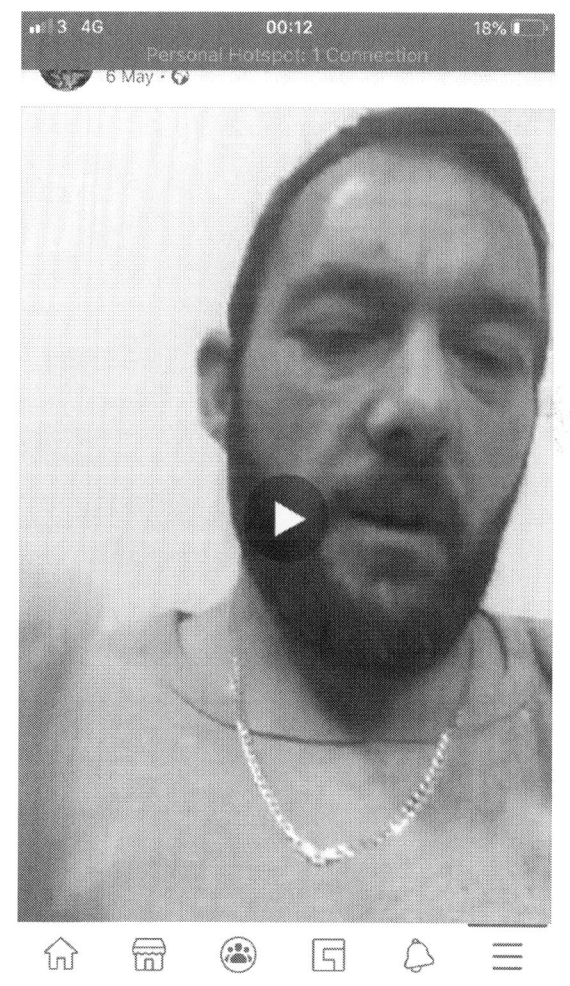

Wednesday. I feel I am literally dying .

.ıll 3 4G　　　　00:56　　　🔒 100% 🔋

Michael Elwood was live.
Posted by Michael Elwood
Wednesday at 18:43 · 🌐

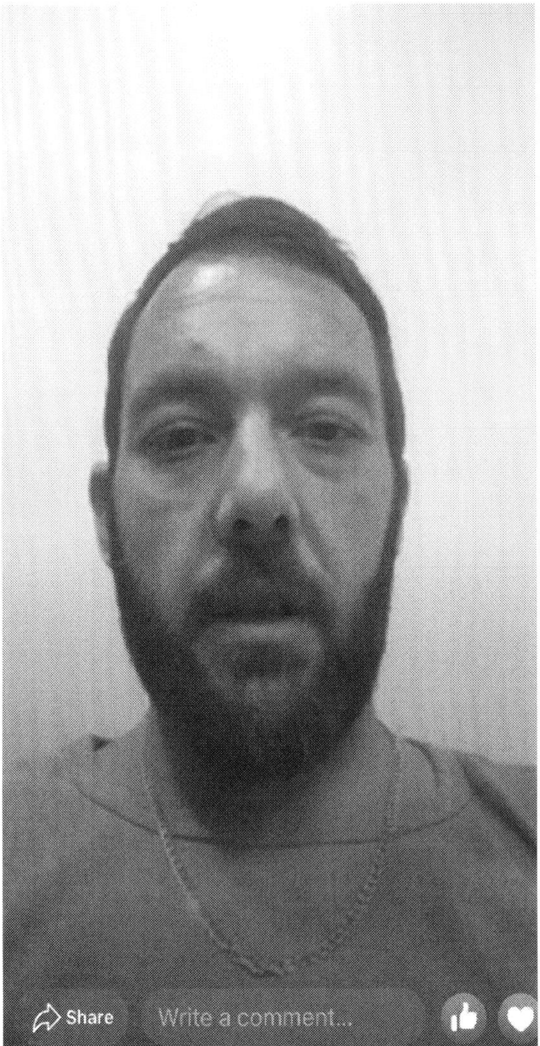
Share
Write a comment...

4 days later and in Roseberry Park

Lost a lot of weight and still very ill.

Two weeks later and recovered, still it was nearly 3 months before totally recovered.

I invite you Cleveland Police to do the right thing and even now finish the investigation. I know you know I am telling the truth and that you took the easy way out. You realised that if you acted in the proper way and did your job the embarrassment it would cause to the force, nationwide no less, not to mention the multiple coppers in court. People like Fred and Rose who would only be in court because of the corrupt elements at Cleveland Police it would not have looked good. They say bad publicity is good publicity but not in this case. I almost understand. Its the truth and embarrassment on the one hand and little old me who everyone thinks is mentally ill already, on the other, I suppose it was an easy decision by those in charge. Fuck the innocent little man and all will be well...I hope it all stops as I don't know how much longer I can keep myself safe and am always looking over my shoulder. What next? Peace hopefully.

However I also believe I deserve answers. I will be sending this book to the chief of Cleveland Police and the Standards and Ethics department in the hope you reverse your decision and do the right thing. Like I say, too many people involved and too much evidence still out there and you only need one of those people to crack. Please come and test what I have left and lets find out what they used. I would love to know what next door told you, interview tapes a secret listen maybe? Wishful thinking more like. I wont give up though and one way or another at least this story will be told...I am still the only one telling the truth and being honest...

To my Girl...I will make it to your door soon. The time is here and I need some loving though I am scared you will reject me. I hope not because you have kept me going all this time and without you I am not sure I would have had the strength to fight this. Even if I don't win your heart at least I will see you again and I hope you are happy to see me,

I will settle for that. You're still single so I hope your waiting, if not for me but your knight in shining armour...which is me...see what I did there? I know nobody will love you like I would and that's the truth. You and your mother are the only two people in the world I trust and the thought of winning your heart and becoming a family would make me the happiest man alive. I love you.

The End?

Nope
Part 5
The Nightmare Continues

Chapter 4

From June the 16th until the 10th of September 2020 it was a rather calm period. It took me the usual 6 weeks to get over my second stay in Roseberry Park and for the medication to wear off. I was still unable to do what most people do like the gym/pub/job for fear of being set up. My daily life had become mundane and I only left home to go to my local shop or a big shop at Aldi once a month. Deciding enough was enough and that my life in Teesside needs to come to an end that no matter what the time had come for me to escape to pastures new. Whist I was looking online on Indeed I came across an advert for lorry driving but the beauty was it was it was 40 miles away and tramping, it meant if I did three weeks I would have more than enough money to leave and start somewhere new. I rang the agency and I got the job because they needed about 20 drivers so I could start anytime, excellent that meant I could wait for my universal credit and get a taxi, yes it would be £50 but because it was tramping it meant I only had to pay it Monday and then Friday home, buzzing...Only, I had a visit...I stupidly answered the door and was greeted by a guy from EDF, shit I owe them a fortune, I had to explain about the job and predictably Fred (Dominic Turnbull) from next door was listening and to stop them putting meters in I had to depart about my new job and that money would be forthcoming soon. I could feel his presence as usual and it was confirmed when at the end of the conversation with the guy, I heard his door quietly shut. Fuck, Fuck, Fuck now everybody who wants to harm me would know I have a tramping job, they would know it was not from around Teesside and it would not take a genius to figure out which company because on indeed at that time there was not many tramping jobs available. I worried and worried and worried about this. How easy would it be to bribe the agency man (they are unscrupulous and devoid of morals generally) to find out my exact location on a night time, given that you are on a tracker and then get a couple of wrong-uns to put WD40 in my air vents (knocks you out cold straight away) smash the window and drag me away? These are worries I face nowadays and I have to admit when it came to the day before the job I was that anxious that I bottled it and let the agency know I couldn't make it. It didn't help that the man at the agency was very pushy and suspicious asking me twice to send all my details even though I had the day he asked me to send them and he rang me a lot but knew my start date so why? He seemed too anxious to get me on the job or its the level of my paranoia, I guess I will never know the answer to that question. So payday on Thursday 20th on a beautiful August day and gutted not to be starting my new job I decide that having not been to a pub in over a year I was going to treat myself to a lovely pint at the Masham pub around the corner from my home, thinking nobody would expect me to do that. So I did and had three lovely and delicious pints of Birra Moretti in the sunshine, amber bloody nectar! I have never ever enjoyed beer more in my life and was only ruined when the lady at the Masham knew who I was and my reputation as a mental patient obviously proceeded me and thought I couldn't pay and blocked the exit in expectation of me trying to flee without paying. If she knew me she would know I would never do that nor would I have been there had I no money. Something very positive did happen before that shaming though and I bumped into somebody important. Only my local MP Matt Vickers! Yes the very guy I helped to get elected with my Facebook antics. I quite tipsy, went over and introduced myself and had a 10 minute conversation with him about this and that and me being me I could not help but let him in on what had been happening to me for the last year! I must have sounded like a right nutter as I always do when trying to tell the story in a short period of time. I said I had tried to contact him for help and that I don't know if he received the emails. He said I was using the wrong email and to send it to his

@parliament email instead, he said send all docs and he will read them! So I did.

Here is my email...

"Hello Matt, do you remember me telling you about the Grant Mitchel post? Just two days after that Cleveland Police and the mental health teams forced their way into my home and after 10 minutes of trying to tell a books worth of a story to complete strangers I was sectioned under the mental health act, pounced on, handcuffed and dragged to Roseberry Park hospital where I was subject to intimidation, secret medicating in my food (because I didn't seem mentally ill enough I believe) and patients being pressured to harm me from outside influences. Why? I had been poisoned back in Sept/Oct for around 8 weeks intermittently, I had also dodged 5 stabbing attempts and made a complaint to the Polices supposed good side the standards and ethics department hoping for some help because I know corrupt elements are involved with my family and have been using their C.I's against me who I know personally, even my family are involved. It's all very big and complicated but I assure you all true, I continued to be poisoned for another two periods and my life is still in danger. I have three pieces of evidence that has the substance in and just need the police to do the right thing. I have asked this question many times...Who do you turn for help when the police are the criminals? You and the IOPC I guess. I have been utterly failed by Cleveland Police.

Cleveland Police then got me sectioned again, when I was close to getting an investigation. They have been abusing the mental health act just to shut me up. It will happen again. Like I told you I have irrefutable proof of the poisoning and with the book, is a guide to an investigation, I just need them to test it. It proves my sanity but at the same time proves Cleveland Police's corruption and skulduggery. That's what it is all about, it is about protecting themselves and the public knowledge of their corruption.

My book although long, if you could read it in your spare time you will see I cannot make this up. Help me please, try and force them to take me seriously. I honestly do not think they can investigate this themselves and need to refer themselves to the IOPC, that way I, for the first time, get treated fairly and their corruption gets uncovered. I am trying to survive and get my life back. Am I mentally ill? Well with what I have been through this last year you cannot blame me if I am a little nuts by this point. Read the book, it is shocking but I assure you, every word is true. I never set out to write a book, it is more a witness statement and wrote itself really because without it I cannot sufficiently tell this story. I wish it was as simple as me suffering paranoid delusions and just need some medication but unfortunately that is not so, I am afraid. I have had to be honest about my past and have had a colourful life but please don't hold that against me...

Please help me Matt as my local MP you may be the only person who really can...

Yours Sincerely and Truthfully

Michael Elwood

With this email I sent quite a lot of documentation and the book and in hope he took me seriously I then started a new complaint with the IOPC and the Standard and Ethics department, remember I still had the backy and bottles of sol that had turned up at the side of my home, not much but enough to prove my story and get that investigation. I was palmed off by the standards department predictably so I decided to write a reply. The excuse that Victoria Finnegan kept giving me was the book was too long to read so I decided to condense it down to a more manageable letter that consisted of 5 and a bit pages and then sent the letter to Victoria, Matt the IOPC and the Gazzette...

06/09/2020 Ref – CO/171/20 IOPC Ref – 2019/128021

Dear Cleveland Police, here we are again. I believe there was some confusion on why I made the latest complaint or rather you have purposely given me the run around again so I am going to help you out and put you right so that there are no misunderstandings in the future and hopefully this time I get taken seriously and you finally refer yourselves to the IOPC in this case. The main reason why I cannot get the IOPC to review my case is because you say you have already dealt with the case previously, insinuating that there are no new aspects. Now Miss Finnegan and you in general Cleveland Police know this to be a false hood, now don't we? The problem with that argument is, yes I did indeed make a complaint under both of the above reference numbers back in November and December 2019 however I did not receive an appeal from the IOPC nor did anything get resolved. Why was that? Well Cleveland Police let me tell you why...It was because you, Cleveland Police, on the 6th December 2019 forced your way into my home without a warrant and attacked me and then sectioned me for 24 days under brutal circumstances and helped greatly by my estranged family and corrupt mental health teams, who are also involved in this conspiracy, I was sectioned in Roseberry Park mental hospital. Why did you do this? Let me tell you why, it had nothing to do with my mental health, you were not worried about that, no you were worried about was your corruption being uncovered and still are, let's be honest now Cleveland Police. The other problem with your argument is you have not taken into account, neigh, purposely ignored, are the recent developments in the case. Why have you not acknowledged that I made an official complaint through the proper channels on the 23rd of April 2020 to report this crime and was again met with your astounding incompetence? I had substantial evidence of being poisoned again for what was then the second period and instead of interviewing me and testing the evidence you instead tried and failed to get me sectioned again. I then went very public and you did eventually come to my home with a warrant and trick me into an ambulance and due to the poisoning effects after a third attempt at killing me by poisoning, rather than take me to hospital, I was again taken to Roseberry Park and sectioned and I was denied medical treatment, though I have to state nothing really happened this second time. My mental health on both occasions has been fine and I needed an investigation not two stays in a mental hospital resulting in actual mental illness from those visits due to the medication I was forced to take by corrupt psychiatrists Dr Edera and Dr Kuma. Another aspect is my first time at Roseberry Park Hospital was a completely planned and set up visit where your corrupt elements (6ft 2in, bald, mid to late 50s, wears expensive suits) and one of your C.I's (Stephen Frost – Linked to Roseberry Park staff member Bethan Story) set up and greatly helped by the staff that work there, I was subject to intimidation, secret medication in my food because I did not seem mentally ill, psychologically tortured and attempts were put on certain patients from outside sources (Corrupt element, Rasheed, last name unknown and Stephen Frost) to murder me while I was in there. Thankfully and to my great relief I won my tribunal and was released. After I was released the second time from hospital I spent a month recovering and then on the 3rd of August I then made an official complaint against Cleveland Police using your complaints proceeder. In the email and compliant documents it clearly states my grievances and if you the police had used any due diligence then why have you ignored every single part of it all? I will tell you why...You, the police know I am telling nothing but the truth and you know an official investigation would indeed uncover every fact I have been stating for nearly a fucking year and it would uncover your corruption. There is simply too much evidence out there for an investigation to fail. Fact. This is all about covering your arses nothing more or less, you know it, I know it, the IOPC know it and so do the people who have been bribed and used against me in the endeavour of ending my life. I don't believe that all of the people involved realised what they were getting themselves into and there are a lot of worried people out there now. Well pointing out to them that what they have got themselves involved in is "attempted murder" and "conspiracy to commit murder" it tends to foster anxiety and worry at the realisation because ultimately a lot of otherwise good people have accepted payment and made a big mistake, which now they realise and regret. Lots of scared and weak people to put pressure on, it is too easy to make the people involved crack. Now this fact brings me on to the money side of things and I will take this opportunity to state that in reality a very considerable amount of money has been spent in this conspiracy. For example there are 4 flats out the back of my home and directly behind my neighbours home (Dominic Turnbull involved and bribed) all four have been bought by my uncle, a Martin Elwood, he is the guy at the top in this real true life conspiracy, it is highly likely he achieved this through a LTD company but here is the thing...he is a wealthy man but all his money are in investments, he would not have £600,000 to buy 4 flats and have them sat there empty for a year, who does that? When he purchased the flats, around August last year I believe, the flats were all occupied but have been empty since then. Now I found this strange for sometime because of the money being lost in monthly rent (£600/£650 x 4 pcm) until I realised that right in front of the 4 flats was how people have been gaining access to my back garden and then my home, you see you could, up to 3 months ago until I extended the fence, access my back garden through the bushes and squeeze behind the shed without being seen, however because I did not realise they were empty until around January 2020 and at this point I did not know my neighbours were involved so just assumed it would be too public in front of the flats and then next doors. However when I realised I remembered that the blinds and windows had been shut for months and the last time I heard doors shutting and activity at the flats was August last year, When I thought about it and around the same time I realised my neighbours were indeed involved and it all clicked and I put it together. It baffled me you see, how people were getting in but nobody noticed, now it all made perfect sense. I sent my nasty uncle a copy of my book around three weeks ago, in a fuck you Martin manor and literally 3 days later blinds and windows were suddenly opening after all this time. Nobody lives there its just someone letting themselves in and making it look like somebody lives there. With that many people involved, I will make a list at the end, it is my estimation that my uncle has spent £800,000 to £1,000,000 on this conspiracy. That is the truth and is money he does not have to burn. Where has it come from? I have my suspicions. What this also tells me is the fact that so many people have taken the money I do not believe that it was in cash, no no, bank transfers in my opinion. Another example of evidence that is out there waiting to be discovered. So many aspects to this case of great woe. What else happened that could not be included in the CO/171/20 – 2019/128021 complaint because it hadn't happened yet? Now there is a good question. What we have to cover here is why I made a proper complaint to Cleveland Police on the 23rd April 2020? You know the complaint you have ignored. By this date I had been poisoned again and with food out of my local shop. I know that sounds unlikely but it is true, basically the corrupt elements, Stephen Frost and my niece Laurencia Wood recruited people who work at the shop and it was just around the time that lock down started. I buy pretty much the same when ever I go to the shop and it was easy for them to set this up with a lack of customers. After 4 meals consumed in around 5 days with the poison in I was quite ill but nowhere near as bad as back in October and that was because the food was cooked through so it was more chronic than acute this time round. For example if you roasted the potatoes a red liquid leaked out of multiple pin size holes. After release from hospital the second time around I, in a paddy at my situation and because I had £60 worth of frozen goods and needed freezer space, I unfortunately threw all the poisoned food away that was saved in my freezer. On 4th of May 2020, after three days of visits by you Cleveland police and the mental health teams I was unable to leave my home because of the evidence that I was protecting. A "friend" of mine, a Laura Calvert offered to go to the shop for me, Laura was the only one from my old friends who had not gotten themselves involved in this conspiracy so I decided to trust her. At 09.30 I put my order in and around 12.30 she delivered the goods. I was highly suspicious but needed the supplies. By the 6th of May and after consuming the milk and tobacco that she brought me I was again extremely ill. Because of your refusal to take me seriously and investigate this case, on the 6th May 2020 you came to my home with a warrant and ambulance and took advantage of my condition and with the promise of medical treatment you Cleveland Police, helped greatly by the corrupt mental health teams, tricked me and I was sectioned again. At the time of my, again illegal incarceration to Roseberry Park, I had so much evidence of being poisoned it was ridiculous really but could I get you to take me seriously? No. You knew I was telling the truth but because this case also exposes your corruption it was imperative to shut me up and get me into hospital and on drugs. My mental health again was not a concern but shutting me up was. This Cleveland Police is the truth of the matter. From the 23rd of April to the 6th May 2020 I tried and tried and tried to get you to help me. You again failed me in every way possible. Now I might not have the evidence that I once had but I have kept the tobacco and receipt and it just needs testing. I would love to know the substance used. Laura will have accepted a substantial payment to do this against me as a lot of people have done. Bank statements and phone records are a must here and alone will prove my claims. There are a lot of soft and weak people involved and they would easily crack in an interview. So lets review. • Between Sept and October 2019 I was poisoned on at least least eight occasions over that time after people were entering my home illegally, involving my family and neighbours, all have accepted money, again bank statements to check! • 24th October 2019, 5 attempts were made to stab me on the streets, two on Darlington road and three attempts on Stockton high street. Set up by your corrupt elements and the C.I's. Gary McCarten, Stephen Frost and Tony Carter. This is where CO/171/20 – 2019/128021 ends because it only covers up to the beginning of December 2019! • 6 th December 2019, my home was illegally and forcibly entered by Cleveland Police and I was attacked and illegally detained under the mental health act. • The Bilsdale Ward at Roseberry Park Hospital was completely set up and the staff and patient used against me. I was subject to intimidation, secret medication put in my food, poisoned food brought in from outside sources, phycological torture and outside pressure put on particular patients to try and murder me. This was set up by your corrupt elements (around 6ft 2in, bald, mid to late 50s, large build and in smart suit) Stephen Frost (C.I), Dr Edera and of course Bethan Story. All have again taken bribe money including many others too, those bank statements again! • In April 2020 as lock down started I was again poisoned four times over a week after eating contaminated food purchased from my local shop. I know which staff members are involved although I do not know their names I can easily identify them. • On the 4th of May 2020 I was delivered by a Laura Calvert goods from a shop that were also contaminated for which I still have evidence of. • On the 6th of May 2020 Cleveland Police, instead of investigating my claims I was tricked and again illegally detained under the mental health act. All to shut me up and solve a problem. • I am constantly dodging set ups on a daily basis and my life remains in a lot of danger. I was even brought more goods on the 20th with poison in. The people involved need me to disappear and seen as though everybody who cared about me has got themselves involved in this conspiracy nobody would notice. My life is hell. I am always looking over my shoulder and unable to do things that normal people do all the time because I would just be set up. The people involved, the connection, alleged crime and whether they have accepted a bribe. Cleveland Police Corrupt Element – Name unknown, 6ft 2in, large build, bald, mid to late 50s in smart suits, a chief inspector I would say and C.I handler. He along with my Uncle Martin is the guy at the top running the conspiracy. Will have accepted money and phone records to be checked. He is as bent as they come. Stephen Frost – Cleveland Police C.I, organised the set up mental health hospital visit, organised poisoning and many set ups. Will have accepted money and phone records and need to be checked, though he is a Cleveland Police sanctioned and protected drug dealer so probably uses a burner phone. Gary McCarten – Cleveland Police C.I, was involved in the attempted stabbings and helped organise, is always trying to set me up and continues to plan for my murder. Tony Carter – Cleveland Police C.I, involved in setting up the stabbing attempts on Stockton High Street. Family Martin Elwood – My uncle. The man at the top. The money man. None of this conspiracy would be happening without him. Spent an unbelievable amount of money on this. Laurencia Wood – My niece, instrumental in getting me sectioned twice, instrumental in all the poisonings, instrumental in recruiting everybody around me. Phone records and bank statements need checking definitely. Carla Wood – My sister. As above People around me involved. Dominic Turnbull – Next door neighbour. Instrumental in the poisonings back in Sept/Oct 2019 and also instrumental in allowing people to access my home. Involved in a few set up attempts and definitely taken money, phone and bank records to check. Darren Wilkinson – Lives across the road. Used as look out for when people entered my home. Taken bribe. Bank records need to be checked. Laura Calvert – Ex-friend, she was used to bring me supplies laced with poison. She has taken a bribe and phone records need to be checked, she could also be charged, not with conspiracy to commit murder but actual attempted murder. Employees at my local shop – Names unknown but can identify quite easily. One man and one women, recruited by Laurencia Wood and Stephen Frost. Both part time workers and highly likely that bank records and pressure from detectives would garner excellent results as both are very weak and low paid people. The Bilsdale Ward Dr Edera – The set up could not have happened if Edera was not involved as he is in charge of the ward. A very shifty and devious character, bank records and phone records are a must. He is a very weak man. Bethan Story – Related through marriage to Stephen Frost (Cleveland Police C.I) and instrumental in recruiting other staff members involved. Taken bribe and phone records need to be checked. John Healy – Staff member recruited by Bethan Story, instrumental in organising intimidation, secret medicating in my food, encouraging the patients who were receiving outside pressure to murder me. Took money and bank statements need to be checked. Peter Armstrong – Recruited by Bethan Story and was instrumental in psychological torture, secret medicating. Bribe taken, statements need checking. Joanne Taylor – Recruited by Bethan Story and involved all the way through. Also taken money. Patients – All though I do not know last names, the patients on the ward at the time would be excellent to interview, half were already involved with the staff and the other half noticed what was going on. There would be a few people to interview and frankly that excites me and I believe would garner great results. Other people close to me. "Friends" - There a lot of my friends involved in this and many have taken money and with varying degrees are involved. I will withhold the names until my interview but plenty of weak people involved and I believe with pressure from detectives would also garner great results. Bank and phone records for connections to Laurencia Wood for example, it would all be very fruitful. I hope this clarifies everything for you Cleveland Police/IOPC and that you do the right thing and refer yourself to the IOPC and start an investigation. This is all true and been happening to me. There are so many situations and attempted set ups that I have left out. If you had given me the respect of reading my witness statement you would know this and see I am telling nothing but the truth. This has all been happening to me and Cleveland Police are so far involved that it is a truly shocking story and obvious why you keep giving me the runaround. I know neither you nor the IOPC could not give a shit about me or my life and the IOPC clearly think it is beneath them to investigate this but I will continue to fight this with every fibre of my being for it is my life I am trying to save. If you had done the right thing back in November/December then this would not be happening to me now. The sheer amount of evidence lost through your ignorance and corruption is staggering, though there is still that much evidence out there that even today an investigation could not be anything other than fruitful but herein lies the problem, an investigation really would uncover your whole sale corruption and ultimately that is why we are at this point isn't it Cleveland Police? I am going to be recruiting a solicitor over this coming week and I do not care if I have to speak to every single one in the country, if that fails I will represent myself and will be suing you unless you do the right thing and refer yourself to the IOPC. Do not forget that I was convicted of speeding under false testimony from PC O'Neil back in July 2019, this is actually what turned your force and its corrupt elements against me. You do not like people who stand up for what is right, clearly. I will put the maximum effort in I promise you. Your treatment of me is nothing short of a scandal of epic proportions and along with the corrupt elements involved you Cleveland Police are as culpable as the people who are trying very hard to murder me. I realised the other day that over three periods in the last year I have been poisoned a total of 20 times! How am I still alive? I do wonder and its not due to the lack of effort now is it? Not to mention the countless set ups and stabbing attempts. Help me, interview me, test my evidence, interview people, check bank records, check phone records and clean your police force up at the same time and DO THE RIGHT THING if you are capable of such a thing. Please re-log this complaint using the information and facts you decided to ignore and start an investigation, it is not to late Cleveland Police. Yours Truthfully and Sincerely

Michael Elwood"

Literally a few days after I sent that letter to everybody I get an email from Matt Vickers chief of Staff...

"Many thanks for your email, and apologies for the delay in responding to you. As mentioned in my previous email, due to the complexity of your case and the amount of correspondence you have sent, we wanted to review your case fully before taking any appropriate action.

Looking into your case, it is apparent that you have not yet received any form of response from the IOPC. As this is the case, and the correct process would be for them to look into your case, I can confirm that Matt has raised your case directly with them and has asked them to provide an update.

Once he has received a response, he will of course be in contact with you.

Kind Regards,
Niall.

Niall Innes
Chief of Staff to Matt Vickers MP - Member of Parliament for Stockton South"

I was elated, I finally felt this was it, though we have been here before haven't we but this time I thought it would be different, I had my MP in my corner and the police surely couldn't ignore me now?

Chapter 5

Since my last visit in hospital I had kept in touch with Lauren Jackson from the psychosis team, she rang me once a week and we had a good chat, I enjoyed these talks and even looked forward to them. On the 8th of September I was in a particularly bad mood and I vented on the phone to Lauren Jackson for a good 30 minutes because a good friend of mine had badly let me down well three good friends really and probably my last ones in Teesside, she sounded off with me. I told her about the letter I had sent and even sent her a copy and I also told her about my MP Vickers involvement suddenly going from angry to excited, I said I expected the police to come around with the mental health teams because now I was getting somewhere again. I ended the call quite worried that I was right because twice it has happened at this point before. Next day I get two massive loud bangs at my door, I ignore them then after a few more loud knocks Lauren rings me, too late darling trust has gone. I waited for them to leave and looked out the front bedroom window, two doctors. The next day same again. I ignored them. Then Friday at 5pm the police came with the two doctors with a warrant to enter my home. Knowing what was happening again I decided there and then that I was unwilling to go back to hospital and would rather be shot instead, such was my absolute dismay at what what was transpiring. So I took the handles off of the garage door and armed with an axe and shield I waited for the police to gain access. Which they did and when an officer opened the internal garage door I lifted my axe in the air and he shut the garage door double quickly "He's got an axe and a shield" I then heard armed response requested on the radios by the coppers out on my drive.

One copper, a PC started a conversation up with me and I told him I would rather be shot than go back to Roseberry Park hospital and be forced medication again. He asked me why I was doing this? So through the door I started to tell him the story of what had been happening and read out the letter I had sent. He called for a Detective. A DETECTIVE! Finally I get to talk to a real copper who can help me! I was excited by this.

Here we meet DS Lyndsey Dale, She befriended me straight away and through my garage door, I told her everything that had been going on. There is a video of this on my Facebook page, feel free to watch it. She promised me she would get the evidence tested and read Prixturious and interview me, I was still reluctant to give myself up because I knew I would be sectioned again. Though because of her promises I did. I thought if she tested all the evidence and read the book it would prove my story and I wouldn't be in hospital for very long.

Chapter 6

I was handcuffed and allowed to gather my belonging and I gave DS Dale all the evidence I had and she promised again to get it tested. I believed her. I was then escorted to my drive and a waiting paddy wagon to be greeted by an evening gazette reporter and all my neighbours, obviously excited by the armed police and bit of drama on the street by the supposed mental patient across the road, Fred and Rose would have loved all the drama and what was happening to me now. I was put in the back and set off too Roseberry Park mental hospital again. I was greeted by two Asian psychiatrists and had to tell the the story of what had been happening. Predictably I was sectioned again for the third time in 12 months.

The only thing that was different was I had wrote that letter and got my MP involved. I did not need to be in hospital. I was again under the care of Doctor Kuma and I refused any drugs. Straight away I emailed DS Dale all the supporting evidence...

"Hello Lyndsey, I am ok, gutted to be in hospital and especially Roseberry park but that is the situation unfortunately. You witnessed the mental health teams and your force abusing the mental health act, it is as simple as that.

Please take me seriously and look into this for me like you promised to. I really hope you were serious and not just telling me what I wanted to hear and you have sent the evidence off for a toxicology report. I am genuine and telling nothing but the truth. Please help me Lyndsey

Yours sincerely and truthfully

Michael Elwood"

This is what I received in reply...

"Hello Michael

I am glad you are okay.

I am going to seek advice from scenes of crime regarding any Tox/forensic submissions to see what the feasibility of this is and I will have a full read of your statement/account as we agreed last night.

Lyndsey

**DS 2007 Lyndsey Dale
CID StocktonTeam"**

The email was the only correspondence that DS Dale afforded me. I had just given all my evidence to the enemy and the enemy had fucked me over...You should have seen that coming Michael...

Now I had nothing left to fight for, with the evidence gone my fight went with it. After 3 weeks I was given an ultimatum by the doctors, take the medication to get out or we will force it on you. Medication I don't need. I relented. After another 4 weeks I was told I was getting 2 weeks leave and then would be discharged. This was, due to my community team, denied. Apparently the want to see the medication change me, from what to what they cannot tell me...I was angry and gutted.

After I was admitted to the PQ ward, which is a special high security ward, the first time on this ward and my second admission to hospital I never once seen a staff member from the Bilsdale ward, not this time though I have seen everyone who was involved in the first visit back in December 2019 and then just after my leave was denied Bethan Story appeared. She was in the office having a right good old catch up with the nurses, I saw red at the sight of this evil women, I called her some not very nice names and stupidly told her I would be coming for John Healy and Peter Armstrong, threats? Not really just me angry and venting. Well they have used that to refer me to what is called a "Forensics Ward" It is a mental health prison basically and yesterday the 23rd of December I was assessed for acceptance to this ward. I was informed that, if accepted I would be on the ward for one year minimum and up to 18 months! I really should have seen the set up with Bethan Story, I fell for it hook line and sinker. FUCK. I find out on the 3rd of December weather or not I get "accepted" I have been on this ward since September and in that time I have been with patients who have threatened the staff directly and even assaulted them and they have not been referred to a forensics ward. I do not suffer any diagnosable mental illness, the doctors are even wrong on the paranoid delusions, I am being set up and fucked over in the worse possible way by every aspect of the establishment in Teesside. My fight is over they have won. I cannot nor will I go to a forensics ward for over a year, something I definitely do not deserve. Remember I am telling the truth and nothing but the truth yet it is I who is being punished without trial or judge and jury. I am dumbfounded but resigned to the decision being made. So what now for Michael Elwood and this sad story of woe? A story of a man who had greatness in him but was oppressed and set up by those who were supposed to love him, help him, guide him? In truth? I cannot do over a year with no internet or any freedoms what so ever, make no mistake the forensics is a prison without trial or jury. I have made the decision to kill myself in my cell using my mattress cover and jamming it in my door. I cannot live this life any more and the torture of being continually fucked over. I have no prospects and no dreams I can see coming true. I am done and just now want the eternal sleep and to be with my Dad, my Mum, Steven and Jane...at least they know the truth.

To Carla and Laurencia Wood, Martin Elwood Paul Dawson, Stephen Frost, Garry McCarten, Tony Carter, Bethen Story, John Healy, Peter Armstrong, Rasheed, Dominic Turnbull (Fred) Darren Wilkinson, Cleveland Police and the Mental Health teams...I hope you all burn in hell for what you have done to me and I haunt all your dreams. All of you against little old me, I did not stand a chance. You are all truly Prixturious...

Authors Notes

Its okay, I did not kill myself in the end because forensics thankfully, would not accept me as I did not meet the criteria. I was at my lowest ebb through all of this because of the set up with Bethan Story on the ward. She accused me of threatening to kill her, she also falsely said I tried to get to her in the office to hurt her, she also said I had searched her on Facebook and threatened her, all the allegations were false and designed to make me get sectioned for 18 months on the forensic wards. The two nurses present backed me up and let it be known she was lying. She really is an evil and despicable women and should have been sacked long ago. I have since realised that my first visit to a mental hospital where I was set up was all about getting me on a forensics ward and when that clearly wasn't working then that's when they started to pressure Baraket to hurt me.

My Uncle Martin confirmed to me the other day he does in fact own the flats at the back of my home. I have seen my cousin there and then heard Martin shout at her that I was watching as she left and said something through the window to him, she ran off at that. Martin Elwood is the top man behind everything that has been happening to me. He is a despicable human being and karma will do for you Martin. You were an evil man when I lived with you and you are an evil man now. Mick Elwood, my father can see you for what you are now.

I was released from hospital after 4 months. I have to state that the staff on the PQ ward, I have very unfairly visited twice now, are all good eggs and never did anything wrong to me. Good people. They know I am telling the truth and I was only released because they put their collective foot down. They also now know Bethan Story as the liar she is. I hope they reported her.

What now for Michael Elwood? I still think I am on borrowed time and no matter where I go or what I do I am doomed. I am going to try though. I have decided I am going to University to study business studies and in a few years get the investment needed to get Parmo's nationwide and create my Dominos style takeaway chain (If Martin doesn't do it first, if he does it will be the straw that broke the camels back and make me the evil one) The location I move too will be a closely guarded secret but it wont take much to find me. I figure if I get a good 6 months of a new life I will be happy. I am going to try at least.

Too Carla and Laurencia Wood, you both have broken my heart. I know you Carla now regret getting involved and are remorseful so I forgive you, though will never speak to you again. Laurencia you are pure evil just like Bethan. I will never forgive you. I hope karma comes for you soon. You and your mum were both blinded by greed and I hope it was worth it.

To Rose, I forgive you too and hope you find the strength to leave Fred. You are a good person and only got involved quite late so I will give you a pass. Fred? Your turn to look over your shoulder my boy along with Uncle Martin, Laurencia, Bethan, Laura Calvert as you are the most evil in this story. I might come for you all one day or I might not. Depends if I survive long enough I suppose. I guess you better get to me first though its not through lack of trying now is it?

To the gangsters and Rasheed, you did nothing that wasn't expected of you. You are sociopathic scum by nature and there is nothing to forgive, though I might come for you 4 too one day...

Wish me luck, whoever reads this, I am going to need it.

The End? I really fucking hope so...

Bonus Material

Not required reading

Only if interested...

The Brexit Article

So do I still think the EU is involved? All I can say is I got right under the skin of Guy Verhofstad and have included an article I wrote and sent out to the papers, well it was intended for Guy's Page to begin with but it never appeared when I tried to upload it though it did disappear so its safe to say Guy has read it. Now whether they are involved I don't know but it is actually possible that Guy and my uncle Martin are connected and this article may have been the moment when my uncle Martin turned. The article was written just after part one when I was still buzzing with inspiration. It was around the time my family started the mental health rumours in August 2019, just before it all kicked off. I love this piece of writing and believe it makes the case for leaving, what every Brexiteer would want to say. I was sick of the negative and insulting actions of the EU against leavers and especially Guy so I decided to start sticking up for leavers and kick back. Now the biggest one "Leavers are that thick they just didn't know what they were voting for" really pissed me off so I wrote a reply. I have to say I may have strayed into troll territory but my reply to something would always be courteous and well thought out in a Good Sir nature and never actually offended really but were clever and true and pointed out the error of their ways. I would always get jumped on by his fans of course and I always replied in a Good Sir manner and even shame a few into apologising to me. I always used facts and figures and was good at it and effective. Until the Facebook comment featured in the story below, no that one went mad. Lots of replies and likes and some good questions so I decided to educate Guy and his fans but it didn't go as planned and the article was never read by them though Guy will have read it and a lot of papers too. I sent it to both Brexit and Remainer papers. Anyway you decide and I hope you enjoy reading it as much as I did writing it...the same as with part one. Big difference in the writing or rather part one and the article are inspired writing as I call it.

The Brexit Bible

I have to start by explaining that I'm not a "Troll" usually, anyway. Accidental Troll? That may just be true after I come across an arrogant, Guy Verhofstad Post shared by his Facebook Page, on my news feed whilst scrolling, the title insinuated that "Britain is fighting for its soul!" I naturally took that to mean "Stay in the EU and save your soul Great Britain" or something along those lines, I wouldn't know because I never get around to actually reading any of his posts because usually just the fact its Guy and the title are

enough to piss me off and make me decide, I have to post something in retort and stick up for us

Leavers. Usually I don't provoke anybody, not this time though..

"Yes and Great Britton will indeed win back it's soul from the soulless and fanatical European Union of which Guy, you are the undisputed poster boy and represent everything that is wrong with the EU. The United Kingdom owes you a great service and gratitude! Every time you appear on UK TVs you gift the "Soul Returning Multi Deal" cause thousands of new ex-remainer recruits...We thank you immensely Guy, we really do."

Here's the thing, I accidentality made the mistake of using Britton spelt with two Ts, instead of Britain. Grammatical mishap you would say? No Big deal you might think? Well not with EU fans it seems, Prejudice borne out of Ignorance, concerning the fact I'm a proud Leaver and have been for over 20 years. A working class boy, youngish, 36, likes a laugh, loves his Queen and his Country and its rich, proud history. Some good, some bad and especially bad, from which are born the lessons that make countries grow. He love's everything that makes Great Britain erm, Great Britain and the British Erm, British. Harpers for the good old days when there was respect and people still had integrity and were proud of it. The "Good Sir" and" My Word is my Bond" ethos, sadly to me, seems to be lost.. A time lost when all those treasured traditions and morals where earned and returned. Ol'school street parties you don't see any longer. The sense of community that feels like it has sadly been lost. I am what you could describe as "The Perfect, Remainer Termed, Stereo Typical, Bigoted, Little, Englander" Yes Remainers that is exactly what we are, every single one of us, Millions of others too, good folk, decent folk, with the ability to think and form an opinion, they knew exactly what they were voting for, just like you or unlike you I think sometimes. All of the prejudiced and Ignorant, assumptions are outrageous. Doctors, Directors, Business Owners, Farmers, Fishermen, Executives, Factory

Workers, Vets, Charity Workers, Self Employed, Retirees, University Students, Artists, Musicians, Actors, Politicians, Black, White, Asian, Immigrants, the list on diversity within the Leave voting community, is endless and all, no matter who you are, you are included in these horrible slurs on Leavers characters. I've lost count of the amount of times we hear our characters dragged through the dirt. "They are too stupid to have known what they were voting for" "Bigoted Racists the lot of them" they cry. "They cannot ever explain why they want to leave!?" These comments made me angry and inspired me to write a reply and challenge the terrible views of the EU and Remainers alike. So I did just that. If a leaver ever gets asked again "Why did you vote leave" Just politely show them this article that resonates and hits the metaphorical nail on the head with the majority of Leavers in my opinion and maybe even some Remainers too, I believe. This will be, of course wishful thinking? Probably but I would like a crack at it, nonetheless. I fully expect, the latter to still attempt to try to argue, mind. Bring it on. Every Brexit Supporting Paper and Magazine should chip in and make a kind donation to the Michael Elwood Entrepreneur fund and print and support this story in solidarity with all the Leavers of this Great Union. Show the World we can have a back bone and regain much lost respect. Let us all unite and really get the Leave cause to where it needs to be and face these Remainers like never before and get the masses Spiritually, re-woken from their politically ignorant slumber. What a way to show Remainers and the World. Every, Brexit Supporting Newspaper, Magazine, Brexit Website, Facebook Page and of course every single Leaver, coming together in Solidarity, in Honour of Queen, Country, Leavers and Democracy. Let's make this Reply to Guy, The EU and Remainers alike, The Brexit Bible for the Leave Masses. All the countries publications coming together in support would be amazing and just what is needed and I think would be the real story, of the story, so to speak and could depart a fair few column inches and make a splash online and on TV news around the World. For if, the Press can come together, bearing in mind you don't really like to even acknowledge each other under normal circumstances, it would make the people of this great country and the world, sit up and take note. The situation is definitely in the top ten of instances that the press should, Indeed work together in a common cause. People would have to take notice. Make people really think about the Issue and as the Press are the public's mouth-piece and support, whist always protecting Democracy and what is right, the Press are perfect to deliver the message and I hope you can see the, play? I'd push it all day long if I was editor of a paper that's for sure. There really are multiple angles and benefits to this Story. Let us take a look. You would be helping the rise of an excellent Writer, Entrepreneur and General Opinionated Gob Shite, One. The Well, Written Arguments, Two. Helps bring awareness to Prejudices and Provokes Old Fashioned Debate and makes Leavers happy to finally be understood and that is what the story invokes all the way through...that and Brexit

Pride, Hopefully, Three. In modern times, how people feel comfortable to abuse a stranger they have never met and only because you have the audacity to share a different view point to them. This is a shocking realisation, with faceless technology it seems we are seeing a serious degradation in human decency, general kindness and respect, Four. Galvanising, Leaver Masses, Five. We give The Ignored and Forgotten Majority a Voice, Six. Selling more papers, Seven. We all receive more Brand Exposure for all of us. Including me, Eight. Remainers forced to pay attention and will be confronted, Nine, Make people believe in the free press again, Ten. Shut Anna Soubry Up, Hopefully, Eleven. the Press Gets to Look Good for a Change and Everybody Wins, Twelve. The Press can claim the accolade of being the bargainers of the rise of Michael Elwood, hope the world's ready? That's the biggest one so I can't number that one thirteen because that's just unlucky, twelve plus will have to do. Let's help Boris and JRM get Brexit done. The Country needs us. Both need a hand as currently they are right up against it. Here is my reply to all the EU, Remainers and Leavers, alike...

Above I added when I sent to the press, below is what I sent to Guy's Facebook Page.

"Hello all. I have to say it seems I might have provoked a reaction from Guy fans and EU lovers alike. I have not ever been a "troll" before and would never set out to be one but good old Guy just brings it out in me. What I didn't expect was the absolute gold that people have written in the comments! I left the post all day and night and I thank you because you made my Sunday morning and I have been absolutely crying with laughter and literally howling! Brilliant! Now I should have known better, I admit. I am a realist and I realise that Guy/EU lovers are incapable of agreeing with leavers and vice versa and that's as concrete as the sun coming up and I apologise unreservedly. I guess if we've learned anything then it's this..."If Mikey Elwood did trolling full time, well, he'd be The Best Troll...In the World..". Deirdre Johnston "Mikey Elwood You are the perfect example of why so many of the fooled voted leave in the first place – uneducated and lacking in critical thinking skills." As for accidentally using Britton instead of Britain, then yes you are correct I am indeed an Uneducated, Bigoted, Narcissistic, Islam-phobic, Xenophobic, Racist and Far Right Little Englander, it seems this is how all of the EU fanatics see the majority of Great Britton's leave voting community. However, if you have this view then really it is you who are the ignorant protagonists in this whole sorry tale. You have to understand that there are really only five million fanatical remain voters in this country. Admittedly a very vocal and powerful cabal, nevertheless they are the minority. It seems after the referendum leave voters lifted their foot off of the gas in satisfaction at the win, content to slip back into a politically ignorant life and normal service was resumed. Letting MPs in like Anna Soubry...Every time I look at this woman and hear her speak I just think to myself "My God she would definitely be a Moscow 'Useful Idiot' in a film" in reality she wouldn't even qualify for that... This allowed remain voting MP's to be voted in by Pissed off and Pride Bruised Remainers to populate Parliament at the proceeding general election. Michael Gove has a lot to answer for here. It has to be said that these fanatical 'not fit for purpose' two bit politicians are even representing staunchly leave voting constituent like me and my pathetic Labour MP for Stockton South Dr Paul Williams. The constituency where I live voted overwhelmingly for Brexit. He has since the election, voted with remain tendencies ever since. When challenged about his blatant treachery he just professes that he knows better than the majority of his constituents. Erm, I beg your pardon you arrogant man? The problem is that the other millions that voted remain are not that fanatical on the EU and can see that the country voted leave and actually just want the democratic result of the referendum to be respected and enacted. Not one of these moderate remain voters and Leavers alike, are pleased with how Brexit has transpired since and just want it bloody sorted. Now! Multi Deal, or Not. Without, I beg you, the horrid Withdrawal Agreement at the least. I still don't know whether to laugh or cry that Mrs May let the EU write it...Mr Gove, MP for Surrey Heath, you are Indeed a twat and I hold you personally responsible for the last 3 years and not you Mrs May. No just you Mickey for enabling Mrs May to have a crack at it in the first place... Everybody in this country, except those five million or so, are sick to back teeth of this sh*t and if no deal means it is finally at an end then so be it. That is the majority attitude in this country and the majority of polls support this view. The 5m Fanatical Remainers, in the London bubble that they live, are totally oblivious, to all of this of course and only listen to people like them. The BBC...On borrowed time with that licence fee! No free licence for over 75's has done for you BBC and you should be thoroughly ashamed you greedy institution. I've had a look at your published accounts and believe within an hour I could save that much money you would be able to pay for the new policy of "Free TV Licenses for the over 65s" I'll do it for free too...I can think of the first deserving £1.75m that can be easily cut from the budget...

Michael McFarlane

"Sue Blower Why is it those of a certain political persuasion can't spell or 'do' grammar? It's almost as though there's an inverse relationship between being right wing / pro-hard leave and levels of intelligence? Fancy that."

David Howe

"Michael McFarlane strange but true.... and then they get offended when it is pointed out that

they're a bit, erm, thick... so patriotic he thinks he lives in Britton"

As I was saying, the BBC, Channel 4, Sky News etc, all are blinded to the rest of the country, stuck in that London bubble and are all mainly remain voting lefties anyway, as is the civil service, all too caught up in Remainer indignation and wrongly believing that is how the rest of the country feel. Not realising we are looking on with dismay and bemusement and would laugh hysterically if I wasn't so f@&king sad and infuriating. Impartial my arse and all of you strangely, share the ridiculous views on the characters of the 17.4m + (many more now I believe) people of an entire nation. You all should be ashamed of yourselves. I'm thinking you especially Gary Lineker and the ex living legend that is Elton John, though grudgingly Big E, I still love your music and that will always be so. Quite...

Peter Emerson-Darnell

"Jason Warne we are not upset just completely disbelieving in the continued gnorance and childish stupidity still being shown by leave voters after over 3 years, which your post typifies!!" Those of you who have just hurled abuse at me, as funny as they are, you all need to realise that insults are the lowest and least intelligent form of debate and I'd counter that in this scenario, it is you my dear friends that are the trolls and not in fact, I...I hope your parents are all really proud..."

Michael Igoe

"David Richard

Gilbertson : I have often noticed the high level of illiteracy and general ignorance in leavers. I wonder if Mikey could tell us in what way the EU is fanatical. I'd like to see an example" Now I will reply to some of the more measured messages...

Big Kieth Unwin

"Mikey Elwood you seem a very clever guy, (Erm) perhaps you could help I've asked so many leavers 2 things,firstly laws can you please let me know a law that we haven't been able to pass because the eu has stopped us that effects our every day life. Secondly could you tell us a mandate from the eu that had adversely affected your life. I wonder do you get up in the morning and say Christ if we wasn't in the eu I could go out and live my life.as you voted out you must be able to pin your reason down or is it the same as 99% of leaver immigration !"

Keith Unwin, you asked some very good and pointed questions and I will do my best to answer as clearly and concisely as I am able, my Good Sir...

"EU Laws and/or laws that have not been able to pass that affected me personally?" I have to start with my experiences in the HGV Industry and

Motorcycling Licensing as perfect examples of EU "Idiocracy" that I like to call it."

The Dictionary of Good Sir.

Idiocracy -

Pronounced with two O's next to one another - Definition - Laws and regulations that make one think "Who the f&£k thought that was a good idea??"...

The HGV industry is on its knees in this country and for many reasons. With the EU Directive Driver Time Regulations AND EU Directive Working Time Regulations you literally need a masters in "Idiocracy" to fathom what the f&£k

you are supposed to be doing or more importantly, not doing at any one time. Any Newbie that stupidly choose this career path, instead of driving and learning the ropes, spends his/hers first 6 months confused and panicking about the most complicated bloody rules the world has ever seen for something that should be really bloody simple! If the Newbie is unlucky enough to get pulled by the biggest most evil, narcissistic, peculiar and gleeful type of arsehole populating the independent body that is VOSA...usually with much needed police protection...then unlucky my boy or girl you are likely to receive a gleefully written up, large fine, yes you, not the company! All the while, being fleeced by your agency, who now shamefully even make you pay to process your own wages, the Bastards! Oh and by the way welcome to the Industry and Happy Hanukkah... Even drivers of 20 years haven't got a scooby half the time in certain situations and even Google won't help you and that's saying something...Don't get me started on the driver CPC, what a waste of time and energy that is and is also an EU directive, it is the biggest example of EU red tape waste that there is. Instead of doing something that makes sense? The biggest that I could see was not making trucker Nav's compulsory and avoid all the bridge strikes that we get. With a Trucker Nav you put in the dimensions, weight and speed of your tractor unit and trailer in the Nav and the device makes sure you don't go down any restricted routes that breach those settings. Though you still get all the pitfalls of any Sat Nav and a bit of common sense is required and sadly missing those two quite important tools means accidents galore. It's currently a "here's the keys and off you go" type Industry, there are a few exceptions like P.D Ports, who nurture and guide new drivers properly. Transport companies like PD who care about their drivers work/home life balance, their driver skills and development, need the credit when it's due. Keep it up. Instead of regulation it should be on the job training and experience and focused on skills and confidence building. Game changer bit of kits and only half of drivers use them shockingly, especially it seems not very many idiot HGV drivers. A company that shall remain unnamed even forbids the use of Trucker Navs! You What?? Most of the good drivers jacked it in years ago. It baffles me why you would not use a Trucker Nav, they really are worth their weight in gold to drivers and transport companies alike. Sometimes it's because older driver are stubborn and think they would not be the same "proper driver" if they used one instead of a old map but they are very experienced and already have been to most places as you do get about a bit. Sometimes its cost, they range from £80 to £600. Though mix a Newbie and Google maps or normal car Sat Nav and you are asking, no positively begging, for it to go wrong... That's just a couple of aspects of the problems in the Heavy Good industry and you can not totally just blame the EU. No, there are many, many other varied factors but namely unscrupulous transport companies and the not very nice and devoid of any scruples, including but not limited to, humanity, integrity, humility...I can lack this sometimes, actually I might not of learnt this one quite yet, I'm working on it though...sympathy or general human decency...Driver Employment Agencies. Some of the girls in the industry haven't quite gone over to the dark side yet but with the men in the Industry it's a prerequisite for the job it seems and are good at keeping testosterone levels naturally high in drivers and on a fresh daily basis... Another good point of the consequences of this cartel like and low paid Industry is the fact the UK has had to bribe, not very skilled and accident prone drivers from elsewhere in the EU with a 10 year British pension! Work in the UK for 10 years and we will pay you £145 a week for the rest of your life! Nice work if you can get it and I don't blame one person who accepted the deal, good luck to you but if the EU did not help with over regulation then maybe there would not be 3 million UK nationals with HGV entitlements not working in the Industry and maybe, just maybe the UK government wouldn't have had to make such ridiculous offers to other EU nationals to entice them to work here? Maybe? You think?

Personally I would of made that offer to UK lorry drivers, that would of been nice wouldn't it? Would sort the chronic driver shortage out in one fell swoop that would, couldn't do that though could they? Let's look to bikes and EU licensing. The motorcycling community has seriously been affected by the EU's directive on motorcycling licensing and the mad hoops that you have to jump through to get through to the Big bike licence. For a young person it has literally quadrupled the price and would take a 17 year old 4 years to get a full licence! That is ridiculous and is stopping new young blood from getting in the motorcycling game. By the time they hit 21 the youngsters have cars, jobs, girlfriends/boyfriends and the initial excitement at 16 on a moped is lost and then so are they. When they look later at what they have to do to gain a full license they are simply put off, it is only the most determined youngsters that persevere or many just don't bother or some end up riding regardless without one and without the benefits of proper experience and training. Though I have to say, I see some very skilled 'outsiders' to the motorcycling community on a daily basis. Seems not having a license to worry about you are, more inclined to ride like you stole it...There's a lesson there somewhere, the Rebels...with a dodgy cause...Usually Whenever I go to a bike meet I get depressed with the average age at these events because it gets higher every year and is heartbreaking and the EU licensing and to a lot lesser extent, a lack of grass route motorsport academies in this country and a generally anti motorcycle public are all shockingly to blame, especially when you think of the congestion and pollution savings benefits over cars. There is one funny EU rule that I came across Keith and that is in one of the manoeuvres that you have to perform in the off road part of the motorcycle test. After you follow cones, set out as a sweeping bend, you have to do an emergency swerve and then an emergency stop between four cones. However, you also have to hit minimum speed just before the emergency swerve. 32mph. Not 30mph, no no, but 32mph and all because some prat at the EU forgot, when writing the legislation, to put mph figures in for the UK in brackets and we have to work to kmh which was 50kph or 32mph...you failed at 31.9 mph WTF! REALLY? I don't know who is more stupid the EU for the oversight or the UK for blindly following this daft, regulation? You really couldn't make this sh*t up Keith! Want it changed? Yeah good luck as now you have to butt heads with the all seeing and all knowing EU Council and another 27 nations...Or maybe the government at the time, didn't give enough of a sh*t to even try?

Derek Angelo Ardito

"David Howe think you

are being very politely BRITISH sir, (in the nicest way) saying " a bit thick" they are tremendously, stupidly , not only thick but ever so ignorant, can't decide what they voted for exactly, or give any reason why other than xenophobia in their superiority complex."

I was in my mid 20s when this happened after I had a driving run in with the law and had to do an extended retest as punishment, I was already quite an experienced biker by then and in practice I couldn't get the required speed in second gear on such a shed of a bike. I got 28 then 30 in the two practice runs and you only get 2 attempts on test. I was on a 100k mile Suzuki GS500 that had seen its best days a long, long time ago and in second gear with such little space I just couldn't get the bloody thing above 30mph. "I approached the start of the 'cones of curves' smoothly tipping in, as I straighten the bike up I suddenly I give the bike full throttle but this time in first gear to ensure I get the acceleration I needed, the bike now suddenly transforms into the young, fast buck that she used to be, instead of the tractor she was in second, as if it was muscle memory from her glorious past, she sets off in a fury of revs and speed. I go through the speed lights and instantly letting the throttle spring back from full throttle to the closed stop, I did the emergency swerve immediately after, quick as a flash, then hard on the front brake, squeezing the leaver as hard as I could, foot pressing down firmly on the rear brake but just enough to get maximum braking without the rear locking, the suspension compressed to maximum then into the emergency stop area, the rear wheel skipping and hopping into the 4 emergency stop cones and...shit I'm not going to make it...trying to scrub as much speed as possible...ssshhhhiiiitttt...with just an inch or two to the furthest two cones, I had made it...Just...I looked over at my instructor, his head in his hands looking like he was coughing but was actually laughing, the extremely bemused looking examiner was laughing too and as I switched the bike off he said it was "Quite possibly a British record if not European but luckily for you my lad, there's no failure for how fast you can perform it...Thankfully" "How fast through the lights did I go like?" "Forty Four miles per hour!!" (70.8 kph) We had a right laugh on the one hour on road part a few weeks later and I was on new machinery too, bonus...it was more a spirited ride out with an old friend than a test after that performance, I passed too with 2 minors...True story... Ken when you say "What laws have we been unable to pass" it instantly makes me think of a misunderstanding of what we mean by regaining sovereignty from the EU. It's not the domestic laws that we've been unable to pass but the regulations that could really benefit this country. With regulations it is really the EU that shapes and runs this country. For example the Steel Industry, Fishing Industry, Farming Industry, Tech Industry, Small Businesses...You could go on and on, the list is endless really but we currently are very restricted on what we can do to help grow sustainable industries like these when we are so hampered by the EU rules we signed up too. Ultimately you cannot create any laws or regulations, that directly contravenes an EU law or regulation/s or one of the main principles of the EU. Like government business financial aid for example and yes Ken that eye rolling word, immigration. When I say regaining Sovereignty what I mean is "Over all control on the shape of this country by the people who live and reside in it and to the best interests of this land and its inhabitants, human or otherwise and while also working towards the Worlds

Interests" Not a cartel of 27 nations who all need different things to each other to thrive and controlled mainly to the benefit of Germany and to a lesser extent France. The EU economic model is a disaster and even Guy himself says the only solution to the, 'Was always going to be, from conception, a known to be completely flawed economic model'...that is a quote from me and not Guy...is by giving ever more powers to Brussels. Basically if you read between the lines he is saying, national governments should just become local EU assemblies and total control over everything, or in other words an EU Super state, is the only solution. Now I'm not trying to scare anybody but the thought of an EU army scares the shit out of me and really you ought to be scared too. There is one good point Keith and silver lining though, it would mean substantially more budget for the UK's military as we need to be 100 steps ahead at all times. Luckily we are already a thousand steps ahead militarily speaking...For the United States of Europe to work, Guy is, I'm afraid, Keith, sadly right in my opinion. Here's the crux Keith, for the EU Super State ideology to happen, the EU needs the UK in lock & stock. It needs the UK to adopt the Euro. It needs control over the London financial markets. It needs access to our industry to redistribute it where it sees fit. It needs its very own central bank in charge of us and controlling our monetary policy. It needs our military expertise and counter intelligence skills to be used for its benefit. It needs total control Keith to succeed in its goal. This would be the result of the UK being in an EU Super State. This is Guys and the EU's open, destination. They don't hide this and it is the ultimate goal of the EU Super State Project. In one go, the EU suddenly becomes the biggest economy in the world and much more powerful than the EU is currently. Looking at the EU hierarchy and how they choose the three presidents. There is not one semblance of democratic process involved. This worries the hell out of me Keith. Can I be the only one to see past history lessons and the easy ways history could be easily repeated again? Did we not learn anything Keith? How do we stop fascists from taking over if the UK is in lock stock and whole? Who would there be to stop it? With the UK in full bore in the EU project then the US doesn't really give two sh*ts about Europe at that point and boom there goes the backup Keith, let's be realistic. We will always be friends with America if we are Independent and for many reasons and I am of the opinion that the "Special Relationship" is kind of crucial to European stability and for the foreseeable future will be required. Now here's the controversial bit, it's my view that the EU needs an independent and strong UK as a deterrent and to be kept honest. That is if you are able to look at those valuable past history lessons and realise maybe, just maybe it's a good thing to not have a Super State with total control over every aspect and facet of every single person and everything single thing in Europe. Ergo it is a good thing the UK leaves the EU and the other 27 nations come to see us as a friendly insurance policy for the citizens of the EU. That would be nice. Let's be honest we don't really have a great track record as a continent now do we? We simply cannot be trusted as a continent to let one institution have that much control over everything. If history teaches us anything then maybe, just maybe that might be, a bad idea that, Keith. No UK involvement? No problem and crack on with the Super State. Good luck too. That's my feeling on it anyway Keith, I hope I've explained my points well enough my Good Sir and I thank you for the questions and hope you found it a good read but in answer to your question about waking up and thinking about the EU...When I get up the first 20mins are spent generally looking at a kettle boil and then I make coffee, then feed the dogs, then drink coffee, all the while with nothing in my brain but white noise. After those 20 minutes of burping, farting and coughing and wondering who the f@&k I am, I then spend around 20/40 mins in the bog of inspiration or despair, depending on what I ate the night before and only actually think about the EU if I happen upon a Guy post in my news feed...though I have been known to wake up whistling "God Save the Queen" and "We are the Champions" strangely...Hope this helps Keith...

Willie Cruikshank

"Mikey Elwood great I am all for it, tally ho and all that, but if you really want to go it on your own, why the need to drag Scotland an N.Ireland with you ?."

Good question and the simple answer is, majority vote rules in the United Kingdom and it's Union. My answer to both is if you would like to go it alone and feel really aggrieved then feel free to have a democratic vote, nothing would really change, in fact England and Wales would highly likely receive a decent windfall in finances and more money per capita! Maybe pay our pensioners a decent weekly, £145 a week, what a disgrace! Cut Vat and Abolish Income Tax! Sounds like quite an exciting scenario when you think about it and should not be feared on that basis. I'm warming to this idea... 60% of Scottish trade is with England and Wales, it's just not going to stop because the Scotts decided to, trade Westminster for Brussels...Nor would trade with the EU, just because England and Wales swapped Brussels for Queen and Country. I find this so Ironic and in equal measures, moronic thinking, I have to say rightly or wrongly but I digress, what the f&@k do I know, really? Britain will always include Scotland and Northern Ireland whether it is on paper or not in my opinion but like any member of any family, eventually you need to fly the coup and make your own way. England and Wales, the family to both of you that we are and always will be, means we bloody well should help you in this noble endeavour in any way we can if that is Indeed your countries democratic wish and who can argue? Always in the knowledge, as any family member would expect, that we are here for you if it ever does go, erm, tits up... A good few people mentioned the ridiculous myth concerning Brexit supporters and their views on, Immigration. I'm not anti Immigration. Nor, are most people. Or are we anti Races. Or anti the Muslim community. Or, anti most things, within reason. No I see the benefits of immigration it just needs to be properly controlled. The People we need, not just anybody. I would also point out that the three million Europeans living in the UK are all welcome and know the major majority, are grafters and if it was up to me I'd give you all passports right now. Immigration, it seems, is massively complex but should be a much better managed issue and past governments have a lot to answer for. The speed at which we have let people in was a bit silly really and rightly or wrongly has changed the landscape of a lot of towns including mine. I see the businesses that immigrants have opened or the jobs filled that they do on a daily. Anybody who comes here for a better life and to contribute has my full backing and bloody good luck to you. But with that welcome does come, a certain responsibility to the culture and hosts of said country. I don't care where you are from or which Imaginary god you love and definitely not bothered one Iota about any humans, pigmentation. No you are afforded the same respect I give to ANY person I meet and are assumed to be a good person no matter who you are and it's your actions that will form my opinion of you and not those other things like race and pigmentations. I am, however going to take offence if you want to destroy British culture and want to make here like there and if that's the case then you should be

made to go back there. Those feelings are natural really...or are they? I'm not so sure in today's times anymore... It's my feeling that it is too late do anything about Tony Blair and his New Labours Multicultural Vision. It's here to stay and we need to live with it. Starting to control Immigration better from Oct 31st is a smart move and a points based system based on our skill requirements is simply a sensible policy. The labour multicultural vision I realise now, with hindsight, it had to happen by the back door under that multicultural banner to feed the worlds capitalist economic growth model that realistically by design, is a unsustainable and a dying economic world model, with no future but that's a whole different debate. I have to say I have met some wonderful people in the immigrant community and I do see the benefits... Someone said about the "Undemocratic way that Parliament was, Prorogued!" That was not undemocratic, my god really? It was a matter of routine and actually only lost a few days debate and the government was quite within its rights as was my dear Queen. The irony is strong on this one... ...no! No! NO!What is undisputedly undemocratic is an openly treasonous, conspiracy to overturn a legitimate referendum vote and a democratic national vote no less, with the goal to remain in the EU by traitorous Remain MP's and their scheming and tricks along with a complete tool of a speaker and the weakest Labour Leader/Man?/Binary/Person/living thing/even down to the molecular level of life forms weakerthangravityeven. Let's not forget you Michael Gove. It was only the biggest vote in UK history to boot too. That should replace the Oxford dictionary definition of "undemocratic". Let's start a petition. I am all for an election before October 31st. I believe it would be another referendum re run and should not be feared. We stand up and shout louder than anybody. Waking the sleeping masses from their blissful, envied and politically ignorant lives! Oh, how we look on in pure jealousy. Let us show this 5 million Remainer cabal what's what in this land and fight for what is right and take back control and starting with the abomination of absolutely treacherous remain MPs in Parliament, especially those who represent leave voting areas, that definitely means you Anna my dear and most definitely you Dr Paul Williams MP for Stockton South, I'll make sure of it. This would be a really good idea and definitely worth the risk. If nothing else it will shut Mrs Soubry up... We as a society really, really do need to look out for Labour postal vote rigging. Very important matter this is, I would say. I do not trust those dodgy Labour Momentum thugs keeping old Jezza in power over in the confused Labour camp. Whether they will just be manipulating the rules or something illegal, I believe some historically, closely contested seats will be won with some skulduggery. I'd get MI5 on the case as this matter is definitely in the public's Interest and I would say exactly what a home grown secret service should defend. Though I have to say, I believe Remainers are actually scared of a General Election or even a Referendum. They know in their own hearts they would get trounced in either scenario but especially in an election as they realise a lot of P45 could be making the way to so many of Remainers constituencies current MP's. That fact, my fellow leavers, scares the sh*t out of them. The only goal is to stay in the EU no matter what. I can imagine gold plated EU jobs are the ultimate goal here probably even promised. The fact Remainers won't get behind a no deal and no deal being the only bargaining chip really just proves how much Michael Gove and Teresa May messed this up and a lot of leavers for "forgetting to vote in the proceeding GE" If they succeed then it is another GE regardless and we leave again but this time with a leave majority parliament, properly representing its democratic people and the will of this country. Sounds nice that does, for a change. Bring it on. This is literally a fight for our right to Govern our own country. For democracy and for even Europe. To Guy I hope you read this. I don't hate you or anything, no you just piss me off for some reason but I think if ever we found ourselves in the same bar, we'd end up having a good piss up you and I. Somebody in the comments section mentioned you should move to England and be Prime Minister... Well I think it's a splendid idea and you should try the Labour party, they would be just the right fit for you Guy. I actually respect you because you clearly believe in your cause so fundamentally and any problems are just that in your mind and can be cured in time...with erm, more power...more control...world domination ...then the Universe...Sorry mate got carried away, you do just bring it out in me though pal, forgive me...Maybe after politics a role as a bond baddy is on the cards? I'd watch it. Alas, I'm not against the EU, I'm just against the UK being in the EU and I love Queen and Country dearly. I just believe in Great Britton more than I ever would a European Super State and that is the unbridled truth of the matter and no one should ever be abused and judged because of that fact. If loving my country makes me a little Englander then I wear that badge and all those other horrid titles with honour and pride, ultimately knowing that they are wrong and you all are wrong about the major majority of leavers. I hope I have portrayed to you that you should not be too quick to judge people, realise that people views are based on experience and the lessons of life and 17.4m people cannot be pigeon holed like they have. Make no mistake we are in this mess because of Remainers and nobody else is to blame. Except Michael Gove. Lastly, I deserve a little credit for leaving my 'Britton' spelt right but the wrong one, booboo for all to see and absolute grammatical error shame that it is...just take it on the chin son...I believe that grammar and correct punctuation always come second to 'just get it wrote down' and as long as your point comes across then f@&k it. Dictionary, of Good Sir, all the way. All you people criticising which comma goes where and that version of that word is wrong...Yeah, Nah F@&k that, you can spend days deciding and debating that sh*t, I see many grammatical errors in print publications and on apps like Sky News, even in the bloody title of the article sometimes and that's the nature of writing something without giving it the proper attention it needs because you know what? Writing is hard! A lot of people that critiqued my grammar actually made more mistakes in their own replies critiquing my grammar! So much irony involved in this story of great woe. You can understand all the mistakes in news apps because writing quickly and accurately on the hop is impossible to get right all the time, though print publications should do better. It all also explains why Big Donald messes his Twatter posts up so much, bless him. You all really do need to pull your grammatical head out of your arse you sad bastards and if you're not already then go get laid...sometimes I really need to follow my own advice, I'm starting to realise...I must say, somewhat happily the grammatical errors were what the majority of people's criticism mostly focused on, though I cannot edit or add a comment and really wanted to put in my original post as an edit and even tried 5 times. Ummmm.

Maybe it's just too long? Probably come to think of it. I do think Guy may have what is now a very early draft that I tried to upload on Sunday night, not wanting to keep my fans waiting like. Probably a good thing as there was a lot of mistakes in that draft and the grammar police would have had a field day. When I pressed update the edited post went somewhere just not onto Guys page...

Adam G Skwierawski

"Mikey Elwood even when you try really hard, you still can't get away from the puzzling choices of "should of" v "should have", "wrote" v "written", etc. The "gramma and spelin" give you leavers away"

Rather than focusing on the content you all focused on spelling and mostly insulted or belittled me, well tried to, at least. I find all this really quite interesting and curious, considering you all delighted in proving your undoubted "Superior Intelligence" to me not even caring 20 other people above your comment have already stated the bleeding obvious but you seem oblivious and wholly focused on portraying how cleaver you are. One can only wonder why? Maybe you have a burning need to matter, feel included, over - compensate for something? Connect with your intelligent brethren? Maybe? Awwww...Me too. Who are you trying to prove this to though, I wonder? Yourself I'd say? Or maybe you're, "Facebook Friends?"...

David Richard Gilbertson

"You can't even spell 'Britain'. Distinctly unpatriotic, as is everything else that Brexiters have done to bring this ruin upon us."

Later Comment...

"Mikey Elwood – you've

spelled 'Briton' wrong, too.

This is the reason you and

17,399,999 of your comrades

should've had your voting
rights permanently curtailed.
I know a number of foreign
nationals who teach English.
Shall I get one to contact you
for tuition? Before they get
deported, that is."
You Smug twat you...Well done
and pat yourself on the back...you're
special.
You all have a Great Evening,
Sincerely too...no I mean it...honestly
Special Mention.
Mike Newport
"Mikey Elwood in the

words of Bob Dylan I hope

that you die

And your Death'll come

soon

I will follow your casket

In the pale afternoon

And I'll watch while

you're lowered

Down to your deathbed

And I'll stand over your

grave 'Til I'm sure that you're

dead"

You should hang your head in shame Mike!"

Jane Horton

"Mikey Elwood just out of interest, what vile behaviour does the EU do that affects you, you or your family personally. How have you been told this will be better for you all immediately after 31st October."

Not sure Vile is the word I would use. Maybe, Jane the answer to the questions you ask, lies in the fact we send great sums of money to the European Union and have not one Iota of a fig what they do with it. Nor, does anybody else know unless you work for the EU council. Ten Thousand people that work at the EU council earn more than our Prime Minister, £150,000 odd! 10,000!! The ridiculous situation of moving the entire bloody EU council to Strasbourg once a month and for four days in some moronic attempt to appease the narcissistic French, who veto the veto to stop the EU having to do this complete waste of time, energy, money, resources and not to mention large carbon foot print. Having to keep doing it because well, France...Have a word will you? C'est la Vie. Hence the reason, no EU accounts are or have ever been signed off by anybody. Ever. The UK pays in £13,200,000,000, per year and gets a rebate of £4.3 billion. By my reckoning we, should be £8.9 billion, up to eight thousand, nine hundred million pounds better off, that's £171,153,846 per week by my calculations or One Hundred and Seventy One Million, One Hundred and Fifty Three Thousand, Eight Hundred and Forty Six Pounds Per Week .That, my dear Jane, is on top of abolishing the EU Vat that we pay on imported goods from outside the EU, which we will be getting more of. It means more money per capita and cheaper goods, to boot. The EU Regulations & Red Tape Revolution is going to help immensely and make us a much more Competitive, Dynamic and Richer country than we would be in the EU otherwise. That scares the shit out of the EU and Remainers that does Jane. Leaving opens a brilliant and exciting new direction and into the land of opportunity and adventure for this country at least. I hope that answers your questions somewhat Jane.

"Mikey Elwood tell me why you voted to leave? You

sound like one of those brain washed idiots we come across a lot on these posts. You've obviously stayed as a baby with the name Mikey. I'm yet to come across an educated Brexshitter."

Much love from Mikey Elwood..."The man who never grew up because he's called Mikey"...lmao,

Thank you Krystyna Owen!

A wise assumption and nailed it my dear. My friends will understand the irony...Brilliant Comments x...

Printed in Great Britain
by Amazon